Essential Management Skills for Pharmacy and Business Managers

Dr. Titus De Silva

Consultant, Pharmacy Practice, Quality Management, Food Safety

BSc (Chemistry), BSc (Pharmacy) Hons. Post-graduate Dipl (Computer Sci),
MBA, PhD, CChem, FRSC, MRPharmS, MPS

CRC Press
Taylor & Francis Group
Boca Raton London New York

CRC Press is an imprint of the
Taylor & Francis Group, an **informa** business
A PRODUCTIVITY PRESS BOOK

CRC Press
Taylor & Francis Group
6000 Broken Sound Parkway NW, Suite 300
Boca Raton, FL 33487-2742

First issued in hardback 2019

© 2013 by Taylor & Francis Group, LLC
CRC Press is an imprint of Taylor & Francis Group, an Informa business

No claim to original U.S. Government works

ISBN-13: 978-1-4665-8258-3 (hbk)

Library of Congress Cataloging-in-Publication Data

De Silva, Titus.
   Essential management skills for pharmacy managers / Titus De Silva.
      p. ; cm.
   Includes bibliographical references and index.
   ISBN 978-1-4665-8258-3 (hardcover : alk. paper)
   I. Title.
   [DNLM: 1. Pharmacy Administration. QV 737.1]

RS100
615.1068--dc23   2013010825

Visit the Taylor & Francis Web site at
http://www.taylorandfrancis.com

and the CRC Press Web site at
http://www.crcpress.com

This book is dedicated to all my teachers for sharing their knowledge and wisdom with me.

Contents

Review of *Essential Management Skills for Pharmacy and Business Managers*

A very comprehensive book that, if thoroughly read, understood, and implemented, will lead to best practice for this industry sector.

The methodology of simply backgrounding management theory and the history thereof through to practical application in the everyday running of a pharmacy or a business is portrayed in a simplistically brilliant manner with complete ease of understanding.

While I am sure the book will meet its intended purpose, I believe it would also make an excellent guide for discussion chapter by chapter for all staff in a pharmacy in group sessions.

I am certain that the use of the book in this matter would lead to

- Greater understanding of each of the player's roles and thinking processes, from which many synergies rather than confrontations could arise
- Good staff relationships better able to direct a constant improvement process

■ In general, moving the pharmacy or a business toward best practice and ultimately greater success

I recommend this book as compulsory reading at least for pharmacy and business management, professional or otherwise, but more particularly as a compressive training manual for all staff in a group environment.

Bruce Craig Munro (CNZM), BSC, BCA, ACA

Former CEO, Penfolds Wines Limited, New Zealand

Executive director specializing in managing corporate recovery, rationalizations, and investment

Director of several public and private enterprises

Chairman of New Zealand Wool Board

Foreword

There is a depressing familiarity about organizations, big and small, that underperform or fail because of bad management, and where individuals are not allowed to realize their full potential. Many of us with years in businesses of all kinds have experienced badly managed organizations from both sides, have learned from our mistakes, and in retrospect, would have done many things differently.

This book aims to address this dilemma as it applies to the management of a retail/community pharmacy. Although this is a specific scenario, it is also a business microcosm that illustrates many of the management issues and principles that arise in organizations of all types and sizes.

The book sets out a number of scenarios arising in a typical community pharmacy, where management issues arise, business objectives suffer, and staff are unable to fulfill their true potential. Many of these initially produce a smile, but this is soon followed by the realization that many of us have been in that situation and have been responsible for, or suffered from, the very same mistakes. The author has extensive management experience over many years in the pharmaceutical industry and in retail pharmacy, and has been able to create scenarios illustrating the kinds of things that most often go wrong. He then uses this to analyze the situation using business management theory and best practice, and finally revisits each scenario to set out how the issue could have been resolved or avoided in the first place.

One clear conclusion is that the vast literature on business management can give a range of answers on important issues, for instance, on the value of performance management in the business workplace and on potential conflicts between technical/legal accountability and business leadership. This book puts these generic issues into the specific context of the community pharmacy and gives sound and valuable advice on how to successfully manage this type of business.

Dr. David Taylor

BSc Pharmacy (Hons)., PhD
Former Director of Product Development, Analytical Development and Project Management of AstraZeneca, UK

Preface

All pharmacy managers are expected to resolve legal, ethical, operational, human resource, and financial issues that affect the organization. In the absence of management skills, managers often struggle to address the range of issues facing them in their day-to-day work and fail to create a patient-focused environment.

I moved from quality control, academia, research, hospital pharmacy practice, pharmaceutical manufacture, and senior management roles to community pharmacy practice. As a staff pharmacist I have continuously used the principles discussed in this book in order to be the most efficient and effective pharmacy professional. However, in my pharmacy career and senior management roles for over 30 years, I have encountered many situations where the managers failed to resolve day-to-day issues satisfactorily because of a lack of management skills. As a result, these issues recurred regularly. I realized that there was a gap to be filled. A book of this kind would have been a great asset as a reference when I commenced my pharmacy career decades ago.

This book is not about financial management of pharmacies. Numerous books have been written on this topic. The aim of the book is to help pharmacist and nonpharmacist managers, aspiring managers, and business managers successfully manage the challenges of the ever-changing competitive pharmacy environment, focus on patient-centered healthcare, and improve management roles in pharmacies and other business operations. Although the scenarios discussed in the book refer to pharmacy practice, the principles of essential management skills can be applied in all practice settings.

Chapters 1 through 5 deal with management principles: from techniques for managing professionals to management theories, managing a pharmacy, and managing change and risk in the organization. These principles are important for all managers regardless of position or practice setting.

Development of staff is discussed in Chapters 6 through 10. Problem solving, conflict resolution, managing stress at work, working as a team, and communication are all essential skills for self-development. It is practically impossible to effectively manage an organization, whether it is a pharmacy or a retail operation, unless we can manage ourselves.

Chapters 11 through 16 are about managing other people. Leadership, delegation, empowerment, and motivation skills are essential for managing the staff in the organization. Pharmacists from all over the world arrive in the UK for employment. Management of diversity has been a topic that has often been ignored. These skills are essential to create a pleasant working environment. Effective management of cultural diversity promotes teamwork among the members of the organization. How performance reviews can be used to achieve a win–win situation, rather than a win–lose situation, is discussed in Chapter 16.

Chapters 17 through 21 deal with the quality management function of pharmacy practice. Although the discussion focuses on pharmacy practice, the principles of quality management can be applied to any practice setting. So far, there are no international standards akin to ISO 9000 that can be applied to pharmacy practice. Hence, the focus is on a pharmacy practice setting. However, this section discusses quality assurance practices in Australia that are applicable to a pharmacy practice. The development of a quality management system is discussed in detail in this section. The quality management system is a dynamic program, and regular audits and reviews are necessary to meet the changing needs of the organization. They are detailed in this section. Dispensing errors and near misses are pharmacy-specific topics. However, principles of handling patient complaints can be applied to any practice setting.

Each chapter includes features that enhance the reader's understanding and application of the principles:

- A brief scenario is discussed to facilitate the application of the principles described in each chapter.
- Comprehensive discussion of the content and theory behind the major concepts enables the development of essential skills.
- References in each chapter provide links to further information on the topic.
- Explanations and applications facilitate the comprehension and application of each concept.
- Scenarios are analyzed using the concepts discussed in the chapters.

Embarking on a management career provides both opportunities and challenges to pharmacists and nonpharmacists aspiring to become better pharmacy managers. I would hope that readers apply these skills as circumstances demand, picking up salient features to guide them in the right direction.

Community Pharmacy Limited and its staff quoted in the scenarios are all fictitious. Any resemblance to real persons, living or dead, is purely coincidental. However, some of the events are based on my own personal experience and observations while working in the pharmacy and business environment in the United Kingdom and New Zealand.

Acknowledgments

Over the years in New Zealand and England I have come to know many colleagues who have shared their knowledge, provided advice, and encouraged me to write this book. I thank them for sharing their knowledge and experience with me.

I thank Dr. David Taylor, the former director of product development, analytical development, and project management of AstraZeneca, UK, for patiently reading through the manuscript, making suggestions, and contributing the Foreword. Dr. Taylor made valuable comments based on his expertise in AstraZeneca in the United Kingdom. I thank Bruce Munroe, the former CEO of Penfolds Wines Limited, New Zealand, for his review of the management skills discussed in the book.

I thank Editwork, New Zealand, and P.S.W. Gunawardena for reading the manuscript and for their suggestions. Also, I extend my gratitude and appreciation to my wife, Anoma, a professional librarian and an archivist, and my sons— Dr. Samitha De Silva, partner and head of technology and outsourcing law at Manches LLP, UK, and Pradeepa De Silva, Windows consumer product marketing manager of Microsoft Australia—who encouraged me to take the challenge of putting my experience in corporate life and management skills into a book. I also thank the organizations I have worked for in senior management roles in Kuwait, New Zealand, Japan, and the United Kingdom for the experience I gained, which helped me accomplish the task. I would be failing in my duty if I do not thank the publishing team at Taylor & Francis for their guidance and support during the preparation of this manuscript.

About the Author

Titus De Silva, PhD gained his pharmacy degree (with honors) from the University of Manchester in the United Kingdom. He has worked in the United Kingdom, New Zealand, Japan, and Kuwait in all sectors of pharmacy practice (hospital, community, academia, research, and industry), and also in the beverage industry. For over 30 years, he held senior management positions in New Zealand, the United Kingdom, and Sri Lanka. Before emigrating to New Zealand, he was the head of the National Drugs Quality Control Laboratory in Sri Lanka. During his time in Sri Lanka, he was a visiting lecturer and examiner at the Faculty of Medicine of the University of Colombo School of Pharmacy. While in Kuwait, he served as a specialist in drug analysis and quality control under its Ministry of Health. In Japan, he was attached to the National Institute of Hygienic Science in Tokyo, where he worked with experts in pharmaceutical science. Organizations he worked for include the Southland Hospital Board (New Zealand), Hoechst Pharmaceuticals (New Zealand), Pernod-Ricard (New Zealand), Eli Lilly Research (UK), Ballinger's Pharmacy (New Zealand), Boots Chemists (UK), and Lloyds Pharmacy (UK).

In addition to his pharmacy qualifications, he has a BSc degree in chemistry, a postgraduate diploma in computer science, and an MBA and PhD in management science. He is a chartered chemist (CChem), a Fellow of the Royal Society of Chemistry (FRSC), a member of the Royal Pharmaceutical

Society of Great Britain (MRPharmS), and a member of the Pharmaceutical Society of New Zealand (MPS).

Pernod-Ricard (previously Montana Wines Limited) owned the largest multiple winery in New Zealand, with wineries in four regions. In his role as corporate quality assurance manager, he was responsible for developing and implementing quality, food safety and occupational safety, and hygiene management systems to comply with international standards. His efforts were rewarded when Montana Wines Limited became the first winery in Australasia to have its quality management system certified to the ISO 9000 standard. In his role, he coached and trained staff for management positions.

Dr. De Silva's expertise has been sought by professional organizations. He has presented numerous papers at international seminars and published a number of papers and articles on quality management, food safety, pharmacy practice, and topics of general interest in management journals and magazines. He was the co-author of the chapter "Hazard Analysis and Critical Control Point" in the book *Handbook of Food Preservation*, published by Marcel Dekker, New York (1st edition) (1999). In the second edition of *Handbook of Food Preservation*, he was the author of the revised "Hazard Analysis and Critical Control Point (HACCP)" chapter and the "Good Manufacturing Practices" chapter (published by CRC Press, Boca Raton, Florida, in July 2007). His book *Handbook of Good Pharmacy Practice* was published in 2011 in Sri Lanka.

He has gained competency as a lead auditor and was a registered auditor in quality management and occupational safety and hygiene. Dr. De Silva was a member of the review board of the Joint Accreditation System of Australia and New Zealand (JAS-ANZ) and a member of its technical advisory council. JAS-ANZ is the sole body responsible for accrediting certifying bodies in Australia and New Zealand. He has also been enlisted as a consultant to United Nations Industrial Development Organization (UNIDO).

In 2004, the New Zealand government awarded him the Queen's Service Medal for services to the New Zealand community.

Chapter 1

Managing Professionals

> Surround yourself with the best people you can find,
> delegate authority, and don't interfere as long as the
> policy you've decided upon is being carried out.
>
> **—Ronald Reagan**

1.1 Scenario

After 20 years of service as a healthcare assistant, Dianne
Watson was promoted to the position of supervisor. Upon
retirement of the incumbent manager two years later, she
became the manager at Community Pharmacy Limited. She
had no formal qualifications or management skills. Six healthcare assistants and the pharmacist, Max Fisher, reported to
her. Being a nonpharmacist lacking in management skills, she
managed by exercising control over her subordinates. Changes
recommended by the pharmacist to streamline the pharmacy
activities were ignored. Her typical reply was: "This is how
we've done it and there is no need to change." Issues relating to pharmacy services were not communicated to higher
authorities, nor were they addressed. At this stage morale was

very low. Ultimately, Max left as he did not see any improvement. Following his resignation, two other pharmacists left in succession for similar reasons. The staff turnover was high.

1.2 Introduction

The above scenario typifies the management of many chain community pharmacies in the United Kingdom. Experience itself does not make one a good manager. Lack of motivation, low morale, high staff turnover, and staff dissatisfaction are some of the outcomes of such situations. Healthcare assistants, counter staff, dispensers, and pharmacists are all essential to run a pharmacy business. However, professionals cannot be managed in the way nonprofessionals such as counter staff are managed. Pharmacists are not a favored class, but appropriate skills must be used in managing them. In a community pharmacy setting, the manager has to carry out numerous activities, and these can only be effective and efficient if appropriate management skills are exercised, especially when other staff are involved.

In the current business environment, professional employees constitute the most rapidly growing sector. With the increase in the number of professionals, the scope of professional employment has also been widening. Professional employees, such as pharmacists, represent a distinct group with attributes of their own. Therefore, it requires managers to understand what the professional employee is, in order to manage the professional and organize the activities effectively.

1.3 Definitions

During the Middle Ages, religious, medical, and legal practitioners provided nonstandard specialized services and were designated as professions. In the medieval period, the term *professional* was associated with divinity and applied to those who professed faith in God. The practice of medicine and pharmacy was not acknowledged as a profession until the late medieval times. It was during the thirteenth century that legal practitioners were recognized as professionals (Ehlert, 2004).

Guy Le Boterf, an expert on competence development, defines a professional (Le Boterf, 2002):

> A Professional is a person who possesses a personal body of knowledge and of know-how which is recognized and valued by the market. Because of this market recognition, the Professional benefits from an advantage not available to other workers: he or she can personally manage internal or external professional mobility, in a specific firm or in the international market. A person who is recognized as a Professional possesses a social standing which is larger than the specific job he or she holds down.

As early as 1927, Henry S. Dennison defined a professional in terms of the following four criteria:[*]

1. The occupation uses trained intelligence and is undertaken after following a course of study and appropriate practice.
2. The occupation applies knowledge and methods of science to study problems.
3. The professional is dedicated to serve the community above self-interest.
4. The professional is bound by a code of ethics.

The criteria defined above relate well to the pharmacy profession. Thus, the word *profession* is associated with a body of

---

[*] Henry C. Metcalf (Ed.), *Business Management as a Profession* (New York: A.W. Shaw Co., 1927), pp. 24–26.

knowledge that is used in the service of others and is based on a foundation of science and a dedication for service (Metcalf and Urwick, 2003). Social scientists define the term *profession* as a career that requires specialized knowledge and skills acquired by successfully completing a course of theoretical and practical study prescribed by a regulatory body. It oversees the entry, training, and service provided to the public by those in the profession. The activities of professionals (such as lawyers, doctors, dentists, and pharmacists) are regulated by their respective councils. For example, the General Pharmaceutical Council of the Royal Pharmaceutical Society of Great Britain is the regulatory body that defines the entry, training, and practice requirement for pharmacists in the United Kingdom.

1.4 Attributes of a Professional

There are certain attributes that distinguish a professional employee from a nonprofessional skilled or unskilled worker. His or her activities, standards, goals, and vision are determined by a set of standards, and these are established by the regulatory body. He or she is sufficiently skilled and qualified to determine the quality of his or her work. Professional employees cannot be directed or controlled, but can be guided, taught, and supported (Drucker, 2007). They have specialized knowledge that enables them to do their work without supervision. Managers who do not possess the same expertise should not attempt to control the technical aspects of the professional (Winsborough and Marshall, 2000). For a professional, business criteria are secondary to the standards of work and its success. Longest (1990) has identified several characteristics unique to health professionals. These can be summarized as

1. Work satisfaction is solely due to their profession.
2. Professional development is part of the profession.

3. Individual efforts are related to their professional goals.
4. They share professional knowledge with their clients and a desire to help others.
5. They are loyal and committed to the profession and its code of ethics.
6. Professional knowledge and competence are important to them.
7. They have an intense desire to learn and update their knowledge.
8. They prefer to work independently.
9. There is a need to be recognized by their clients.

The American Pharmacists Association Academy of Student Pharmacists (APhA-ASA) and the American Association of Colleges of Pharmacy (AACP) Council of Deans task force defined professionalism as "active demonstration of the traits of a professional" (Sorensen et al., 2010). In terms of pharmacy professionals, these traits are as follows:

1. Appropriate knowledge and skills expected of a pharmacist, for example, knowledge of pharmacy practice and management skills, which are necessary to discharge the duties
2. Commitment to professional development by participating in continuing professional development (CPD) activities
3. Commitment to provide the services that enhance patient care
4. Takes pride in the profession and gains respect from patients and the healthcare team
5. Maintains covenantal relationships with the patients and the community
6. Creative and innovative
7. Conscientious and trustworthy
8. As defined by the code of ethics, accountable for his or her work
9. Does not compromise ethical standards for profit
10. Demonstrates leadership qualities

In addition, pharmacists have eight qualities that distinguish them from other professionals (Settineri, 2010):

1. Attention to detail in their work
2. Effective communication and counseling skills
3. Very effective in teamwork
4. Efficient planning and organizational skills
5. Keen on keeping abreast of pharmacy knowledge and professional development
6. Knowledge of computer-based activities
7. Reliable as a professional
8. Have initiative

1.5 Needs of a Professional

If professionals are to be recognized as effective and productive employees of organizations, there are certain needs that must be satisfied. Drucker (2007) has identified five such needs:

1. Business objectives should reconcile with professional standards, and these should provide the managerial vision of the organization. The professional's contribution to the organization must be recognized.
2. Professional employees often have only a few opportunities for promotion. Promotion of professionals to administrative positions is not without failure. However, promotional positions that recognize professional work and are equal to administrative positions in the organization offer better rewards for professionals.
3. Because professional activities are not directly linked to financial objectives, financial incentives to professionals are often ignored. The organizations must recognize that a professional employee can make as great a vital contribution in his or her role as a manager can.

4. Professional employees need high performance standards and goals. However, they cannot be supervised. Rather, the manager has to provide support, assistance, and protection to carry out their tasks. The organization must have opportunities for a professional to move from one position to another using his or her expertise.

5. The contribution of a professional should be recognized both inside and outside the company. Professional employees with long service have prestige in the organization. Young employees who wish to extend their horizon in professional activities in universities should be encouraged.

1.6 Leadership Style

In a community pharmacy environment, the hierarchy of management structure is shown in Figure 1.1. The style of communication between the various staff in the organization depends on the level in the ladder of hierarchy. Communication between the CEO and his or her subordinates is almost

Figure 1.1   Management hierarchy.

exclusively in financial terms. This can be described as the "language of money." On the other hand, managers communicate with the line staff in operational terms that can be described as the operational language. Therefore, the managers and the pharmacist have to understand both the language of money and the operational language. In dealing with professionals such as pharmacists, managers should realize that they are not line staff, and hence use the appropriate communication style.

When supervising professionals, the leadership style of the supervisor is an important consideration. Leadership styles can range from an authoritarian style without any subordinate participation to a democratic style enabling full participation of employees. Appropriate leadership style depends upon the personalities, expectations, and situational and environmental issues. Most of all, the manager must bring to the position and demonstrate a definite concept of leadership (Longest, 1990). Discussing the leadership style with the employees will improve communication, expectations, and understanding.

1.7 Techniques for Managing Professionals

When managing professionals, the following strategies can be helpful (Woodruff, 1995; Winsborough and Marshall, 2000):

1. Clarify expectations. Define the tasks to be accomplished, leaving room for creativity and innovation. Discuss with the employees their professional and career expectations.
2. Provide protection and support to deliver expectations.
3. Encourage professional development activities.
4. Acknowledge and recognize them as professionals.
5. Give credit where it is due and avoid taking credit for their good work.
6. Encourage flexibility to promote innovation and creativity.

7. Ensure top management is aware of their professional contribution to the development of the organization.
8. Resolve mistakes in an open manner and allow them to correct their mistakes.
9. Do not pretend to possess technical knowledge that you do not have.
10. Provide regular feedback. Be constructive in criticisms. Do not blame professionals for your mistakes.
11. Set SMART goals that are:
    - Specific
    - Measurable
    - Achievable
    - Realistic
    - Timely

1.8 Dealing with Performance Issues

In the modern pharmacy practice environment, pharmacists as professionals work under a great deal of stress to perform and meet unrealistic targets. Performance suffers and mistakes are made. Performance issues can arise when professionals do not take initiatives, do not complete assignments on time, do what they are told by the manager even when they know that it is wrong, criticize the organization for their failure and frustration, abuse company assets, and obstruct the efforts of co-workers. An effective manager is able to identify professionals who have performed below the expected standard so that they can be supported. The manager should motivate his or her staff, inspire improvement, and develop a program to help them become more efficient. Some guidelines for dealing with performance issues are (Woodruff, 1995)

1. Identify the reasons for poor performance. Commend the professional on areas of good performance. Agree on areas for improvement.
2. Explain how improvement can benefit the professional and the organization.
3. Discuss various means of improving the performance. Respect the opinion of the professional.
4. Agree on a plan of action. Set a timeline. Be available to provide guidance and support when necessary.
5. Document the performance improvement plan.
6. Follow up according to the timeline and provide feedback.

The performance review must be a positive experience for both the manager and the professional. It is a win–win situation. Positive reinforcement and immediate recognition for good work are effective tools in managing professionals. The relationship between the manager and the professional is an important one. Progress can only be achieved when both partners mutually support each other to meet common goals.

1.9 Revisiting the Scenario

Managing professionals require special management skills. Unfortunately, in most chain community pharmacies, the promotion of healthcare assistants to managerial positions without providing management skills has created a culture of incompetence. As demonstrated in the scenario described in the beginning, the person promoted to the managerial position has not been given an opportunity to develop management skills such as leadership, communication, conflict resolution, problem solving, etc. The remainder of the book explores these essential skills for managing a pharmacy.

References

Drucker, P.F. (2007). *The practice of management.* Oxford: Elsevier.

Ehlert, D.A. (2004). Managing professionals. In A.M. Peterson (Ed.), *Managing pharmacy practice* (pp. 39–55). New York: CRC Press.

Le Boterf, G. (2002). *Développer la compétence des professionnels.* Paris: Editions d'Organisation.

Longest, B.B. (1990). *Management practices for the health professional* (4th ed.). Norwalk, CT: Appleton-Lange.

Metcalf, H.C., and Urwick, L. (Eds.). (2003). *Dynamic administration: The collective papers of Mary Follett.* London: Routledge.

Settineri, H. (2010, April). Hire a hirer. *Retail Pharmacy,* 32–33.

Sorensen, T.D., Traynor, A.P., and Janke, K.K. (2010). Inviting scholarhip in leadership in pharmacy. *Innovations in Pharmacy,* 1(1), 1–5.

Winsborough, D., and Marshall, B. (2000). The art of managing professionals. *Chartered Accountants Journal,* 79(3), 60–66.

Woodruff, D.M. (1995). Supervising professional employees. *Hydrocarbon Processing,* 74(10), 141–143.

Chapter 2

Management Theories

The conventional definition of management is getting work done through people, but real management is developing people through work.

—Agha Hasan Abedi, banker

2.1 Introduction

Management theories evolved during the latter part of the nineteenth century following the industrial revolution in Western nations. Political, educational, and economic organizations were always looking for techniques that would enhance customer satisfaction. Rapid changes in the environment were taking place in the economic, cultural, and technical operations. Small production facilities that employed skilled workers were replaced by large factories employing a large number of semiskilled and unskilled workers. Change from small-scale to large-scale production imposed numerous challenges. The leaders were technically oriented and were not able to manage the social problems that occurred when people worked together as teams. It was therefore necessary for the managers

Table 2.1 Evolution of Management Theories

Period	Theory
1890–1940s	Scientific management theory:
	F. Taylor (1856–1915)
	F. Gilbreth (1868–1924)
	L. Gilbreth (1878–1972)
	H. Gantt (1861–1919)
1890s–1980s	Administrative management theory:
	H. Fayol (1841–1925)
Early 20th century	Behavior management theory:
	M. Weber (1864–1920)
	E. Mayo (1880–1949)
1940–1990s	Management science theory:
	A. Maslow (1908–1970)
	D. McGregor (1906–1964)
1950–2000	Organizational management theory

to find better ways to utilize the resources and increase the efficiency by combining worker skills and tasks. The evolution of management theories is shown in Table 2.1.

Management theories can be classified into four types (Kanjilal, n.d.; Jones and George, 2008; Smit et al., 2011):

1. Classical management approach
2. Behavioral management approach
3. Management science approach
4. Organizational environment approach

2.2 Classical Management Approach

The classical management approach is concerned with increasing the efficiency of the organization by improving the performance of workers. Its focus is managing the organization. The theories on classical management evolved during the mid-eighteenth century and continued into the nineteenth century. The three approaches of classical management are (1) scientific management, (2) administrative management, and (3) Weber's theory of bureaucracy (Jones and George, 2008; Mark and Saenz, 2011; Tripathy and Reddy, 2007).

2.2.1 Scientific Management

Scientific management is a systematic study of the relationship between workers and their tasks aimed at refining the work process to increase efficiency (Smit et al., 2011). Frederick W. Taylor (1856–1915) found that the time needed to produce a unit of output could be reduced by specialization and division of labor. He discarded the rule-of-thumb knowledge and introduced scientific techniques. Taylor formulated four principles to increase efficiency:

Principle 1: Study how the workers perform tasks, collect their informal knowledge, and test new ways of improving the process.

Principle 2: Record how new tasks are performed and develop rules and standard operating procedures (SOPs), so that all workers perform the tasks in a consistent manner.

Principle 3: Recruit workers based on their skills and abilities and train them to perform the tasks as stipulated in SOPs.

Principle 4: Establish a reasonable level of performance for a given task and reward those who exceed the performance requirements.

2.2.1.1 Benefits and Limitations of Taylor's Approach

Taylor's approach contributed to the way tasks were performed in the organization. It created awareness that tools and physical movement associated with a task can be made more productive. Ability and training were recognized as essential to do a job properly. Managers were encouraged to seek "one best way" to perform a job, thereby developing a rational approach to solving the organization's problem.

However, several problems manifested as managers began to implement Taylor's scientific management principles. As time needed to produce a unit of output decreased, more tasks were added to the workers. Because of the specialization, fewer workers were needed and layoffs could not be avoided. The jobs were monotonous and staff turnover increased. Taking instructions from several supervisors created confusion in the workplace. Economic incentives did not always motivate workers. There was no one best way to do a job because individuals vary in the way they work with the same care and promptness. Taylor's focus was on the process rather than on the workers (Tripathy and Reddy, 2007).

Principles of Scientific Management have been used to streamline the activities and service of KFC, Honda, Canon and Intel. Through time and motions studies KFC improved its services to customers (Hellriegel et al., 2002, p. 51).

Following Taylor's work, Frank Gilbreth (1868–1924) and Lilian Gilbreth (1878–1972) refined his techniques and formulated a new time and motion study. They analyzed each task into several component tasks, found better ways to perform each component task, and reorganized the component tasks so that the entire task could be completed more efficiently. However, the workers were dissatisfied with the new arrangements because the tasks were boring and monotonous. Scientific management focuses on the employee of the organization. While its benefits of productivity and efficiency are clear, it overlooks the social needs of the employees (Jones and George, 2008).

Henry Gantt (1861–1919) studied work scheduling and control and developed the Gantt chart to improve the efficiency of the organization. Even today, the Gantt chart is used for work planning and scheduling (Kanjilal, n.d.).

2.2.2 Administrative Management

Administrative management focuses on creating an organization structure that leads to a more efficient and effective organization. The organization structure defines the task and authority relationships in the organization that control the utilization of resources to achieve its goals.

Henry Fayol (1841–1925) formulated 14 principles that are essential for the efficient management of the organization:

1. Job specialization and the division of labor increase the efficiency of the organization.
2. Authority and responsibility: The managers have the right to give instructions and orders, and expect subordinates to follow those instructions and orders.
3. Unity of command: Workers should receive instructions and commands from only one supervisor.
4. Line of authority: The length of the chain of command from the top management to the bottom should be limited.
5. Centralization: The authority should not be vested in top management.
6. Unity of direction: The managers and the workers should be guided by a single plan of action.
7. Equity: All the staff should be treated with dignity and respect.
8. Order: The organizational positions should be created to maximize the efficiency of the organization, and the staff should have prospects of promotion.

9. Initiative: The management should encourage innovation and creativity by the staff.
10. Discipline: All workers should work toward the same goals of the organization.
11. Remuneration and personnel: The employees should receive fair payment for the work.
12. Stability of tenure of personnel: Long-term employees can make a vital contribution to improve the efficiency of the organization.
13. Subordination of individual interest to common interest: Employees should be aware of how individual performance affects the performance of the entire organization.
14. Esprit de corps: The managers must endeavor to improve morale among the staff to promote mutual trust and understanding so that all staff work in a harmonious environment.

Some of these principles have declined from the management scene. Administrative management principles focus on the manager of the organization. They define a clear structure and professionalism of managerial roles. However, the principles are applicable to the internal activities of the organization and overemphasize the rational behavior of managers (Jones and George, 2008; Mark and Saenz, 2011).

2.2.2.1 Benefits and Limitations of Fayol's Approach

At the time Fayol formulated his principles, they were widely accepted among managers and writers. His principles were embodied in the book *Onward Industry* (which was later revised and renamed *Principles of Organization*), written by two General Motors executives, James D. Mooney and Alan C. Railey. Later, Colonel L. Urwick, a distinguished executive and management consultant, wrote *Elements of Administration,* based on the principles of Taylor, Fayol, Mooney, Railey, and other management theorists. Fayol's work inspired a new school of thought known as management process school, which recognized that management is a dynamic process of planning, organizing, staffing, directing, and controlling.

Several limitations are also evident in Fayol's work. His work creates small work groups that work in a disjointed manner without due regard for the wider picture of the organization. There is no provision to use individual abilities. The principles increase specialization, resulting in increased overhead costs. Some of his principles are contradictory; for example, unity of command and division of labor cannot be applied simultaneously. Managers also realize that the principles cannot be applied in all situations. In addition, the principles were not tested empirically. The principles of specialization, chain of command, and unity of direction are not compatible with employees' social and psychological needs. Organizations are considered closed systems (Tripathy and Reddy, 2007).

2.2.3 Weber's Theory of Bureaucracy

Max Weber (1864–1920) postulated his theory of bureaucracy at the time of the German industrial revolution. His theory was based on the following (Jones and George, 2008):

1. Authority is vested in the manager of the organization.
2. The position of a worker is based on his or her performance.
3. Authorities and responsibilities of a position should be clearly specified.
4. Rules and standard operating procedures are written to enable all activities to be adequately controlled.
5. The structure of the organization is based on hierarchy.

2.2.3.1 Benefits and Limitations of Weber's Approach of Bureaucracy

The concepts have been applied to large organizations that required functional specialized staff to train and control individuals with different backgrounds and to delegate special responsibilities and functions to them.

There are numerous limitations to Weber's approach. Employees strictly adhere to rules for fear of penalization. They follow the letter of the law, ignoring the spirit, and are discouraged to make decisions. Often, new goals are substituted instead of the ones for which the organization was created. Resource allocation then is a problem. Clients' queries are categorized into a few broad categories, ignoring the differences between the categories. Clients of bureaucratic organizations have no right to appeal because supervisors are biased toward the opinion of their subordinates. Organizations have informal groups, and they are ignored in bureaucratic organizations. Informal groups are essential for an organization. Rigid structure imposed by bureaucratic organizations is not compatible with the changing economic and social environment. Mature employees of any organization make a vital contribution to its progress. The bureaucratic structure ignores the mature employee's needs, such as independence, initiative self-control, opportunity to use the skills and experience, and information to plan for the future (Tripathy and Reddy, 2007).

An example of an organization which has been able to overcome the problems of bureaucracy is United Parcel Service delivering more than 12.4 million packages daily throughout the world. Its success is due to the efficiency and consistency of its services. There are eight hierarchical levels in the organization. Rules, regulations and the policy manual enable the staff to carry out their tasks in a consistent manner (Hellriegel et al., 2002, p. 48).

2.3 Behavioral Management Approach

The behavioral approach (Jones and George, 2008) focuses on the human relation approach of the organization. Mary Follett (1868–1933) recognized the importance of behavior of managers toward the workforce. The organization can be more effective and efficient if the workers' efforts are recognized, and if they are allowed to participate in development work. Because the workers have the knowledge and skills required for the job, they should be in control, and not the managers. Follett also promoted cross-functional communication. At the time Follett presented the human relations approach to management, it was recognized as radical.

Whole Foods, a supermarket chain that sells natural foods, applied Follett's ideas that shaped its management practices. Typically, each store employs between 60 and 140 employees organized into various teams to promote a sense of cooperation. Each team is accountable for their work and meet monthly to discuss problems and resolve issues (Hellriegel et al., 2002, p. 54).

2.3.1 Hawthorne Studies

Hawthorne studies were conducted by Elton Mayo (1880–1949) and associates in order to increase the efficiency of the organization by improving job specializing and the type of tools used. These studies were conducted at the Hawthorne Institute of Western Electric from 1924 to 1932. Three types of studies were conducted:

1. Illumination: Effect of illumination on work efficiency.
2. Group study: How the attitude of employees toward the manager affects the work.
3. The importance of human behavior toward work.

The human relations movement gathered momentum during this period, and the two studies that focused on the human relations aspect of management were Abraham Maslow's (1908–1970) motivation theory and Douglas McGregor's (1906–1964) theory X and theory Y.

2.3.2 Maslow's Motivation Theory

Abraham Maslow classified basic human needs into five categories in a hierarchical order: physiological, security, affiliation, esteem, and self-accomplishment (Dima et al., 2010). His theory was based on the concept that people have well-defined needs. The most basic needs to be satisfied first are physiological needs, such as food, water, air, etc. Physiological needs lead to needs for security in a safe environment, that is, a shelter, comfortable temperature for living, etc. The next level of needs is social satisfaction. People need to coexist in a social environment sharing each other's vision and objectives. When the need for affiliation is satisfied, human beings need to be appreciated by others for their position in society and their contribution toward it. The highest need is self-fulfillment, the desire to achieve the maximum potential. This level is continuously changing because of changes in external conditions and challenges imposed by them.

2.3.3 McGregor's Theory X and Theory Y

McGregor studied how the assumptions of behavior and attitudes of workers affect the way they behave in the organization (Jones and George, 2008). He proposed two sets of assumptions: theory X and theory Y.

According to theory X, man is inherently lazy, dislikes work, avoids responsibility, and tries to do as little as possible. Managing such people needs close supervision to control their behavior with reward and punishment. On the other hand, theory Y assumes that people are not inherently lazy and do not avoid work and responsibility. Given the opportunity, they will do their best to satisfy the needs of the organization.

2.3.3.1 Benefits and Limitations of the Human Relations Movement

The human relations movement recognizes the social needs of individuals. Improved work conditions do not always correlate with an increase in production. Work production norms are established by the group and not by the informal group. Monetary rewards do not always affect one's work. Nonfinancial incentives are also important. An employee-centered democratic participative style of leadership is a hallmark of the human relations movement and is more effective than the task-oriented leadership style. The dominant unit of the human relations movement is the informal group.

The human relations movement is not without limitations. Only human variables are considered important. No one single solution satisfies people of diverse social groups with incompatible values and interests. This approach focuses on symbolic rewards, ignoring material rewards. Informal groups encourage affiliation and affection but have no effect on tasks that can be repetitive, monotonous, and uninteresting. The human relations approach is production oriented and not employee oriented, as it claims. Socializing programs, such as picnics and social events, and providing subsidized meals, do not improve the well-being of employees. A leisurely attitude of employees does not encourage quick decision making. It places unrealistic demands on the supervisor. The assumption of this approach that satisfied workers are more productive is incorrect, and in fact attempts to improve production by improving working conditions, and the human relations skills of a manager do not improve productivity as expected (Tripathy and Reddy, 2007).

2.4 Management Science Theory

The management science theory is an approach to management that utilizes a variety of quantitative techniques to help managers make the best use of resources in the organization. It is an extension of Taylor's work of measuring the worker-task mix. There are many branches of management science, each of which specializes in a particular field (Jones and George, 2008).

Quantitative management deals with mathematical techniques that enable managers, for example, to quantify inventory levels, identify new locations of factories, and how best to invest the money.

Operations management utilizes various techniques to improve the efficiency of the operations of the organization.

Total quality management (TQM) is an approach that manages the quality of the resources, processes, and the final product to achieve efficiency and quality of the final product.

Management information systems (MIS) help managers design information systems that monitor the internal and external environments that impact the performance of the organization, thereby providing a means to meet future challenges.

2.5 Organizational Environment Theory

In a competitive global economy, the survival of the organization depends upon the ability to acquire and utilize resources. Therefore, systems must be in place to meet the challenges of the external environment. The resources in the organizational environment include raw materials, skilled labor, customers who buy products and services, and financial organizations. The organizational environment theory considers how managers can control the relationship with the external environment. The significance of the external environment became clear when the open systems and contingency theories were developed in the 1960s (Jones and George, 2008).

2.5.1 Open and Closed Systems Theories

In the 1960s, Daniel Katz, Robert Kahn, and James Thompson studied how an organization is affected by the external environment. The organization was considered an open system—one that acquired resources from the external environment and transformed them into goods and services that are then sold to the customers in the external environment. The resources are raw materials, labor, and money. After acquiring the resources the process of transformation begins with tools, techniques, and machinery to produce the output as goods and services. It is described as an open system because it interacts with the external environment.

On the other hand, a closed system is not affected by the external environment, and it ignores the influence of the external environment on the organization (Jones and George, 2008). The organization fails to acquire the necessary resources and loses control, leading to dissolution of the organization. In a community pharmacy, the pharmacy manager acquires medicines and other goods, employs pharmacists, technicians, and healthcare assistants, and dispenses or sells medicines to customers. Skilled managers ensure that all components of the open system work together as a team to promote effectiveness and efficiency.

2.5.2 Contingency Theory

In 1960s, Tom Burns and G.M. Stalker of the United Kingdom, and Paul Lawrence and Jay Lorsch of the United Stated, formulated the contingency theory. The basis of this theory is that there is no one best way to organize. The main assumption of this theory is that the organization's ability to obtain much-needed resources depends on the external environment. So, the structure of the organization and the control methods are contingent on the characteristics of the external environment (Jones and George, 2008).

The operations of a community pharmacy are affected not only by the ability to obtain medicines and products from wholesalers in a timely manner, but also by the unavailability of some medicines due to manufacturing problems, competing pharmacies delivering better or additional services, not embracing new technology, etc. Rapid changes in the external environment create more problems of acquiring the resources. Therefore, the managers must coordinate the control mechanisms to respond to the environment quickly and effectively.

Fayol and Weber's principles even today provide a clear set of guidelines to enable managers to create a work environment that promotes the efficient and effective use of the organization's resources. Hawthorne studies demonstrated the impact of people's and managers' emotions and thoughts on the performance of the organization. From these studies emerged the human relations movement and organizational behavior. McGregor's study enables managers to design an appropriate work setting depending upon the assumptions of attitudes and behavior of the workers. Fields of management science provide tools and techniques to improve the quality of decision making, thereby increasing the efficiency and effectiveness of the organization. Managers can model the activities of the organizations using the open system view and create synergy among the various units to enhance the performance of the workers as well as the organization. As formulated by the contingency theory, there is no one best way to model and lead an organization. Theories of management are guidelines that managers can use to create a harmonious work setting compatible with the structure of the organization.

References

Dima, I.C., Man, M., and Kot, C. (2010). Use of Abraham Maslow's motivation theory or setting consumer's satisfaction and non-satisfaction. *Polish Journal of Management Studies*, 2(1), 132–138.

Hellriegel, D., Jackson, S.E., and Slocum Jr., J.W. (2002). *Management: A competency based approach*. Singapore: Thomas Asia Pte. Ltd.

Jones, G., and George, J. (2008). *Contemporary management* (6th ed.). Berkshire, UK: McGraw-Hill Higher Education.

Kanjilal, U. (n.d.). *Management theories and principles: Their application in libraries and information centres* (BLIS 02). Indira Gandhi National Open University. Retrieved May 21, 2011, from http://www.youtube.com/watch?v=ncEStUcDF-I.

Mark, S.M., and Saenz, R. (2011). Management essentials for pharmacists. In M.A. Chisholm-Burns, A.M. Vaillantcourt, and M. Shepard (Eds.), *Pharmacy management: Leadership, marketing and finance* (pp. 21–47). Mississauga, Ontario: Jones and Bartlett.

Smit, P.J., Cronje, G.J. de J., Brevis, T., and Vrba, M.J. (2011). *Management principles: A contemporary edition for Africa*. Lansdowne: Juta Legal and Academic Publishers.

Tripathy, P.C., and Reddy, P.N. (2007). *Principles of management* (3rd ed.). New Delhi: McGraw-Hill.

Chapter 3

Managing a Pharmacy

Good management is the art of making problems so
interesting and their solutions so constructive that
everyone wants to get to work and deal with them.

—Paul Hawken, *Natural Capitalism*

3.1 Scenario

Since the introduction of the responsible pharmacist regulations, Steve has logged in as the responsible pharmacist (RP).
Very soon, Steve realized that Dianne did not possess formal
qualifications or management skills to manage a pharmacy.
Although he was the RP, Dianne intervened in every decision in the pharmacy. She had the habit of jumping from one
task to another without completing a task. Arbitrary targets
were set for medicine use reviews (MURs) and repeat prescription service without any consultation with the pharmacy
staff. Dispensers and technicians were interviewed by Dianne
without giving Steve an opportunity to talk to the candidates.
Staff shortages were not resolved, and he often had to take up
issues with the area manager. Dianne was not able to manage

conflicts effectively and always needed the assistance of the area manager. Staff morale was extremely low.

3.2 Introduction

Managing a community pharmacy is a unique experience. Although RP regulations require the RP to be accountable to all pharmacy operations, conflicts arise as in the scenario quoted above, when the manager is a nonpharmacist. The primary focus of a nonpharmacist manager is financial considerations. Being a healthcare provider, the manager of a community pharmacy is accountable to the professional body and to the customer. He or she has to comply with the code of ethics. On no account should financial motives override ethical considerations. Therefore, the pharmacy business is different from all other commercial enterprises. Graduate pharmacists who are in management roles have adequate skills and training to meet the challenges of the ever-changing commercial environment while balancing ethical considerations. All pharmacy managers must balance commercial skills with duty of care for the patients they serve.

3.3 Definitions

Management: Mark et al. (2011) define management as follows: "Management is the art of maximising productivity by using and developing growth."

Professionalism: Refers to the views, standards, and behavior of a person engaged in tasks related to his or her profession.

Leadership: Northouse (2010) defines leadership as "a process whereby an individual influences a group of individuals to achieve a common goal."

Management and leadership are complementary just like the two sides of a coin. The former focuses more on the operational activities of an organization, whereas leadership inspires and influences others to achieve goals.

3.4 Management Styles

Management styles deal with the development of people. There are two main management styles (Media Selling, n.d.): autocratic and democratic. The features of the autocratic style of management are as follows:

- Seeks power and glory
- Excludes subordinates when decisions are made
- Expects obedience from subordinates
- Works best in an environment where formal, rigid rules are enforced

Those who demonstrate the autocratic style of management can be exploitative or benevolent. An exploitative autocrat exploits subordinates and shows no concern for people or their problems. Such managers do not ask for input from their subordinates and are not fair and reasonable in their decisions. A benevolent autocrat will seek input from the staff in order to confirm his or her decisions. There is only one way of doing things: only his or her way.

The managers who demonstrate a democratic style of management exhibit these characteristics:

- Seek input from others and consult when decisions are made
- Interested in the welfare of people and humanistic
- Base decisions on consensus of opinion
- Give credit where it is due
- Are informal in approach and tolerant of conflict

A consultative democrat listens to the input from subordinates and makes changes, if necessary, and takes responsibility for the final decision, whereas a participative democrat makes decisions on group consensus.

A study conducted in the United States on managerial behavior found that 90% of the managers spend their time in ineffective activities and only 10% spend their time in a purposeful and committed manner (Bruch and Goshal, 2002). Managers are not expected to achieve the impossible, but they are expected to exceed expectations to meet the company's objectives. Those who are committed and purposeful share two traits: focus and energy.

The managers who are focused concentrate their attention on tasks ahead and ensure their completion. They are generally proactive and therefore do not respond unnecessarily to every issue that comes in their way. Distractions do not draw their attention. All options are considered before any action is taken. Because they undertake few activities at a time, tasks get their full attention. Energy refers to the total commitment to the task, and these two traits are complementary. Focus without energy results in unnecessary execution of activities and may lead to burnout. Energy without focus leads to being busy without any purpose and could result in failures.

3.5 Types of Managers

Based on the above traits, managers can be classified into four types (Bruch and Goshal, 2002): procrastinators, disengaged, distracted, and purposeful.

Procrastinators: Have low levels of both energy and focus. In fact, 30% of the managers fall into this category. They are good at performing routine tasks without any initiative. Generally, procrastinators do not attempt to enhance their performance or deal with strategic issues.

Disengaged managers: About 20% of the managers exhibit this quality. Although they are fully focused, they lack sufficient energy. Such managers are often exhausted and frequently suffer from burnout. They are not committed to tasks, and problems are ignored, assuming that they do not exist. Disengaged managers do not like their jobs and hence are easily stressed out.

Distracted managers: Some 40% of the managers are distracted. They have high levels of energy but lack focus. Hence, there is a need to feel busy without any proper purpose. Development of strategy is not their forte. They commit themselves to multiple tasks because of their short-sightedness and therefore often have to resort to firefighting. As a result, the tasks do not reach completion. Lack of interest leads to the failure of tasks.

Purposeful managers: Only 10% of the managers in the United States fall into this category. They have high levels of both energy and focus. Purposeful managers are aware of what they need to achieve, and therefore they reach their goals effectively. Decisions are based on sound judgment with proper time management. Stress does not distract them from achieving their goals because they are able to manage stress successfully. External environment does not divert their attention. Much-needed resources are carefully planned without leaving any room for the external environment to influence their goals.

3.6 Traditional Roles of a Manager

The traditional roles of management are planning, organizing, directing, coordinating, and controlling (Peterson, 2004; Smit et al., 2011).

3.6.1 Planning

The planning process aims to (1) minimize risk and maximize efficiency, (2) achieve future success, (3) resolve potential problems, and (4) make the best use of available resources. Main activities involved in planning are preparation of the budget, identifying staff requirements and resources, and determining the hours of operation. There are five steps in planning: (1) conduct a SWOT analysis to determine strengths and weaknesses, (2) review mission, (3) develop a vision, (4) determine the objectives, and (5) create and implement the plan.

Strategic plans aim at long-term objectives. The pharmacy manager may decide to recruit more patients for the repeat prescription service. In order to achieve this, consultations should take place between the General Practitioners (GPs) and the pharmacist. The entire dispensary team should be trained to support the service, and a public service campaign should commence to create awareness among the patients. Short-term planning is aimed at resolving day-to-day operations.

3.6.2 Organizing

Organizing is the second role of a manager. It involves assigning responsibilities and allocating tasks to be accomplished within a time frame. The organizing chart may have to be reviewed in keeping with the responsibilities or may have to be created if it does not exist.

3.6.3 Directing

Directing is the most important function of a manager. It requires excellent interpersonal skills. Directing involves leading, delegating, and motivating the team to achieve the objectives of the organization.

3.6.4 *Coordinating*

A wide variety of activities take place in a pharmacy. The role of the manager is to coordinate these activities in an efficient and effective manner to produce the desired result. Corrective actions may have to be taken as and when necessary. Preventive actions must be implemented to prevent problems from occurring. Above all, the manager has to create a harmonious environment to obtain the maximum benefit from the team that performs a variety of tasks.

3.6.5 *Controlling*

The role of controlling involves monitoring the performance against the established standards. All deviations from the standard are addressed. Various control measures are used to monitor the performance. The performance of the staff is measured through performance reviews. Expenses in the pharmacy are controlled through budget reports. Monthly dispensing reports can be used to monitor the dispensing activities in the pharmacy. Customer satisfaction reports indicate the extent of satisfaction of customers for the services provided in the pharmacy.

3.7 Management Skills

Skill is defined as one's own ability to transform knowledge into action. Hence it is related to his or her performance. Skill is not something inborn. Skills are acquired through practice and learning from one's personal experiences in the work environment. A pharmacy manager must possess these skills (Fincham, 2011; Tripathy and Reddy, 2008):

- ■ Technical and professional skills
- ■ Conceptual and intellectual skills

- Ethical skills
- Human resource skills

3.7.1 Technical and Professional Skills

Technical and professional skills of a pharmacy manager involve proficiency in the activities in the dispensary and shop floor. When the pharmacy is managed by a nonpharmacist, he or she supervises the shop assistants and the pharmacy staff, including the pharmacist and the dispensary technicians. The activities in the pharmacy are foreign to a nonpharmacist manager, and hence misunderstandings often arise. In this situation, the manager's role is mainly to support and satisfy the requirements of the pharmacy staff. A nonpharmacist manager has to understand the nature of the job that subordinates have to perform.

3.7.2 Conceptual and Intellectual Skills

Conceptual skills refer to the ability to perceive the future of the organization, meet challenges imposed by changes in external forces, be creative and innovative, conceptualize the organization's and one's own role, and set goals for oneself and the staff.

The development of intellectual skills involves the acquisition of perception, judgment, and reasoning to enable a pharmacy manager to interact successfully with the commercial environment and respond to challenges effectively. An opening of a new pharmacy in the vicinity or a medical center with dispensing facilities imposes new challenges that may adversely affect the future of the organization. In the role of a manager, one has to learn the concepts, rules, and routines of the pharmacy.

3.7.3 Ethical Skills

Ethical skills are important skills that a pharmacy manager has to acquire. Although the pharmacy is a commercial enterprise, financial gain should not override ethical considerations. In all situations, a manager has to understand right from wrong. A pharmacy manager must always have the patients' interest at heart. Coercing patients to agree to participate in an MUR to satisfy arbitrary targets for financial gain is not justified.

3.7.4 Human Resource Skills

A pharmacy manager supervises staff at all levels, from counter staff to pharmacists. Therefore, human resource skills are vital to create a harmonious work environment where people enjoy their work. He or she should be able to interact with all the staff, irrespective of level. The ability to handle one's own emotions and being sensitive to others' feelings are important human resource qualities. Excellent communication skills are required to create an atmosphere that facilitates communication. Most of all, a pharmacy manager has to examine his or her own concepts and values that enable him or her to develop more useful attitudes.

Other skills relevant to the pharmacy practice are (Institute of Pharmacy Management, 2010)

- Awareness of healthcare and other issues relevant to those managed by the pharmacy manager
- Principle skills and contributions of other healthcare workers
- Awareness of the roles and policies of local healthcare agencies, such Primary Care Trust (PCT), family planning, etc.
- Understanding the needs of patients, the public, careers, and staff
- Knowledge of risks involved with medicines and legal, financial, and professional issues
- Working knowledge of controlling the financial aspects of the business
- Knowledge of change management

- An understanding of the culture of the organization and its people
- Awareness of the structure of the organization and the lines of responsibility
- Knowledge of good employment practices and human resource skills
- A thorough awareness of laws affecting the business and its employees

3.8 Pharmacy Manager's Roles

The essential roles of a pharmacy manager are leading, managing, and supporting the team to meet the objectives of the organization. These are the key roles:

1. Lead, train, and develop the team to improve their performance and meet the organization's goals.
2. Develop and manage customer service to meet the business standards of the organization.
3. Ensure that the standard operating procedures (SOPs), all regulatory requirements, and ethical standards are met by the staff.
4. Promote the delivery of services such as MURs and others to maximize service income without compromising ethical standards.
5. Maintain effective relationship with GPs, local healthcare agencies, and care homes.
6. Ensure adequate staff levels and other resources are made available to deliver effective healthcare.

3.9 Revisiting the Scenario

It is clear from Dianne's attitude toward the staff that she lacks management and human resource skills. Her actions typify the behavior of an exploitative autocratic manager. She is easily distracted, and none of the jobs that she undertakes reach completion. Although Dianne has energy, she lacks focus and would benefit from human resource and management skills training.

References

Bruch, H., and Goshal, S. (2002). Beware of the busy manager. *Harvard Business Review*, 80(2), 62–69.

Fincham, J.E. (2011). Basic management principles. Retrieved May 4, 2011, from http://faculty.mercer.edu/jackson_r/Ownership/chap02.pdf

Institute of Pharmacy Management. (2010). Management for pharmacists: Draft guidelines. Retrieved June 12, 2010, from http://www.ipmi.org.uk/images/documents/news/management-for-pharmacists.pdf

Mark, S.M. and Saenz, R. (2011). Management essentials for pharmacists. In M.A. Chisholm-Burns and A.M. Vallancourt and M. Shepard (Eds.), *Pharmacy Management, Leadership, Marketing and Finance* (pp. 21–46). Sudbury, MA: Jones and Bartlett.

Media Selling. (n.d.). *Leadership* (Chap. 6). Retrieved February 8, 2012, from http://mediaselling.us/MSM_Chapter6-Leadership.pdf.

Northouse, P.G. (2010). *Leadership: Theory and practice*. Thousand Oaks, CA: Sage Publications.

Peterson, A.W. (2004). Introduction to management. In Andrew W. Peterson (Ed.), *Managing pharmacy practice: Principles, strategies and systems* (pp. 1–10). Boca Raton, FL: CRC Press.

Smit, P.J., Cronje, G.J. de J., Brevis, T., and Vrba, M.J. (2011). *Management principles: A contemporary edition for Africa*. Lansdowne, South Africa: Juta Legal and Academic Publishers.

Tripathy, P.C., and Reddy, P.N. (2008). *Principles of management* (4th ed.). New Delhi: McGraw-Hill.

Chapter 4

Managing Change

There is nothing more difficult to take in hand, more perilous to conduct or more uncertain in the success than to take the lead in the introduction of a new order of things.

—Niccolo Machievelli

4.1 Scenario

The pharmacy manager, Dianne Watts, was away on long-term sick leave. In her absence, Maureen Wright assumed duties as pharmacy manager until Dianne's return. Maureen, who is also a nonpharmacist, has been a relief manager for several years. Within a week of assuming duties, she announced several changes that she intended to make. Shelving of bags of dispensed medications was done by healthcare assistants as and when time permitted, leaving time for dispensers to do their work uninterrupted. Dispensers were made responsible for shelving. Maureen instructed the responsible pharmacist to perform six medicine use reviews (MURs) per week. Waiting time, she said, was too high and she wanted that reduced by

25%. She set an arbitrary target for signing up patients for the repeat dispensing service. There was no consultation on these matters with anybody in the pharmacy. Because there was no employee participation, the staff were extremely disappointed with the manner in which the changes were introduced. When the staff protested, her reply was: "Unless these changes are made, you'll have to look elsewhere for jobs."

4.2 Introduction

Change is inevitable. The world around us is changing rapidly in response to physical, biological, and economic forces of the environment we live in. Impermanence was known even in ancient times. According to the Greek philosopher Heraclitus (c. 535–c. 475 BCE), "nothing is permanent except change." In the healthcare sector, changes are happening in all activities, starting with the development of medicines to the delivery of medications to patients. Pharmacists are not immune from changes happening in their profession. However, they are very slow to embrace change (Royal Pharmaceutical Society of Great Britain, 2008) because of their apathy, inward focus, and passive approach. In the community pharmacy sector, changes affect the pharmacists, dispensers, healthcare assistants, and managers. Therefore, the managers must demonstrate leadership to manage change and take the organization forward.

4.3 Definitions

Change: The process of effectively managing the transformation of a business to improve the way it works in order to meet the challenges imposed by the organization and the external environment.

Change management: "The coordination of a structured period of transition from situation A to situation B in order to achieve lasting change within an organisation" (Connelly, 2008).

4.4 Triggers

Changes may be triggered by a multitude of factors both within and outside the organization (Huczynski and Buchanan, 1991; Newton, 2007; Costello, 1994). They can be classified as internal triggers, external triggers, and anticipatory triggers. The need to modify the employees' attitudes, motives, behaviors, knowledge, skills, training, and the relationships among the employees induces internal triggers. These changes can be accomplished by

- Improving job design, skills, and responsibilities
- Having an innovative or broader range of products and services
- Improving the infrastructure, such as buildings, factories, and machinery
- Enhancing information technology
- Modifying and improving processes and procedures
- Reducing the cost of operations
- Enhancing the skill base
- Improving customer service
- Altering the organizational structure

In order to remain competitive, organizations have to respond to threats from the external environment, such as variation in competition, new products and resources, changes in customer behavior, improvements in technology, new or amended legislation and regulations, new trends such as a healthier lifestyle, and more care for the environment. These are external triggers.

Anticipatory triggers are threats due to anticipated developments and trends that can affect the business of the organization. In a community pharmacy setting, the establishment of care homes in the vicinity and delivery of medications to elderly patients may trigger new services that the organization has to cope with.

4.5 History of Changes

During the past 200 years or so, the globally traditional agricultural society has transformed into an industrial society. We have taken for granted several changes that have taken place during this period, such as

■ Proliferation of factories
■ Discovery of new medicines resulting in longer life expectancy
■ Better disease control
■ Increase in global population
■ Improved and new modes of communication
■ Developments in information technology

4.6 Three Components of Change

Change has three components: (1) scope, (2) depth, and (3) duration (Allan, 2008).

4.6.1 Scope

Changes occur at three levels: (1) organizational level, (2) individual level, and (3) group level. At the organizational level, changes affect working conditions, job divisions, training and experience, and hierarchical divisions. Changes that affect job security, motivation, challenges, and advancement opportunities occur at the individual level. Group level changes affect the norms, cohesiveness, role relationships, and interpersonal relations.

4.6.2 Depth

There are many ways to categorize change, depending upon the extent of the change and whether it is top down or bottom up. Therefore, it is important to understand the intended outcome, the path of achievement, and the political and cultural environment of the organization. Three types of change are commonly described in terms of the magnitude of intended change: (1) developmental, (2) unplanned, and (3) planned (Harrington and Terry, 2009).

4.6.2.1 Developmental Change

Developmental change is a planned process that is predictable. Tasks to be changed are identified at each stage of the process. It is not a radical change. What already exists is continuously improved. Expanding the medicine supply program for care homes is an example of a developmental change.

4.6.2.2 Unplanned Change

Unplanned change can be favorable or unfavorable, desirable or undesirable. These changes are forced or spontaneous. Forced changes occur in response to emergent situations. Opening a new pharmacy in the vicinity requires a new strategy and changes to maintain the customer base. Unplanned spontaneous changes are random and unpredictable. The long-term illness of an employee requires changes in the roles and responsibilities of existing employees until the situation is resolved.

4.6.2.3 Planned Change

Planned change is closely associated with the planning process. The goals of change and the intended outcome are known and predictable. The change agent takes a leading role in this process. There are four types of planned change: (1) incremental, (2) rapid, (3) transactional, and (4) transformational (Anderson and Anderson, 2009; Haberberg and Rieple, 2008, Harrington and Terry, 2009).

4.6.2.4 Incremental Change

This type of change involves a stepwise change to reflect the changes in the environment. They are generally long term and apply to the competitive position, value chain, or architecture. In a community pharmacy setting, extension of services to include blood pressure monitoring and blood glucose monitoring are incremental changes that do not require fundamental changes to the organization's strategy and values.

4.6.2.5 Rapid Change

These changes, although planned, are carried out quickly to respond to an immediate need. They are implemented without considering the consequences. A backlog of unfilled prescriptions due to staff shortages requires rapid adjustment to the rota to satisfy the needs of patients.

4.6.2.6 Transactional Change

These changes are simple and predictable. Established goals are achieved by redefining and clarifying roles and responsibilities, management practices, policies and procedures, task requirements, and individual skill requirements. Transactional change is known as a first-order change that does not alter the fundamental form or functions of the unit.

4.6.2.7 Transformational Change

Transformational change is a second-order change that is complex and unpredictable. Sweeping and radical changes are needed to the mission, strategy, and culture of the organization. The management has to introduce new ways of thinking and improve the skill base. Policies and procedures must be completely modified to achieve the intended changes.

4.6.3 Duration

The time needed to accomplish the change depends upon the scope and depth of the intended change (Allan, 2008). Short-duration changes require the utilization of much-needed resources rapidly. Furthermore, the skill base may not be adequate to accomplish the change. The level of resistance among co-workers is highest with short-duration changes. They disrupt the daily activities of the operation that cannot be stopped for the change to take place. Short-duration changes are rapid and take only days or weeks. A new computer program to monitor patient medication records must be introduced rapidly in order to avoid disruption to dispensing in the pharmacy.

On the other hand, intermediate-duration changes require months to accomplish the goals. Upgrading dispensers to obtain recognized qualifications requires months of hard work.

Long-term changes have a higher risk of not achieving the goals because of the complexity of the changes and the need to tie up resources for long periods. Changes in culture require many years to accomplish the intended change objectives.

4.7 Methods of Achieving Changes

There are four methods for achieving changes: (1) structural, (2) cost cutting, (3) process, and (4) cultural (Harvard Business

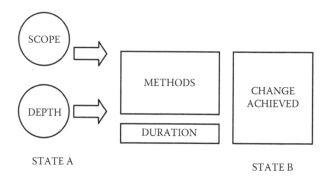

Figure 4.1   Interrelationship among change components.

Essentials, 2003). Figure 4.1 shows the interrelationship among the components of change.

4.7.1 Structural

Structural change refers to the reorganization of the organization structure to maximize efficiency and performance. This may also include mergers, acquisitions, consolidation, and diversifying the operations. In a retail chain, instead of all pharmacies supplying medications to care homes, one or two pharmacies may be allocated to provide this service.

4.7.2 Cost Cutting

When cost-cutting changes are implemented, nonessential activities are eliminated. Layoffs usually occur. Rota may be rearranged to reduce overtime. Pharmacists may be pressured by the management to reduce waiting times.

4.7.3 Process

All business operations are reviewed with a view to reduce costs, improve efficiency and reliability, and achieve faster operations. Standard operating procedures (SOPs) may be reviewed to improve all dispensary activities. Computer systems may be upgraded to improve efficiency.

4.7.4 Cultural

These changes affect the human aspect of the organization and activities between the management and the employees. It involves a shift from an autocratic style of management to a participative style of management. This is the most difficult change to achieve. Pharmacists and dispensers may be involved in the decision-making process with improved communication.

4.8 Resistance to Change

It is a common myth that people resist change. People do not resist change. People resist being changed. Generally, people feel comfortable in their jobs, relationships with colleagues, and expertise. Even when they are dissatisfied with their jobs, they are threatened by changes that affect them. There are seven possible sources of resistance to change (Longest, 1984).

4.8.1 Insecurity and Fear

Changes disturb the comfort zone and cause uncertainty and inconvenience for those affected by the change. These feelings of insecurity lead to a fear of the new and unknown. It is particularly so when the change is imposed by the top management. Individuals doubt whether their competence and skills can cope with the changes.

4.8.2 Social Issues

Changes alter the interrelationships among the co-workers. An individual may have to work with new employees; a close co-worker may be moved to another location or given a promotion. People who support the change management program are closer to the management than others, causing a rift among the co-workers. Their position or the status symbol is threatened.

4.8.3 Economic Issues

Changes that involve technological advances cause disruption by being able to achieve more work faster with fewer people. The jobs of individuals are threatened. Job losses and reduced earnings disrupt the family environment.

4.8.4 Stability

People who work in an organization that has a stable history will themselves feel stable in their jobs. Even minor changes may seem disruptive and radical.

4.8.5 Impact on Business Units of the Organization

Most changes have an impact on other parts of the organization. Central IT (information technology) department employees may have doubts about their position when technicians are given skills and training to resolve computer software issues.

4.8.6 Inconvenience

Changes, however minor, cause inconvenience, and extra effort is needed to make adjustments. The status quo is threatened because individuals have to learn new skills and discard old habits.

4.8.7 Unions

Wherever there are labor unions, the representatives oppose changes suggested by the management even though the change may bring benefits to the organization.

4.9 Overcoming Resistance to Change

There will always be some resistance to any change that
affects the work of individuals. Before the change takes effect,
it is necessary to overcome resistance. Here are a few tips
(Huczynski and Buchanan, 1991):

Management issues:
- Encourage ownership by those affected by the change.
- Demonstrate total commitment to the project from
  top management.
- Involve those affected by the change in decision making.
- Demonstrate empathy to those who oppose the
  change and dispel their fears.
- Clarify all aspects of the change to prevent misinter-
  pretation and misunderstanding.
- Promote trust and confidence in the relationships
  among individuals.
- Have a flexible approach to the change process and be
  prepared to make amends as and when necessary.

Issues relating to the change:
- Change should be perceived as reducing the current
  problems.
- Change should not bring about a departure from cur-
  rently held values and ideals.
- Change should pose new challenges to the employees.
- Change should have the support of all individuals at
  all levels.

People issues:
- Job security and employees' autonomy should not be
  threatened by the intended change.

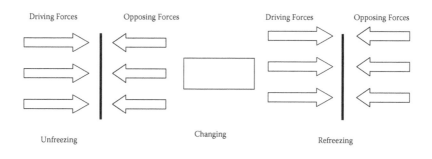

Figure 4.2   Lewin's model of change process.

4.10 Lewin's Change Process Model

A number of models have been proposed to explain the process of change. These models consider the reasons for change, the steps necessary to bring about change, and the manager's input during the change.

A much-quoted model of the change process is Kurt Lewin's three-stage model (Figure 4.2) (Williams et al., 2002). The model has three phases: (1) unfreezing phase, (2) changing phase, and (3) refreezing phase.

During the unfreezing phase, a need for change is identified. This is followed by the changing phase, during which the driving forces are strengthened and resistance forces are weakened. The organization then settles into a new equilibrium during the refreezing phase. Although there are some drawbacks, Lewin's model is useful to understand how changes occur.

4.11 Managing Change

4.11.1 Longest's Plan

There are numerous approaches to manage a change effectively. Longest (1984) proposed the following six-step plan to make a change:

1. Recognize the need to change.
2. Identify the problem and define intended outcomes.
3. Develop alternative methods of achieving the change by involving those who are affected by the change.
4. Select the best strategy to make the change happen.
5. Implement the change. Ensure that employees have a clear vision of the change and outcome. Involve the individuals in the implementation process with minimum disruption. Provide guidance and support to overcome resistance to change and fear.
6. Evaluate the outcome: Initiate changes, if necessary, following feedback from those affected by the change.

4.11.2 Kotter's Eight-Step Plan

Kotter (1996) proposed an eight-step plan compatible with the Lewin model of change process.

Unfreezing steps:
1. Eliminate complacency.
2. Form a guiding coalition.
3. Create a clear vision for change.
4. Communicate the vision to all those employees affected by the change.

Changing steps:
5. Empower employees to implement the change.
6. Establish short-term goals.
7. Encourage additional change.

Refreezing step:
8. Consolidate the changes.

4.11.3 Pettinger's Four-Step Plan

Pettinger (2004) describes four phases to achieve a change:

Phase 1: Exploration. The exploration phase involves the recognition of the current state and identifying the desired change. The required change is explained and communicated to those affected by the change. At this stage it may be necessary to engage external sources to manage the change.

Phase 2: Planning. Necessary data and information are collected and evaluated. Priorities are identified and resistance overcome. It is necessary to gain support and approval from the affected individuals. Develop an action plan and goals.

Phase 3: Implementation. Implement the plan and demonstrate early gains. Evaluate the outcome and encourage feedback from those affected by the change. Make adjustments to the action plan, if necessary.

Phase 4: Integration. The new change is integrated into the current systems and methods. Enhance skills and provide the necessary training. Establish a new reward system to promote a successful change.

4.11.4 Newton's Nine-Step Plan

A more comprehensive plan has been suggested by Newton (2007). It involves nine steps, from identifying the need to preparation for future changes.

1. Establish the basics. A qualitative analysis of the status quo is carried out, and the sources of changes, changes required and challenges, and impact on the people are explored. Different approaches to the change are considered.

2. Establish objectives and targets. This step requires triggers to be identified and objectives to be defined. Output measures and targets are identified. It is necessary to understand

the gap between the current state and the intended change. A method of overcoming resistance to change is developed.

3. Build the change team. A change agent is appointed, and he or she has to build a core team to implement and manage the team. In a community pharmacy, the team members may come from the healthcare team or the pharmacy team in the dispensary. The change agent has to assess the support and identify those who have reservations about the change.

4. Plan the change. During the planning stage, an action plan is developed, and roadblocks are identified and resolved by the core team. The plan includes the task schedule, resources required, the cost of the change, quick wins, and the benefits to the team. Approval is gained by top management.

5. Assess the impact of change. The team members and the activities affected by the intended change are identified. All those affected by the change must have a clear idea of the response to change. If necessary, the plan is adjusted and enhanced.

6. Implement the change plan. The action plan is followed to ensure that all individuals are performing the scheduled tasks as described. All issues that arise during the implementation phase are resolved. When the change has been successfully accomplished, the achievements are celebrated.

7. Consolidate the change. Following the implantation of the change plan, individuals have to adapt to the changes. The manager has to provide support to the staff during this period. Mistakes that have been made in planning or implementation are quickly addressed.

8. Encourage communication.

9. Prepare for the next change.

4.11.5 Change Management Models in Health System Pharmacy Practice in the United States

Since 1985, health system pharmacy practice in the United States has been focusing on clinical practice. During the same period, considerable progress has been made in drug distribution and control programs, modernizing information systems, and training of pharmacy technicians. However, these changes have not been applied consistently, thereby leading to a variety of practice models.

The progress in the past 25 years has been process driven rather than outcome driven. The changes were based on the incremental development of new services or programs that did not focus on departmental goals. The American Society of Health-System Pharmacists (ASHP) 2015 Health System Pharmacy Initiative established a clear vision based on outcomes of medication use in patients. Several change models have been proposed to implement organizational change. The models applicable to the pharmacy environment are as follows (Ray and Breland, 2011):

1. Kotter's eight-step model
2. Sutevski model
3. The Institute of Healthcare Improvement specific improvement acceleration model
4. Denver (Colorado) Health and Hospital Authority toolkit for redesign and healthcare model
5. U.S. Health Resources and Service Administration Patient Safety and Clinical Pharmacy Services Collaborative change package

Details of the Kotter's model are presented in Section 4.11.2. The descriptions of other models are shown in Table 4.1.

In the 1990s, Montana Wines Limited, the largest winery in New Zealand, embarked on a major challenge of developing and implementing an effective quality management

Table 4.1 U.S. Health System Pharmacy Practice Models

Sutevski Model	*IHI Model*	*DHHA Model*	*PSPC Change Package*
Decide on what and when to change	Appoint a project team	Establish the readiness for major redesign	Commitment to develop organizational relationships that promote safe medication use systems and optimize health outcomes
Create a plan for implementation	Establish aims for change	Establish the structure for change	Measure improvements
Identify factors that can cause resistance	Establish measures to monitor	Collect external data related to the redesign	Build an integrated healthcare system across healthcare providers and settings that result in safe and optimal health outcomes
Minimize the impact of the factors on the change process	Select changes that can lead to improvement	Gather internal data	Develop and implement safe medication practices

(continued)

Table 4.1 (continued)   U.S. Health System Pharmacy Practice Models

Sutevski Model	IHI Model	DHHA Model	PSPC Change Package
Implement the change process	Trial changes	Select appropriate tools to implement redesign	Establish a patient-focused medication use system
Celebrate achievements	Review, if necessary, and implement changes		
Monitor results			
Commence the process again			
Note: Adopts PDSA to make improvements	Note: Intended to be used along with other change programs	Note: Pharmacy department should take the initiative to develop its own plan for change that would result in cost savings and process improvement	Notes: Change package describes the details, and the package incorporates most elements of other change management models

Note: IHI, Institute of Healthcare Improvement specific improvement acceleration model; DHHA, Denver (Colorado) Health and Hospital Authority tool kit for redesign in healthcare; PSPC, U.S. Health Resources and Services Administration Patient Safety and Clinical Pharmacy Services Collaborative change package; PDSA, plan-do-study-act.

system (QMS). The task was led by the corporate quality assurance manager. During the development phase, major obstacles had to be overcome. The first challenge was a culture change, which required the staff to think in terms of quality in all their operations. Series of in-house training sessions were conducted to develop the concepts of quality among all the staff, from senior executives to floor staff. This was followed by empowerment, enabling the workers to check their own work and make decisions. The engineering team was busy developing engineering manuals and preventive maintenance programs. Operations manuals were prepared and updated with input from the staff. At the end of the program, the workers were proud of their achievements, and the supervisor said, "Before the program we were merely workers. But now we feel we are part of the company." A gap analysis was carried out to fulfill the requirements of the QMS, and eventually in 1993, Montana Wines Limited became the first winery in Australasia to get its QMS certified to the ISO 9000 standard.

The success of the program was due to a major culture change achieved through commitment, dedication, and involvement of all the staff.

4.11.6 *Proposed Structure for Change Management*

The elements in these models can be integrated to form a practical approach to the management of change. The suggested approach is shown in Table 4.2.

4.12 The Competencies of a Change Agent

The change agent's role is to plan and implement the change successfully. They are leaders with a broad vision

Table 4.2 Change Management Plan

Phases of Change	Activity
Exploration	• Identify the need to change • Identify the problem through a problem-solving exercise • Define intended outcome • Develop options for achieving the change and select the best option
Planning	• Identify the triggers • Identify those affected by the change • Establish standards to measure the current state and the outcome • Prepare a plan for implementation—establish the task schedule, resources required, cost of the change, quick wins, and benefits to the team
Implementation phase 1: Unfreezing (Lewin's model)	• Establish a sense of urgency • Form a guiding coalition • Establish a clear vision of the change and the direction • Communicate the vision to those affected by the change
Implementation phase 2: Changing (Lewin's model)	• Empower employees to implement the plan • Encourage new ideas and make changes as necessary • Identify roadblocks and remove them • Gain top management support and commitment • Establish short-term goals • Avoid celebrating success too early • Consolidate the change and improvements into current methods, policies, and procedures
Implementation phase 3: Refreezing (Lewin's model)	• Integrate the change into the culture of the organization to become a part of "the way we do things here"

capable of delivering the outcome in all situations.* Fifteen competencies are listed under five clusters: (1) objectives, (2) roles, (3) communication, (4) negotiation, and (5) managing. An effective change manager should utilize these competencies appropriately.

The objectives cluster includes sensitivity to personnel and market conditions, ability to identify and specify the goals clearly, and flexibility to respond to changes when necessary. The roles cluster competencies are team building ability, networking skills, and ability to work effectively in an uncertain environment. Communication skills, interpersonal skills, personal passion in expressing plans and ideas, and ability to motivate others are competencies in the communication cluster. Under the negotiation cluster are the change agent's ability to sell the plans to others, negotiate for resources, and resolution of conflicts. The managing cluster includes political awareness, ability to influence others, and taking a broader view of the priorities.

4.13 Why Change Management Fails

Case studies of organizations that have been successful in implementing changes show that changes take a considerable amount of time, and bypassing crucial steps creates a perception of illusion and speed with disappointing results. Critical mistakes in any of the phases will retard the progress already made. Kotter (1995), who has monitored more than 100 companies, describes eight reasons for the failure of change management:

---

* D.A. Buchanan and D. Buddy, *The Expertise of the Change Agent: Public Performance and Backstage Activity* (New York: Prentice Hall International, 1992), in A. Williams, S. Woodward, and P. Dobson, *Managing Change Successfully* (London: Thomson Learning, 2002), p. 280.

1. No sense of urgency. Organizations do not realize the urgency to address the competitive situation, market position, and technological advances. These organizations find it difficult to escape from the comfort zone and are lulled into a false sense of security.

2. Not establishing a guiding coalition. The head of the organization or the business unit should demonstrate total commitment to the change process. The guiding coalition of small companies may include 3 to 5 members, whereas in larger companies 20 to 50 members may form the coalition. Members of the coalition should include a senior manager. A board member, customer representative, or even a union leader may also be included. Without an effective guiding coalition, the change process will not progress.

3. Lack of vision. Without a clear vision, the efforts of the change process will lead to confusion and incompatibilities, and will progress in the wrong direction. A clear vision communicates the change to customers, stakeholders, and employees. It will demonstrate the direction of change.

4. Lack of communication. Communication is an essential part of the change process. Unless the vision is clearly communicated to the staff, they do not perceive the benefits of the change. Employees are prepared to make sacrifices when they realize the benefits of the proposed change.

5. Not removing the obstacles. The progress of a change process is never smooth. The vision may be clear, and it may have been clearly communicated, but obstacles may appear. There may be people who are not supportive or are dissatisfied with the organization structure itself or the impact of the change on performance appraisal. The obstacles should be identified and removed at early stages in order to empower people and maintain credibility of the outcome.

6. Not creating short-term wins. The benefits of the change will be realized after a considerable length of time. Most

people would like to see benefits within one or two years. Unless there are short-term gains, the support and efforts diminish over time. A successful change management plan includes yearly goals and offers of rewards for the efforts.

7. Celebrating success too soon. After a few years of effort, the managers are tempted to celebrate victory over the benefits gained. Stability of the change cannot be achieved unless the change itself is integrated into the culture of the organization. Initiators of the change, in their enthusiasm, celebrate victory to gain support from the resistors. The resistors perceive the victory as an end to the change process already in progress. The change thus comes to a halt.

8. Not integrating the change into the corporate culture. Change is stabilized only when it is integrated into "the way we do things here." Unless new behavior is compatible with the norms and values, the change degrades as soon as the pressure for change is removed.

4.14 Revisiting the Scenario

Maureen's management of changes is obviously flawed. The proposed changes have not been discussed with the responsible pharmacist or the dispensers, who could make a valuable contribution to the proposed changes. Arbitrary targets have been set without consultation. Her threatening behavior has made the situation worse. A recommended plan to reduce waiting times is shown in Table 4.3.

Changes made without the participation of those affected by the change are ineffective and temporary. If the targets are unrealistic, a state of confusion will prevail in the workplace.

Table 4.3 Change Management Plan for Reducing the Waiting Time for Dispensing Prescriptions

Activity	Response
Need to change	Patient satisfaction, reduce backlog of unfilled prescriptions, increase turnover of prescriptions
Expected problems	See Chapter 20 (interruptions, labeling errors leading to relabeling, near misses causing refilling of the prescription, etc.)
Intended outcome	Reduce waiting time to 8 minutes
Options	Generate options for resolving each of the problems through participation of all members
Triggers	Complaints from patients, backlog of unfilled prescriptions, need to increase the turnover of prescriptions to remain competitive, need to increase income, lack of time for activities such as counseling
Those affected by the change	Pharmacists, dispensers and healthcare assistants, patients
Establish standards	Define methods to measure waiting times
Prepare a plan	Describe the tasks, roles, responsibilities, and intended outcome
Urgency	Emphasize the need for urgency
Guiding coalition	Pharmacists, dispensers, and pharmacy manager
Vision	Develop a clear vision
Communicate	Communicate the vision through all available means, clarify doubts
Empower employees	Manager (change agent) encourages participation of all members of the coalition and decision making
New ideas	Encourage members to propose new ideas

(continued)

Table 4.3 (continued)   Change Management Plan for Reducing the Waiting Time for Dispensing Prescriptions

Activity	*Response*
Identify roadblocks	Identify obstacles to the change and remove them
Management support	Total commitment from the pharmacy manager ("walk the talk")
Short-term goals	Monitor daily waiting time to measure progress
Avoid early celebration	Wait until the goals are achieved
Consolidate	Update current procedures, policies, and goals
Integrate the changes	Make the new procedure a part of the way prescriptions are dispensed

References

Allan, L. (2008). *Managing change in the workplace: A practical guide*. Victoria, Australia: Business Performance Pty.

Anderson, L.A., and Anderson, D. (2009). *Awake at the wheel: Moving beyond change management to conscious change leadership*. Retrieved January 14, 2010, from http://www.beingfirst.com/resources/pdf/AR_PDF_AwakeAtTheWheel_v2_091123.pdf

Connelly, M. (2008). *Definition of change management*. Change-Management-Coach.com. Retrieved January 23, 2013. From http: //www.change-management-coach.com/definition-of-change-management.html

Costello, S.J. (1994). *Managing change in the workplace*. New York: McGraw-Hill.

Haberberg, A., and Rieple, A. (2008). *Strategic management: Theory and application*. Oxford: Oxford University Press.

Harrington, N., and Terry, C.L. (2009). *LPN to RN transitions: Achieving success in your role* (3rd ed.). Philadelphia: Lippincott Williams and Wilkins.

Harvard Business Essentials. (2003). *Managing change and transition*. Boston: Harvard Business School Publishing.

Huczynski, A., and Buchanan, D. (1991). *Organizational behaviour* (2nd ed.). Hertfordshire, England: Prentice Hall.

Kotter, J.P. (1995, March–April). Leading change: Why transformation efforts fail. *Harvard Business Review*, 73(2), 59–67.

Kotter, J.P. (1996). *Leading change*. Boston: Harvard Business School Press.

Longest, B. (1984). *Management practices for the health professional* (3rd ed.). Reston, VA: Reston Publishing.

Newton, R. (2007). *Managing change step by step: All you need to build a plan and make it happen*. Halow: Pearson Education.

Pettinger, R. (2004). *Contemporary strategic management*. Basingstoke, England: Palgrave Macmillan.

Ray, M.D., and Breland, B.D. (2011). Methods of fostering change in the practice model at the pharmacy department level. *American Journal of Health-System Pharmacy*, 68, 1138–1145.

Royal Pharmaceutical Society of Great Britain. (2008). Meetings: Pharmacists are seeing themselves as their own worst enemy when it comes to embracing change. *Pharmaceutical Journal*, 280, 173.

Williams, A., Woodward, S., and Dobson, P. (2002). *Managing change successfully*. London: Thomson Learning.

Chapter 5

Managing Risk

The man who does things makes many mistakes,
but he never makes the biggest mistake of all—
doing nothing.

—Benjamin Franklin

5.1 Scenario

Ann has been the most senior technician in the community
pharmacy. There are two other technicians in the pharmacy.
Ann informed Dianne of her intention to undergo a major
operation that required her to be away for about eight weeks.
Leave has already been granted to another technician. The
manager did not arrange for cover. Steve, the pharmacist, was
concerned about the staff shortage, and he raised his concerns
with Dianne. She was not willing to arrange cover, saying,
"There is no money in the budget." Steve, being the responsible pharmacist, raised the issue with the area manager, who
promised to look into it. During this period, Steve was not
able to complete the prescriptions by the end of the day. This
created a backlog and patients had to wait for long periods

to collect their medications. Repeat prescriptions from the surgeries could not be filled on time. Patients who visited the pharmacy were frustrated and complained to the manager. A large number of patients recalled the prescriptions and visited nearby pharmacies. Cover was arranged when Dianne realized that the pharmacy was losing business, but it was too late. The patients who left never returned.

5.2 Introduction

In our day-to-day work, we are challenged by decisions that involve risks. Financial risk in the banking sector is well known. In terms of investments, the higher the gain, the greater is the risk. Risks of injury are associated with many sports. In the pharmacy profession, pharmacists are well aware of the risks associated with their work in dispensing, counseling, checking, etc. Dispensing errors can have fatal consequences. Incorrect advice to patients carries a risk of harm to the patients. Therefore, systems and procedures must be in place to manage effectively the risks associated with the work.

5.3 Definitions

NASA, in its independent verification and validation program, under *Guidelines for Risk Management* (NASA, 2009), defines the terms associated with risk management as follows:

Risk: Risk is the measure of the potential inability to achieve an expected outcome within defined parameters of safety, cost, schedule, and technical characteristics. It has two components: the likelihood of occurrence and the consequence of failure (for example, wrong advice given to a patient may have serious consequences).

Risk acceptance: A risk can be accepted when the benefit outweighs the risk that may occur, which cannot be avoided or reasonably mitigated with further action. A General Practitioner (GP) may weigh the benefits of a treatment against the possible adverse effects.

Risk analysis: Risk analysis is the process of defining and analyzing the extent, likelihood, and occurrence of a risk.

Risk attributes: Risk attributes defined in the risk management plan are the probability, impact, and time frame within which the risk can be avoided or mitigated. These attributes provide useful information to make informed decisions.

Risk classification: Risk classification is the process of categorizing risks according to (1) the severity and their consequences and (2) shared characteristics or relationships.

Risk identification: Risk identification is the process of examining and documenting the risks of each element of a process or a project that may impact on the activities in the pharmacy or workplace.

Risk management: Risk management is an approach to prevent or mitigate a potential risk through identification, analysis, mitigation, planning, and tracking of root causes and their consequences.

Risk management planning: Risk management planning is the process of developing and documenting an organized, comprehensive, and interactive strategy for analyzing the root causes of potential risks, developing plans to prevent or mitigate risks, performing continuous risk assessment, and allocating resources.

5.4 Type of Risks

Pharmacists employed in community pharmacy practice face two types of risks: (1) professional risk and (2) business risk (Nutan, 2006). Professional risks refer to dispensing errors, wrong advice, failure to detect prescribing errors, etc. On the other hand, business risks affect business activities and the profit. Staff shortages may force the dispensing activities to be stopped until the problems are resolved. Opening another pharmacy in the nearby vicinity carries the risk of losing patients to the new pharmacy.

5.4.1 How Do Mistakes Happen?

Risks occur because of individual failure or system failure. Table 5.1 shows how these can occur (CPPE, 2005; Dornan, n.d.).

Rule-based mistakes are due to the failure to apply the rules relating to pharmacy activities, for example, failure to follow dispensing and checking procedures, report incidents, determine expiry dates, remove outdated products, or check whether a patient is allergic to the medication. They can also happen when the wrong rule is applied, the correct rule is misapplied, or in situations for which there are no rules. Knowledge-based mistakes occur because of lack of knowledge (knowledge of drug interactions), lack of skills (not competent to check blood pressure), lack of sufficient knowledge for counseling, etc.

5.5 Continuous Risk Management Process

Continuous risk management (CRM) is a structured management approach consisting of processes, methods, and tools for managing risks in the environment (Dezfuli, 2010; Siu, 2004). It is a disciplined proactive program that includes

- A continuous assessment of what could go wrong by determining the current performance against the expected performance
- Estimating the likelihood and consequence of identified risk through analysis

Table 5.1 Sources of Unintended Errors

	Individual Failure		System Failure
		Mistakes	
Slips and Lapses	*Rule Based*	*Knowledge Based*	*System Failure*
Forgetfulness Inattention Interruptions Burnout Depression Stress Communication issues	Wrong rule is chosen, the rule is misapplied, or there are no rules	A situation for which no solution exists, lack of knowledge of the situation, misinterpretation of the problem	Poor or ineffective working conditions Unclear procedures and policies Poor IT facilities Failure of equipment

- Planning for risk disposal and handling the risk, developing mitigation plans, and establishing monitoring requirements
- Monitoring the effectiveness of the implemented strategies
- Controlling risk by evaluating monitored data to verify the effectiveness of mitigation plans

The five steps in the CRM process are shown in Figure 5.1.

Step 1: Identify risks. Identify the risks and state them in terms of conditions and consequences, including the context: what, where, when, how, and why.

Step 2: Analyze the risks. Evaluate the risk on the basis probability impact and severity. Determine the time frame within which actions need to be taken. Classify and group similar risks and prioritize for action.

Step 3: Plan. Determine the approach (research, accept, mitigate, or monitor) to deal with the risk. Prepare a detail plan that includes responsibilities, tasks, goals, time frame, and budget estimates. Execute the plan.

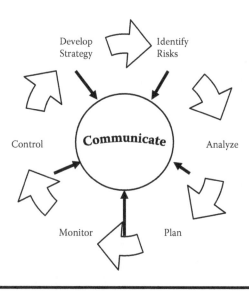

Figure 5.1   Continuous risk management process.

Step 4: Monitor. Track the activities and organize risk data, reports, and results. Verify and validate mitigation action.

Step 5: Control. Analyze the data to determine the effectiveness of the plan. Review, if necessary, to replan or close the risk. Execute the control plan.

Communication is an essential part of the CRM program, and essential risk status must be communicated to the entire team. A system for determining and tracking of risk decisions has to be implemented.

5.5.1 Identification of Risks

Several tools can be used to identify risk in the pharmacy. Team effort produces better results than individual efforts. Deficiencies in the following 10 key system elements can lead to risks of making mistakes (Hahn, 2007):

1. Patient information
2. Drug information
3. Dispensing: labeling, application of the label, bagging, and handing over to the customer
4. Communication issues
5. Storage of drugs, verification of expiry dates, and removing outdated drugs from the shelf
6. Acquisition of appliances and monitoring their use
7. Working environment
8. Staff training and skills
9. Patient education
10. Risk management

Inadequate knowledge of the following can also lead to mistakes:

■ Contraindications
■ Drug interactions

■ Drug allergies
■ Drug dosages
■ Drugs that have a narrow therapeutic range
■ Patient knowledge

Several approaches can be used to identify risks in the workplace (NASA, 2009; Tague, 2005), such as

■ Brainstorming
■ Tests and verification
■ Pause-and-learn sessions
■ Previous analysis of risks
■ Historical data
■ Lessons learned
■ Checklists
■ Informal notifications

5.5.1.1 Failure Modes and Effects Analysis (FMEA)

FMEA (Tague, 2005) is a stepwise approach for identifying all possible ways and modes of causing errors and defects and studying the consequences of failure. The risks are prioritized according to the severity, frequency of occurrence, and ease of detection.

5.5.1.2 Fault Tree Analysis (FTA)

According to this technique, the undesired effect is taken as the root of a logic tree (Tague, 2005). Various combinations of hardware and software and human errors that could cause this effect are added to the logic tree as a series of logic expressions. When real numbers are assigned to the failures, future failure probability can be calculated.

5.5.1.3 Probability Risk Assessment (PRA)

PRA is a technique that has been used to evaluate the safety of the designs of high-hazard, low-risk systems in nuclear industry and chemical processing plants. It is now being used in the medical field to improve patient safety. The process involves the identification of the outcome to be prevented, determining the initiating events, and assessing the frequencies of occurrence. The combinations of events that could cause failure are then identified. Analysis of data provides the probabilities of risks (Wreathall and Nemeth, 2004).

5.5.1.4 Risk Statement

When the risks are identified, a risk statement should be prepared for each risk. The statement should be brief, clear, and simple. It should include one event and one or more consequences, and a context statement that should identify what, when, where, and how. Some examples of risk statements are given below.

5.5.1.4.1 Risks due to Interruptions

Taking telephone calls while picking medicines from the shelf by the staff in the dispensary is likely to cause interruptions, and there is a risk that the staff will pick (1) the wrong medicine, (2) the correct medicine but the wrong strength, or (3) the wrong brand of medicine.

5.5.1.4.2 Risks due to Rule-Based Mistakes

Rule misapplied: Instructing pharmacists to meet targets for medicine use reviews (MURs) is likely to put pressure on pharmacists, and there is a risk that they will perform MURs on patients who will not benefit from them (for example, a patient who has been taking 25 and 50 µg levothyroxine once daily for over eight years).

Rule not applied: When there is a shortage of staff at the counter, it is likely to put pressure on the staff to hand over medicines without checking the full name and address, and there is a risk that the medicine is handed over to the wrong patient.

No rule: In the absence of a proper place to stack crates of medicines received from the warehouse, it is likely that these crates are stacked obstructing the passage of staff in the dispensary, and there is a risk that the staff will suffer some injury.

5.5.1.4.3 Risks due to Knowledge-Based Mistakes

Staff who do not have knowledge of allergy due to penicillin are likely to dispense a prescription for a penicillin, and there is a risk that the patient who is known to be allergic to this drug will be given amoxicillin.

5.5.1.4.4 Risks due to System Failure

Adverse weather conditions such as snow or computer failure are likely to cause a breakdown of the ordering system of medicines from the warehouse, and there is a risk that there will be a shortage of some medicines.

5.5.2 Risk Analysis

Pharmacists are responsible for a range of activities in the pharmacy, from supply of medicines to patient counseling. Risks are involved in both these activities as well as with medicines themselves. Risk analysis is a complex process of risk assessment that includes an assessment of the ability to prevent or mitigate the risks, their likelihood of occurrence, and the potential impact on personnel and the organization (Mooney, 2010). The effectiveness of existing controls determines the likelihood of the occurrence of the risk and is based on previous experience of the risk, knowledge, and the expertise of the team. A scoring system is ideal for assessing the likelihood and impact (consequence) of a risk (National Patient Safety Agency (NPSA), 2008; Mooney, 2010). The higher the degree of controls in place to manage risks, the lower the likelihood score (Table 5.2). The impact on personnel, property, and regulations is scored on a scale of 1 to 5, with 5 being the critical impact (Table 5.3).

Each identified risk is scored on the basis of likelihood and impact. The risk rating R = Likelihood score × Consequence score. The significance of the risk rating is evaluated using the risk assessment matrix in Table 5.4. The risk rating (low, moderate, high, or extreme) determines the level in the business unit responsible for the action plan and its implementation. For example, risks with a "low" risk rating require the attention of a member of the pharmacy team. Those risks classified as "moderate" are resolved by the team. Action plans for "high" risk events are determined by the manager of the unit. Information relating to risks rated as "extreme" must be escalated to the senior management team for necessary action and follow-up.

Care must be taken in the application of the scoring system. The likelihood of occurrence of a risk can be scored on the basis of the frequency or probability of happening. For example, the likelihood of handing over the medication to the wrong patient due to staff under pressure cannot be scored on the basis of probability (i.e., on a weekly or monthly basis). It is more meaningful to allocate a score of 3 or 4 on the basis of frequency. Similarly, appropriate criteria must be selected to assess the impact score. In the example cited above, personal privacy infringement or violation of procedures is more consistent with the mistake. The possibility of a patient using the medication must be treated as a separate risk. Although past incidents or previous experiences are good indicators, they should be applied with caution.

Table 5.2 Likelihood of Risk (Broad Descriptors of Frequency)

Likelihood Score	1	2	3	4	5
Descriptor	Rare	Unlikely	Possible	Likely	Almost Certain
Frequency (how often might it/does it happen)	This will probably never happen/recur	Do not expect it to happen/recur, but it is possible it may do so	Might happen or recur occasionally	Will probably happen/recur, but it is not a persisting issue	Will undoubtedly happen/recur, possibly frequently

Likelihood of Risk (Time Frame Descriptors of Frequency)

	1	2	3	4	5
Frequency	Not expected to occur for years	Expected to occur at least annually	Expected to occur at least monthly	Expected to occur at least weekly	Expected to occur at least daily

Likelihood Scores (Probability Descriptors)

	1	2	3	4	5
Probability (will happen or not?)	<0.1%	0.1–1.0%	1–10%	10–50%	>50%

Source: Reproduced with permission from National Patient Safety Agency (NPSA), 2008. Copyright © National Patient Safety Agency.

Table 5.3 Consequence of Risk

| Domains | Consequence Score (Severity Levels) and Examples of Descriptors | | | | |
	1 *Negligible*	*2* *Minor*	*3* *Moderate*	*4* *Major*	*5* *Catastrophic*
Impact on the safety of patients, staff, or public (physical/ psychological harm)	Minimal injury requiring no/ minimal intervention or treatment No time off work	Minor injury or illness, requiring minor intervention Requiring time off work for <3 days Increase in length of hospital stay by 1–3 days	Moderate injury requiring professional intervention Requiring time off work for 4–14 days Increase in length of hospital stay by 4–15 days RIDDOR[a]/agency reportable incident An event that impacts a small number of patients	Major injury leading to long-term incapacity/ disability Requiring time off work for >14 days Increase in length of hospital stay by >15 days Mismanagement of patient care with long-term effects	Incident leading to death Multiple permanent injuries or irreversible health effects An event that impacts a large number of patients

(continued)

Table 5.3 Consequence of Risk (continued)

	Consequence Score (Severity Levels) and Examples of Descriptors				
	1	*2*	*3*	*4*	*5*
Domains	*Negligible*	*Minor*	*Moderate*	*Major*	*Catastrophic*
Quality/ complaints/ audit	Peripheral element of treatment or service suboptimal Informal complaint/inquiry	Overall treatment or service suboptimal Formal complaint (stage 1) Local resolution Single failure to meet internal standards Minor implications for patient safety if unresolved	Treatment or service has significantly reduced effectiveness Formal (stage 2) complaint Local resolution (with potential to go to independent review) Repeated failure to meet internal standards	Noncompliance with national standards with significant risk to patients if unresolved Multiple complaints/ independent review Low performance rating Critical report	Totally unacceptable level or quality of treatment/service Gross failure of patient safety if findings not acted on Inquest/ ombudsman inquiry Gross failure to meet national standards

(continued)

Table 5.3 Consequence of Risk (continued)

Domains	Consequence Score (Severity Levels) and Examples of Descriptors				
	1	*2*	*3*	*4*	*5*
	Negligible	*Minor*	*Moderate*	*Major*	*Catastrophic*
		Reduced performance rating if unresolved	Major patient safety implications if findings are not acted on		
Human resources/ organizational development/ staffing/ competence	Short-term low staffing level that temporarily reduces service quality (<1 day)	Low staffing level that reduces the service quality	Late delivery of key objective/ service due to lack of staff	Uncertain delivery of key objective/service due to lack of staff	Nondelivery of key objective/ service due to lack of staff
			Unsafe staffing level or competence (>1 day)	Unsafe staffing level or competence (>5 days)	Ongoing unsafe staffing levels or competence
			Low staff morale	Loss of key staff	Loss of several key staff
				Very low staff morale	

(continued)

Table 5.3 Consequence of Risk (continued)

Domains	*Consequence Score (Severity Levels) and Examples of Descriptors*				
	1	*2*	*3*	*4*	*5*
	Negligible	*Minor*	*Moderate*	*Major*	*Catastrophic*
			Poor staff attendance for mandatory/key training	No staff attending mandatory/key training	No staff attending mandatory training/key training on an ongoing basis
Statutory duty/ inspections	No or minimal impact or breach of guidance/ statutory duty	Breach of statutory legislation Reduced performance rating if unresolved	Single breach in statutory duty Challenging external recommendations/ improvement notice	Enforcement action Multiple breaches in statutory duty Improvement notices Low performance rating Critical report	Multiple breaches in statutory duty Prosecution Complete systems change required Zero performance rating Severely critical report

(continued)

Table 5.3 Consequence of Risk (continued)

	Consequence Score (Severity Levels) and Examples of Descriptors				
	1	2	3	4	5
Domains	Negligible	Minor	Moderate	Major	Catastrophic
Adverse publicity/ reputation	Rumors Potential for public concern	Local media coverage—short-term reduction in public confidence Elements of public expectation not being met	Local media coverage—long-term reduction in public confidence	National media coverage with <3 days service well below reasonable public expectation	National media coverage with >3 days service well below reasonable public expectation; MP concerned (questions in the House) Total loss of public confidence

(continued)

Table 5.3   Consequence of Risk (continued)

| Domains | Consequence Score (Severity Levels) and Examples of Descriptors | | | | |
| | *1* | *2* | *3* | *4* | *5* |
	Negligible	*Minor*	*Moderate*	*Major*	*Catastrophic*
Business objectives/ projects	Insignificant cost increase/schedule slippage	<5% over project budget Schedule slippage	5–10% over project budget Schedule slippage	Noncompliance with national 10–25% over project budget Schedule slippage Key objectives not met	Incident leading >25% over project budget Schedule slippage Key objectives not met
Finance including claims	Small loss risk of claim remote	Loss of 0.1–0.25% of budget Claim less than £10,000	Loss of 0.25–0.5% of budget Claim(s) between £10,000 and £100,000	Uncertain delivery of key objective/ loss of 0.5–1.0% of budget Claim(s) between £100,000 and £1 million Purchasers failing to pay on time	Nondelivery of key objective/loss of >1% of budget Failure to meet specification/ slippage Loss of contract/ payment by results Claim(s) >£1 million

(continued)

Table 5.3 Consequence of Risk (continued)

Domains	Consequence Score (Severity Levels) and Examples of Descriptors				
	1 *Negligible*	*2* *Minor*	*3* *Moderate*	*4* *Major*	*5* *Catastrophic*
Service/business interruption environmental impact	Loss/interruption of >1 hour Minimal or no impact on the environment	Loss/interruption of >8 hours Minor impact on environment	Loss/interruption of >1 day Moderate impact on environment	Loss/interruption of >1 week Major impact on environment	Permanent loss of service or facility Catastrophic impact on environment
Impact on the safety of patients, staff, or public (physical/psychological harm)	Minimal injury requiring no/minimal intervention or treatment No time off work	Minor injury or illness requiring minor intervention Requiring time off work for <3 days Increase in length of hospital stay by 1–3 days	Moderate injury requiring professional intervention Requiring time off work for 4–14 days Increase in length of hospital stay by 4–15 days	Major injury leading to long-term incapacity/disability Requiring time off work for >14 days Increase in length of hospital stay by >15 days	Incident leading to death Multiple permanent injuries or irreversible health effects An event that impacts on a large number of patients

(continued)

Table 5.3   Consequence of Risk (continued)

| | Consequence Score (Severity Levels) and Examples of Descriptors | | | | |
	1	2	3	4	5
Domains	Negligible	Minor	Moderate	Major	Catastrophic
			RIDDOR/agency reportable event	Mismanagement of patient care with long-term effects	
			An event that impacts a small number of patients		
Additional examples	Incorrect medication dispensed but not taken	Wrong drug or dosage administered, with no adverse effects	Wrong drug or dosage administered with potential adverse effects	Wrong drug or dosage administered with adverse effects	Unexpected death
	Incident resulting in a bruise/graze	Physical attack such as pushing, shoving, or pinching, causing minor injury	Physical attack causing moderate injury	Physical attack resulting in serious injury	Suicide of a patient known to the service in the past 12 months
	Delay in routine transport for patient		Self-harm requiring medical attention	Grade 4 pressure ulcer	Homicide committed by a mental health patient
				Long-term HCAI	

(continued)

Table 5.3   Consequence of Risk (continued)

	Consequence Score (Severity Levels) and Examples of Descriptors				
	1	2	3	4	5
Domains	*Negligible*	*Minor*	*Moderate*	*Major*	*Catastrophic*
		Self-harm resulting in minor injuries	Grade 2/3 pressure ulcer	Retained instruments/ material after surgery requiring further intervention	Large-scale cervical screening errors
		Grade 1 pressure ulcer	Healthcare-acquired infection (HCAI)		Removal of wrong body part leading to death or permanent incapacity
		Laceration, sprain, anxiety requiring occupational health counseling (no time off work required)	Incorrect or inadequate information/ communication on transfer of care	Hemolytic transfusion reaction	Incident leading to paralysis
			Vehicle carrying patient involved in a road traffic accident	Slip/fall resulting in injury such as dislocation/ fracture/blow to the head	Incident leading to long-term mental health problem
			Slip/fall resulting in injury such as a sprain	Loss of a limb	Rape/serious sexual assault
				Posttraumatic stress disorder	

(continued)

Table 5.3 Consequence of Risk (continued)

Domains	Consequence Score (Severity Levels) and Examples of Descriptors				
	1	2	3	4	5
	Negligible	Minor	Moderate	Major	Catastrophic
				Failure to follow up and administer vaccine to baby born to a mother with hepatitis B	

[a] Reporting Injuries, Diseases, and Dangerous Occurrences Regulations (RIDDOR)

Source: Reproduced with permission from National Patient Safety Agency (NPSA), 2008. Copyright © National Patient Safety Agency.

Table 5.4   Risk Scoring (Consequence × Likelihood)

	Likelihood				
	1	2	3	4	5
Likelihood Score	*Rare*	*Unlikely*	*Possible*	*Likely*	*Almost Certain*
5 Catastrophic	5	10	15	20	25
4 Major	4	8	12	16	20
3 Moderate	3	6	9	12	15
2 Minor	2	4	6	8	10
1 Negligible	1	2	3	4	5

Source: Reproduced with permission from National Patient Safety Agency (NPSA, 2008). Copyright © National Patient Safety Agency.

Note: For grading risk, the scores obtained from the risk matrix are assigned grades as follows:
1–3: Low risk
4–6: Moderate risk
8–12: High risk
15–25: Extreme risk

5.5.3 Planning

The output of this step is an updated risk index and an action plan. The risks that have been analyzed are prioritized on the basis of severity and impact in areas such as safety, security, and reliability that would obstruct successful implementation. The planning team must be aware of risks that pose the greatest threat to the organization, the staff, and patients' safety. Prioritizing is a continuous process that takes into account the changing circumstances or external influences that can change the established priorities. The risk index (Table 5.5) can be used to track and prioritize risks based on the severity, time frame for action, impact on safety, security, activities, and organization. After the priorities have been established, an action plan must be prepared for each risk specifying whether

Table 5.5 Risk Index

Risk Description	Likelihood Score	Impact Score	Risk Rating Score
Crates of medicines stacked obstructing the passage of staff in the dispensary	Daily occurrence (5)	Minor injury (2)	High (10)
Performing MURs on patients who do not benefit	Will probably happen (4)	Minimum infringement of code of ethics (1)	Moderate (4)
Obstructions on motorways	Recur occasionally (3)	Temporary to some activities (1)	Low (3)
Not removing outdated products	Will probably happen (4)	Significant risk to patient; complaint escalated to local authorities (4)	Extreme (16)
Dispensing errors (see risk statement for details)	Recur occasionally (3)	Gross failure of patient safety (5)	Extreme (15)

Note: Low risk = administrative action, planning, delegating, ordering items, etc.; moderate risk = action within weeks; high risk = action within days; extreme risk = immediate action.

to accept the risk or address the risk by (1) avoiding the risk, (2) transferring the risk, or (3) mitigating or controlling the risk (Health Service Executive, 2008).

Accepting the risk: The organization may opt to accept the risk without taking any action for a variety of reasons:
1. The risk is very low and has no significant impact on the organization, staff, or patients.
2. No control option is available or not within the control of the organization. For example, new legislature may impose risks to some activities.
3. The benefits outweigh the risks. A patient who shows only skin reaction allergy to penicillin may be prescribed a penicillin for a life-threatening illness by the GP after taking precautions to counteract the ill effects of penicillin.

Avoiding the risk: The organization may decide to take any action to control an unacceptable risk by using an alternative methodology in order to implement the same activity, which is less risky.

Transferring the risk: This implies the transfer of the risk to a third party for insurance or indemnity cover. The cost of such a cover depends on the assurance that the organization can give in terms of a claim being made. The insurer would require information regarding the nature of the risk, the controls in place to mitigate the risk, and the claims history so far.

Mitigating the risk: This process reduces the risk to an acceptable level. If the risk cannot be eliminated completely, it is mitigated by substituting the materials or processes or redefining the policies and procedures.

The action plan should specify the following (Table 5.6):

1. Risk description
2. Impact

Table 5.6 Action Plan

Risk Description	Impact	Current Controls	Are Current Controls Adequate?	Action	By Whom	By When	Completion
Crates of medicines stacked, obstructing the passage of staff in the dispensary	Injury	None	No controls	1. Advise staff to be cautious 2. Locate a safe area to stack crates	Manager	Within 1 week	Done on....
Performing MURs on patients who do not benefit	Violating clause 2.2 of the code of conduct, ethics, and performance	None	No controls	Perform MURs on suitable patients only; justify on the basis of the code of conduct	Pharmacist	Next MUR	Done on....

(continued)

Table 5.6 Action Plan (continued)

Risk Description	Impact	Current Controls	Are Current Controls Adequate?	Action	By Whom	By When	Completion
Obstruction on motorways	Temporary disruption of activities	None	No controls	Order sufficient stocks of fast-moving items when adverse weather conditions are expected	Pharmacy technician	Before the expected disruption	Done…
Not removing outdated products from the shelf	Dispensing outdated products	Stock takes	No, stock takes not done regularly	Perform stock takes regularly; remove outdated products immediately	Pharmacy team	Immediately	Done…

3. Current controls in place
4. Effectiveness of current controls
5. Action
6. Person responsible
7. Time frame
8. Completion date

5.5.4 Tracking

The purpose of the tracking step is to monitor the progress of the action plan by collecting and analyzing accurate, timely, and relevant risk information (NASA, 2009; Siu, 2004). It is a proactive approach that enables further action to be taken before a risk becomes a problem. Tracking also enables the team to close the risk, if it has been effectively resolved. Analysis of risk information is useful to determine whether (1) additional risk handling options are necessary, (2) risk handling strategies need updating, or (3) known risks must be reassessed. Risk may change over time, and therefore repeated assessment of risks is necessary to manage the risks effectively.

5.5.5 Control

The final phase of the CRM cycle is control. At this phase the reports are analyzed, decisions are made, and the control decisions are executed (NASA, 2009; Siu, 2004). Control decisions are made by the senior management. During risk control, the following strategies are implemented:

1. Close the risk.
2. Continue as planned.
3. Develop a new or an updated risk mitigation plan.
4. Invoke a contingency plan if the risk has been a problem.

5.6 Communication

Communication within the team and with external authorities is essential for the management of risks in the organization. The team can provide valuable information on potential risks and their resolution. The decisions must be discussed with the team at each stage of the CRM cycle. The escalation to top management is necessary to obtain extra resources for resolving the risk or initiating action with statutory authorities.

Risk management should be an essential part of training for all pharmacy professionals. All activities of the pharmacy are directed toward patient safety. Therefore, by assessing the risks and implementing strategies to deal with risks, they can be managed proactively. Risk assessment is only beneficial if the action plan is effectively implemented, and this phase is the most difficult but most important part.

The NPSA (2004) provides guidelines for patient safety in the document *Seven Steps to Patient Safety*:

1. Create a safe culture.
2. Lead and support the staff.
3. Integrate risk management activities into daily pharmacy practices.
4. Encourage reporting of all incidents.
5. Communicate effectively with patients, the public, and the staff.
6. Promote learning from safety lessons.
7. Assess risks regularly and implement activities to prevent harm.

5.7 Why Do Risk Management Programs Fail?

In this environment of Internet and globalization, the world has become a complex system of relationships and other independent factors. As a result, forecasting ordinary events,

let alone low-probability, high-impact events, has been difficult. The low-probability, high-impact events are called black
swan events, and the aim of any risk management program is
to minimize the impact of unknown events. Risk management
programs fail due to six mistakes (Taleb et al., 2009):

1. Assuming that extreme events can be predicted.
   Organizations generally focus on possibilities of exposure
   to extreme events. A more useful approach is to focus
   their efforts on managing the impact of low-probability,
   high-risk events instead of trying to predict the actual
   cause of a potential risk event.
2. Assuming that studying the past will help us manage risk.
   Businesses often use previous occurrences of events to
   predict the occurrence of future events. However, major
   black swan events are difficult to predict. The probabilities in the real world cannot be predicted using numbers
   and statistical tools. There is no such thing as a typical
   failure. Organizations must be prepared to face the impact
   of random events.
3. Failure to listen to advice on what should not be done.
   Business managers often focus on increasing profit mar-
   gin instead of avoiding losses. However, companies can
   become successful and will be able to meet the challenges of the competitive environment by preventing
   losses. Risk managers should treat loss avoidance and
   earning profit with the same degree of significance.
   Therefore, it is beneficial to integrate risk management
   activities into profit centers with profit-generating activities, particularly if organizations are vulnerable to black
   swan events.
4. Assuming that risk can be measured in terms of standard deviation. Statistical tools such as regression models,
   R squared values, and betas are inaccurate methods of
   measuring risk. Precise measurement of risk will make
   the organization prepare for the most probable event. But

the most probable event in the current socioeconomic environment is not always the one that usually occurs. Application of standard deviation complicates risk measurements, making them difficult to interpret.

5. Failure to appreciate that mathematical equivalence and psychological equivalence are different. In addition to mathematical complications of risk measurement, various methods of communication can confuse listeners, even if the same numbers are used. For example, if the pharmacy manager tells the staff, "We had only two dispensing errors last month," they are more likely to consider the occurrence as a nonserious situation, considering the very large number of prescriptions dispensed per month. However, if the manager says, "We had two dispensing errors last month; both resulted in hospitalization of the two patients," the staff will take the two errors as critical events. Therefore, when providing risk information to stakeholders and managers, it is important to describe the risk in a manner such that its true measurement is clearly understood.

6. Belief that efficiency and maximizing shareholder value do not tolerate redundancy. Business managers do not realize that optimization makes the organization more susceptible to changes in the environment. If organizations cannot cope with changes, the net result is redundancy. When companies use leverage, it makes the companies and the economic system more fragile. Organizations that "overspecialize" their production find it difficult to adapt to changes in the economic environment. Having less debt makes the companies more flexible to change with times, while maintaining an efficient business operation. Therefore, it is important for executives to concentrate on optimizing profits and providing a variety of products and services, instead of depending on a single avenue of revenue.

5.8 Case Study of a Successful Risk Management Program

In 2008, Milestone Centers, Inc. received the Negley Chairman's Award for the best risk management plan, including policy and practice for its submission, "Developing a Five Component Risk Management Programme in a Behavioural Health Organisation" (Milestone Centers, 2008).

Milestone, a community-based behavioral health provider in western Pennsylvania offering a comprehensive service to people with behavioral and intellectual challenges, has been in operation for 38 years, employing more than 400 people. Annually, it serves over 3,500 consumers located throughout 20 counties in Pennsylvania. It provides a variety of services, including treatment, clinical services, day programming, residential programs, home-based services, employee training, case management, and specialized deaf services.

Milestone Centers' risk management program was a proactive approach aimed at decreasing costly events in all aspects of the agency. In order to account for all risk events that could interrupt the provision of services, Milestone developed a five-component risk management program that promoted safety, accountability, and a continuous improvement process. The program was initiated with a three-stage process:

Stage 1: Establish an oversight committee.
Stage 2: Develop and implement a five-component risk management program.
Stage 3: Create a culture of life safety and risk management among the associates and consumers.

5.8.1 Stage 1: Oversight Committee

The Risk Management Committee (RMC) was established to develop, implement, and maintain an agency-wide risk management program. The RMC reported to the executive director and the board of directors, and it represented a diverse cross section of associates. The RMC established a five-component risk management program.

5.8.2 Stage 2: Five-Component Risk Management Program

1. Incident Management Committee (IMC). IMC was set up to establish a reporting system and review incidents in the agency and to develop and implement preventive and proactive measures. It identified trends, assessed isolated incidents, communicated to the appropriate committee for the development and implementation of intervention, established policies and procedures, trained supervisory associates, and developed a system of documentation.

2. Policy and Procedures Work Group (PPW). The role of the PPW was to create accountability and establish a standard format for policies and instructions. All policies and procedures were made accessible to all associates.

3. Health and Safety Commission (HSC). The HSC had a multitude of roles. In order to promote safety practices throughout the organization, the HSC was made accountable to develop, implement, and provide training on all aspects of safety. The HSC was also responsible for compliance and licensing arrangements, and locating, identifying, and correcting safety and health hazards.

4. Quality Assurance Committee (QAC). The QAC implemented a company-wide quality assurance program in which each department established its goals and objectives and reported the results to the QAC for monitoring, reviewing, and feedback.

5. Corporate Compliance Committee (CCC). The corporate compliance officer interacted with the four other com-

mittees, addressed the issues, and revised the corporate compliance plan and policy.

5.8.3 Stage 3: Creating a Culture of Life Safety and Management Risk

An essential component of the risk management program was to instill a culture of life safety among all associates and consumers. This was done by completing safety and risk training, addressing issues that arose via trend analysis, providing feedback and suggestions, and reporting incidents to avoid future occurrences. Achievements were celebrated. Consumers were provided with information on how to report problems and concerns.

5.8.4 Outcome

Fiscal: No citation following the annual audit.

Corporate compliance officer: Did not have to intervene in any compliance issues.

Consumer survey: Ninety-one percent of consumers who responded claimed that Milestone ensured privacy of their information, 8.6% indicated room for improvement, and the rest did not respond.

Workers' compensation: Annual workers' compensation insurance cost decreased from $193,442 in 2005 to $167,598 in 2007. The number of injuries decreased from 54 (2005) to 51 (2007).

Customer service: An independent survey found 100% satisfaction in the areas of access, acceptance, perceived choice, and overall satisfaction. Eighty-five percent of the customers were satisfied with the information provided to the customers. All issues were addressed through the quality assurance program.

5.9 Revisiting the Scenario

In the scenario cited in the chapter, a staff shortage has been recognized as a problem. However, there was no attempt to resolve the issue until the situation became critical. The risk can then be defined as follows:

> When there is a shortage of dispensing staff, it is likely that the staff working in the dispensary will encounter a heavy workload, and there is a risk that the patient will be given (1) wrong medicine, (2) correct medicine but wrong strength, (3) correct medicine with a wrong label, (4) wrong brand, or (5) another person's medicine.

The likelihood score is 3 (possible) on the basis of frequency (might recur occasionally). The consequence score is 4 (major) on the basis of significant risk to patients, if unresolved. The risk rating is thus 12 (high risk) and requires the attention of the manager (see Table 5.5). The action plan for managing the risk of shortage of staff in the dispensary is shown in Table 5.7.

Table 5.7 Action Plan for Managing the Risk of Staff Shortage

Risk Description	Impact	Current Controls	Are Current Controls Adequate?	Action	By Whom	By When	Completion
Shortage of staff	Dispensing errors (see risk statement for details)	Staff cover when available	No	1. Request extra staff[a] 2. Inform patients that they have a longer waiting time 3. Take regular mental and physical breaks 4. Read scripts carefully 5. Take time to check 6. Reduce interruptions	Pharmacy manager	Immediate	Done on …

[a] Responsible pharmacist is responsible for the safe and effective operation of all the activities in the pharmacy.

References

CPPE. (2005). *Risk management*. Manchester: School of Pharmacy and Pharmaceutical Sciences.

Dezfuli, M. (2010, September). *NASA's risk management approach*. Workshop on risk assessment and safety decision making under uncertainty, Bethesda, MD.

Dornan, T. (n.d.). *Final report. An in-depth investigation into causes of prescribing errors by foundation trainees in relation to their medical education*. Retrieved February 1, 2011, from http://www.gmc-uk.org/FINAL_Report_prevalence_and_causes_of_prescribing_errors.pdf_28935150.pdf

Hahn, K. (2007). The "top 10" drug errors and how to prevent them. Retrieved February 12, 2011, from http://www.medscape.org/viewarticle/556487

Health Service Executive. (2008). Risk assessment tool and guidance. Retrieved January 10, 2011, from http://www.hse.ie/eng/About/Who/OQR012_20081210_v4_Risk_Assessment_Tool_and_Guidance_incl_guidance_on.pdf

Milestone. (2008). Developing a five component risk management programme in a behavioural health organisation. Retrieved August 21, 2012, from http://www.mhrrg.com/Milestone08Chairman.pdf

Mooney, C. (2010). An introduction to risk management. *European Journal of Hospital Pharmacy Practice*, 16, 68–70.

NASA. (2009). *Guidelines for risk management. Independent verification and validation programme* (Document S3001, Revision B). Retrieved February 12, 2011, from http://www.nasa.gov/centers/ivv/pdf/209213main_S3001_-_Rev_C.pdf

NPSA. (2004, August). *Seven steps to patient safety* (2nd print). Retrieved January 23, 2013, from http://www.npsa.nhs.uk/search/?q=seven+steps

NPSA. (2008). *A risk matrix for risk managers*. Retrieved February 23, 2013, from http://www.nrls.npsa.nhs.uk/resources/?entryid45=59833

Nutan, R. (2006). The management of risk in the pharmacy. *Business Management*, P3, 19–22.

Siu, T. (2004). *Risk-eye for the IT security guy. GSEC practical version 1.4b (options) 1*. SANS Institute. Retrieved February 12, 2011, from http://www.sans.org/reading_room/whitepapers/threats/risk-eye-security-guy_1380

Tague, N.R. (2005). *The quality toolbox* (2nd ed.). Milwaukee: Quality Press.

Taleb, N.N., Goldstein, D.G., and Spitznagel, M.W. (2009). The six mistakes executives make in risk management. *Harvard Business Review*, 87, 78–81.

Wreathall, J., and Nemeth, C. (2004). Assessing risk: The role of probabilistic risk assessment (PRA) in patient safety improvement. *Quality and Safety in Health Care*, 13, 206–212.

Chapter 6

Problem Solving

When a problem comes along, study it until you are completely knowledgeable. Then find that weak spot, break the problem apart, and the rest will be easy.

—Norman Vincent Peale,
author of *The Power of Positive Thinking*

6.1 Scenario

Community Pharmacy Limited receives a large number of prescriptions from surgeries for repeat dispensing. One of the dispensers is already on long-term stress leave. Another dispenser has taken leave for an operation. The pharmacy is thus short-staffed. Dianne often employs locum dispensers who are not fully conversant with the dispensing program in the computer. Pharmacists work under constant stress. Repeat prescriptions are piling up, and when the patients visit the pharmacy to collect the medicines, they are not ready. The healthcare assistants have to spend a considerable amount of time trying to locate the prescriptions among the huge pile. When confronted, Dianne's reply is: "Everybody has to work harder, and it is difficult to get good dispensers."

6.2 Introduction

The situations cited above are common in chain pharmacies receiving a large number of prescriptions for repeat dispensing. Excellent problem-solving skills are essential for resolving such issues. One of the serious mistakes that an untrained manager does is to jump into a solution without identifying or analyzing the problem. The solutions arrived at in this manner are short-lived and bound to be failures.

The *Cambridge Advanced Learners' Dictionary* (2008) defines a problem as a situation, person, or thing that needs attention and needs to be dealt with or solved. A solution is defined as an answer to a problem. A problem has several features (Newstrom, 2007): (1) it is an unresolved issue or something that causes concern, (2) its nature raises complex issues, and (3) its resolution requires considerable skill. Problems often arise when there is a difference between the expected outcome and the current performance.

Problem solving involves decision making, and it is an important managerial skill. Resolution of the problem depends on the quality of the decision-making process, and by improving its quality, effective solutions can be achieved (Chapman, 2010).

Unskilled managers often attempt to resolve problems by reacting to them. Owing to time constraints, short-term decisions are made that seemed to work before. This process results in an endless cycle of recurring problems and unskilled decisions (McNamara, 2003).

Pharmacy managers are under a considerable amount of stress because of the expectations of the patients, the need to meet targets that are sometimes unrealistic, and the requirement to comply with current legislation. Under stressful conditions, problems often occur. They may occur as a result of a previous decision, for example, selecting an untrained and unskilled person or by incidents beyond the control of the manager, such as the inability to deliver an order because of a fire in the warehouse. Solving the problem in a logical manner enables the managers not only to resolve problems effectively, but also to anticipate and prevent problems from occurring (Liraz, n.d.).

A well-known example of creative problem solving is the story of Post-it® slips (3M Company, 2002). Spencer Silver of 3M developed a unique adhesive in 1968, which formed a temporary bond with the surface to which it was attached. He could not find a use for it until 1973, when Arthur Fry, while turning the pages of a hymnbook in church, dropped the scrap paper bookmarks on the floor. His imagination captured the idea of Silver, and after overcoming various technical problems, the Post-it slip was born. Spencer knew the potential of his discovery when he remarked, "My discovery was a solution for a problem to solve."

6.3 Process

In the process of solving a problem, the cause or causes of the deviation between the expected outcome and the actual condition must be identified. Current problems require corrective action, whereas potential problems need preventive action. There are several techniques for solving problems. One such technique is the Osborn-Parnes model (Creative Education Foundation, 2010). This model involves creative problem solving, and it is a way of thinking and behaving (Mitchell and Kowalik, 1999). According to this model, the problem-solving process involves six steps:

1. Object finding: Attempting to identify a situation with its concerns and challenges.
2. Fact finding: Gathering all the data relevant to the situation.
3. Problem finding: Attempting to identify all the possible problem statements and selecting the most appropriate one for resolution.
4. Idea finding: Listing all the possible solutions to the problem.

5. Solution finding: Selecting the most appropriate solution.
6. Acceptance finding: Attempting to gain consensus and develop an action plan for implementation.

Following the implementation of the action plan, it must be monitored for its effectiveness. If the solution is not successful, it must be amended using the six steps above. However, a more rigorous approach involves nine steps, which is a fundamental approach to problem solving and decision making (Newstrom, 2007). The following steps are involved in this process:

1. Define the problem clearly and specifically.
2. Gather all the data relevant to the situation.
3. Identify all the possible causes for the problem.
4. Select the most likely cause or causes that resulted in the problem.
5. Generate solutions to the problem at hand.
6. Evaluate the solution for feasibility.
7. Choose the best option.
8. Generate an action plan.
9. Implement the plan and monitor its effectiveness.

Steps 1 and 2 are problem-identifying steps, and steps 6 and 7 are decision-making steps. This process demonstrates how problem solving and decision making are interlinked.

6.3.1 Identification of the Problem

Identification of the real problem is crucial to finding the causes of the problem. The problem itself should not be confused with its symptoms. For example, in the scenario cited in Section 6.1, the delay in delivering the medication to the patient is a symptom of the problem and not the problem itself. In order to fully identify the problem, it is necessary to find out how the problem occurred, its nature (for example, people, operational, or technical) and significance, and the type of problem (for example, a current problem, a potential problem, or a previous problem that requires attention to prevent it from occurring again).

In the scenario, the problem occurred when the patients started complaining about the delay in receiving their medication. This is an operational issue and is very significant, causing anger among the patients. The delay is a current problem, which has not occurred previously. Therefore, the problem statement could read: "The repeat prescriptions from the surgeries cannot be dispensed on the same day, thereby causing delay and piling up."

6.3.2 Collection of Data

Collection of data is the fact-finding step of the process. All the data that relate to the problem are assessed and reviewed (Creative Education Foundation, 2010). This involves finding out who is involved, and when and where and why it happened. It is also necessary to establish whether any more problems are caused by the situation. A list of all the facts and data is prepared, which should also include any assumptions, feelings, and perceptions. The facts presented should be verifiable, and assumptions should be clarified and validated as part of the process.

6.3.3 Identification of the Causes of the Problem

At this stage, it is essential that all the causes leading to the problem are identified using the input from all the staff. Usually, there is a tendency to jump into solutions without identifying the root cause. This should be avoided because it can lead to the treatment of symptoms rather than the problem itself. A multiple-cause diagram, shown in Figure 6.1, is a useful tool for identifying all the causes of the problem (Cameron, 2005).

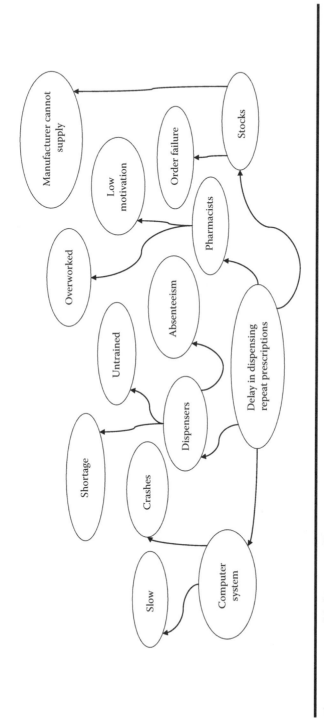

Figure 6.1 Multiple-cause diagram.

In the 1990s, a large winery in New Zealand engaged the services of a top-class label designer from Italy to redesign labels for a range of upmarket wines for export. The labels were very attractive, and the marketing department was thrilled with the outcome. However, shortly after the introduction, a problem was detected; the labels were badly damaged during transport. Marketing staff promptly expressed their dissatisfaction and instructed the production team to resolve the issue quickly. The quality assurance (QA) team visited many outlets to assess the nature and extent of the problem. Some labels were torn, some were scuffed, and others were damaged, destroying their beauty. Samples brought from the market were analyzed with the aid of a multiple-cause diagram. The team was able to identify three major causes for failure: (1) incorrect technique of inserting the bottle in the box, (2) faulty design of the divider separating the bottles, and (3) poor coating on the label. Improving the technique of inserting the bottle in the box eliminated the first problem. The engineering team redesigned the divider, allowing room for the section to move when the bottle was inserted. The third problem was more difficult to solve. The company's QA team assisted the label printer to conduct trials on new coatings, and eventually a new coating was developed that withstood severe transport trials.

The above example illustrates how the multiple-cause diagram was used to solve a major problem with effective teamwork.

6.3.4 Selection of Causes

Using the information gathered in step 1, sift through all the causes to recognize the most probable cause or causes. This can be achieved through a process of elimination of unlikely causes. To test a cause for likelihood, return the factor to the original state and judge whether it would make a difference. For example, in Figure 6.1, absenteeism of dispensers has been cited as a cause. Ask yourself whether it is more frequent than before the occurrence of the problem. In this manner, most probable causes can be identified.

6.3.5 Generating Solutions

There are several approaches to generate solutions. One such widely used approach is brainstorming, which involves all the staff. This is a technique for generating ideas in a nonthreatening environment. The problem is explained to the group, and each member is encouraged to contribute as many solutions as possible. All ideas are accepted without criticism. An idea that may sound silly may stimulate further ideas.

6.3.6 Evaluation of the Solution for Feasibility

In this step, the pros and cons of each solution are determined. It may be useful to devise a set of criteria for evaluation. For example, some of the criteria are the cost of implementation, ease of implementation, timeliness, effect on patients, effect on the organization, impact on the problem, etc. Evaluate all solutions using the selected criteria.

6.3.7 Selection of the Best Options or Options

This is the decision phase of the problem-solving process. Select the best option or options that have the best chance of success. The advantages and strengths of the chosen option or options should outweigh the weaknesses.

6.3.8 Generation of the Action Plan

The problem-solving process is incomplete unless the solution or solutions are implemented. Therefore, an action plan must be designed in detail. The details may include the tasks to be accomplished, who will drive them, the time frame, and any other relevant details.

6.3.9 *Implementation and Monitoring*

Managers must ensure that the decisions are properly carried out within the given time frame. Support and resources should be provided to implement the plan effectively. The final step of the process is follow-up, which is often ignored. Without the monitoring step, it not possible to determine whether the solutions have been successful. The staff may not agree with the manager's perception of success, and therefore their feedback is critical and is one of the most important tools in successfully carrying out the solutions.

6.4 Barriers for Implementation

There are a number of obstacles that may arise during the course of implementation. Being aware of the obstacles makes it possible to devise ways to overcome them. Some of the obstacles are (1) nonreceipt of resources to carry out the action plan; (2) other situations that may cause a diversion; (3) procrastination; (4) power struggle among the manager, dispensers, and pharmacists; and (5) resistance to change.

The resistance to change is a human characteristic. However, it must be borne in mind that people do not resist change, but resist being changed. Therefore, for the problem-solving exercise to be successful, teamwork is very essential.

6.5 Systematic Problem Solving: Xerox® Case Study

Systematic problem solving (SPS) depends on scientific methods for analyzing problems without guesswork. It is based on the philosophy and methods of quality improvement (Garvin, 1993), and underlying ideas are as follows:

- The first idea is Deming's plan, do, check, act cycle.
- The second idea is fact-based management that relies on data and not on assumptions.
- The third idea is the use of simple statistical tools such as histograms, Pareto charts, correlations, and cause-and-effect diagrams to organize data and demonstrate relationships.

For the problem-solving session to be more effective, employees must adopt a disciplined approach in their thinking. Attention to detail is important because accuracy and precision are important factors. In 1983, senior executives of Xerox initiated the company's Leadership through Quality program. According to this program, employees were trained in small-group activities and problem-solving techniques (Garvin, 1993). Four different tools were provided to accomplish the activities:

1. Generating ideas and gathering information through brainstorming, interviewing, and surveying
2. Reaching consensus by list reduction, rating forms, and weighting votes
3. Analyzing and displaying data using cause-and-effect diagrams and force field analysis
4. Planning actions using flowcharts and Gantt charts

Xerox's six-step problem-solving model was as follows:

Step 1: Identify and select problem(s):
  Consider what requires changing.
  Many problems are considered.
  Generate one problem statement and agree upon one desired state.
  Perform a gap analysis.
  Describe the desired state in measurable/observable terms.
Step 2: Analyze the problem:
  Identify the obstacles to reach the desired state.
  Many potential obstacles are identified.

Identify key causes and verify.

Document and rank key causes.

Step 3: Generate potential solutions.

Determine how the desired change can be achieved:

Many ideas are generated to solve the problem.

Clarify potential solutions.

Document the solution list.

Step 4: Select the best solution:

Identify criteria for evaluating potential solutions.

Ideas necessary to implement and assess the selected solution are considered.

Agree upon criteria for evaluating solutions.

Agree upon implementation and evaluating plans.

Make a plan for monitoring the change.

Decide on measurement criteria to evaluate solutions.

Step 5: Implement the solution:

Check whether the established plan is followed.

If necessary, generate and implement contingency plans.

Solution is implemented.

Step 6: Evaluate the solution:

Determine whether the solution has been effective.

Agree upon the effectiveness of the solution.

Identify continuing problems, if any.

Verify whether the solution has been effective or whether it is necessary to address continuing problem(s).

The result of this process has been a common system and a dependable company-wide approach to problem solving.

6.6 Revisiting the Scenario

In the case cited in Section 6.1, the manager has to face up to several problems without avoiding them. The situation is unlikely to improve unless the problems are identified and addressed. In fact, if they are not resolved, the situation will deteriorate further, causing frustration and dissatisfaction among the staff. Using the multiple-cause diagram shown in Figure 6.1, the manager, together with the staff, should resolve the issue.

References

3M Company. (2002). *A century of innovation* (1st ed.). 3M Company.

Cambridge advanced learners' dictionary (3rd ed.). (2008). Cambridge, MA: Cambridge University Press.

Cameron, S. (2005). *The MBA handbook* (5th ed.). Essex, England: Prentice-Hall.

Chapman, A. (2010). Problem solving and decision making. Retrieved June 19, 2010, from http://www.businessballs.com/problemsolving.htm

Creative Education Foundation. (2010). What is CPS? Retrieved June 19, 2010, from http://www.creativeeducationfoundation.org/?page_id=41

Garvin, D.A. (1993). Building a learning organisation. *Harvard Business Review*, 71(4), 78–91.

McNamara, C. (2003). *Field guide to leadership and supervision for non-profit staff* (3rd ed.). Minneapolis, MN: Authenticity Consulting, LLC.

Mitchell, W.E., and Kowalik, T.F. (1999). *Creative problem solving* (3rd ed.). New York: SUNY-Binghamton Press.

Newstrom, J.W. (2007). *Supervision* (9th ed.). New York: McGraw-Hill.

Small Business Management. (2008). Problem solving techniques: How to solve a problem. Retrieved January 23, 2013, from http://www.bizmove.com/skills/m8d.htm

Chapter 7

Conflict Resolution

Courage is what it takes to stand up and speak.
Courage is also what it takes to sit down and listen.

—Winston Churchill

7.1 Scenario

A few weeks after Max Fisher commenced work as a pharmacist at Community Pharmacy Limited, one morning Dianne Watts, the manager, invited him to the small tearoom. After he entered the room, she closed the door behind her. In the room, the area manager (nonpharmacist) and another pharmacist who accompanies the area manager were waiting for him. Max had no idea what the meeting was about. Without exchanging greetings, the area manager said, "We are here to look into some issues raised by your staff."

"I've no idea what the issues are," said Max.

"That's why we are here to investigate," said the area manager.

He listed a series of issues, and all the time Dianne was silent. These issues had never been brought to Max's attention. There was no proper discussion. Instead, the pharmacist who accompanied the area manager outlined what should be done to resolve the issues. The area manager warned that Max was still under probation and wanted him to sign a document that included an action plan that had already been decided without any input from Max.

7.2 Introduction

Conflict among people and groups is unavoidable. By itself, conflict is not a problem. The real problem is how it is managed. When managed correctly, it can have a positive influence on the people concerned and the organization.

7.3 Definitions

Conflict: A successful conflict resolution leads to trust and openness. It is a situation between two or more people or groups whose actions or intentions are perceived as threats by another person or a group who cares about the situation. For a conflict to occur, a number of conditions must be fulfilled: (1) two or more people should be involved, (2) the situation is of interest to both parties, and (3) the perception of one party is seen as a threat to the other party.

Conflict resolution: The process that parties go through to resolve the conflict.

Conflict management: The management of the conflict resolution process to ensure satisfactory resolution of the conflict.

7.4 What Conflict Is Not

Disagreement, indecision, and stress-induced situations are not necessarily conflicts (Dana, 2001). A disagreement between two managers on the interpretation of audit results of a project is not a conflict. A situation where a person is indecisive about going to a technical institute or going abroad is not a conflict. Stress-induced situations where one is torn between continuing to work or giving up the job are not conflict situations. They can be resolved by using problem solving, decision making, or appropriate stress management tools.

7.5 Types of Conflict

To manage a conflict successfully, one has to identify the type of conflict. There are five most common types of conflict in the workplace (Holmes, 2010): (1) interdependence, (2) differences in style, (3) differences in background/gender, (4) differences in leadership, and (5) differences in personality.

Interdependence: One person needs the assistance of another person to complete the task. The pharmacist depends on the dispenser to assemble and label medications written on a prescription for him or her to check according to the standard operating procedures (SOPs). However, the dispenser may give priority to putting the stock away, thereby delaying the dispensing process. The situation gives rise to a conflict.

Differences in style: The pharmacist who wants to avoid errors may take time to check prescriptions accurately, whereas the manager (nonpharmacist) who wants to reduce the waiting time may instruct the pharmacist to check the prescriptions quickly, thereby leading to a conflict situation.

Differences in background/gender: Conflicts may arise due to differences in educational background, personal experiences, ethnic group, gender, or political preferences.

Differences in leadership: A pharmacist working under a nonpharmacist manager lacking in management skills and qualifications may not be comfortable with an autocratic style of manager. Consultative and democratic styles of leaders often conflict with managers who are autocratic.

Differences in personality: The most common types of conflict arise because of differences in personality. The deeds and motives of one person may be perceived as a threat by another person because of emotions and character.

7.6 Skills Necessary for Conflict Resolution

Four skills are essentials for a successful outcome of a conflict resolution session: (1) listening, (2) questioning, (3) nonverbal communication, and (4) negotiating (Ramsey, 1996).

7.6.1 Listening

Listening skills determine one's ability to manage a conflict. Most people speak at the rate of 100 to 125 words per minute but think at a rate of 400 to 500 words per minute (Plunkett, 2003). The faster thinking ability allows us to interpret and criticize while listening. However, active listening enables us to secure information, including emotions and feelings, through attention, observation, asking appropriate questions for clarity, and paraphrasing what has been said to indicate that the speaker has been understood correctly. It requires a conscious effort to be aware of what is being communicated without interruptions, assumptions, guessing the intentions of the speaker, and responding too quickly. People who listen actively (1) think with those involved and respond appropriately, (2) are nonjudgmental, (3) pay attention to content and feelings, and (4) respond to what is being said (Plunkett, 2003).

7.6.2 Questioning

Good questioning skills can help the manager understand the situation, ascertain the root cause of the conflict, understand the feelings and emotions, and determine what is required to resolve the issue or issues. Closed questions such as "Did you tell her that she is incompetent?" require only a yes or no answer, or leading questions such as "You did tell him to shut up, did you not?" should be avoided at all costs. Probing and open-ended questions are the most effective types of questions. The following statement is an example of a probing question: "You said the dispenser shouted at you in front of the patients. Please explain this further so that I can understand the situation."

The above statement gives the listener the opportunity to clarify the situation. Consider the following open-ended question: "Why do you feel the manager resents your opinion?" Here there is a need to explain why the manager resents his opinion. A simple yes or no answer is not appropriate.

7.6.3 Nonverbal Communication

During a conflict resolution session, important information is conveyed through nonverbal communication. This communication is expressed in various forms, such as eye contact, facial expression, tone of voice, posture, touch, and gestures (Segal et al., 2009). These signals assist the mediator to respond in a manner to build confidence and trust, and reach the root cause of the problem. A heated exchange of words can be diffused through nonverbal communication, such as a calm tone of speech, reassuring touch, or facial expression. Physical expressions such as nodding the head up and down, tapping the table with fingers, tapping the foot, raising the eyebrows, rolling the eyes, and tight-lipped frowning should be avoided, as they are easily misinterpreted across various cultures.

7.6.4 Negotiation

Negotiating is the process by which the parties involved in the conflict meet together in order to resolve their differences and reach an agreement. Each party gives up those needs that are least important to it, thereby achieving a win-win situation. The art of negotiating involves (Patten, 2009)

1. Research: Gather all the information and speak to parties involved, if necessary.
2. Prepare: Identify the goals, negotiating points, opinions, relationships, consequences of losing or winning, and who has the power and possible solutions. Bring the right people and review your case often.
3. Plan your approach: Identify the strengths and weaknesses of your case.
4. Identify the best alternative to a negotiated agreement.
5. Be open-minded and listen.
6. Communicate clearly and precisely.
7. Make the first offer.
8. Listen carefully and respond to all the objections.
9. Do not reveal your weaknesses, but focus on strengths.
10. Confirm the agreement both verbally and in writing.

7.7 Conflict Resolution Process

There is no universal formula for resolving conflicts. Daniel Dana (2001) suggests a three-step plan for resolving conflict. On the other hand, Dudley Weeks (1992) suggests an eight-step plan for managing conflicts successfully. The resolution essentially depends on the structure of the conflict. By following a series of steps, it is possible to manage the conflict at the earliest opportunity (Peterson, 2004). Barbara Bulleit (2006), in a white paper on effectively managing team conflict, proposes a five-step plan to resolve a conflict. Sometimes, the two parties can themselves resolve the issues without a third person's intervention. If it does not work, the manager has to intervene as a facilitator. Conflicts involving the manager as a party must be resolved with support from a human resources division or an external agency.

Step 1: Bring the parties together to build a mutually beneficial partnership. The correct atmosphere is essential to defusing a threatening situation. The manager should stress that all are important members of the company, and they need each other to carry out the work effectively. The parties should understand that it is possible to work together as a team to find a mutually beneficial solution to improve the relationship and deal effectively with the issues facing them.

In the scenario cited in Section 7.1, Dianne should have invited Max, the pharmacist, and the other member of the team who raised the issues together to find a mutually acceptable solution.

Step 2: Define the problem. Defining the problem accurately sets the correct path for resolving the conflict. Often, it is the most difficult part of the process because each party may have a different perspective on the problem. The facilitator or the manager should remind the parties that they work as a team.

Having identified the problems in the scenario cited in the chapter, the team arrives at the following problem statements:

– Waiting time is too long to dispense prescriptions.
– Conducting medicine use reviews (MURs) when the pharmacy is busy interrupts dispensing.
– Questioning the dispensers when they are busy causes distractions.

Step 3: Gather and analyze the data. At this stage, it is essential to gather data on what is actually occurring: facts that can be substantiated, measured, and not based on opinions or hearsay.

In the scenario, data showing that the waiting time has increased, how the manner of conducting MURs is affecting the business, and how questioning the dispensers affects their performance should be presented.

Hard facts must be shown and opinions cannot be accepted as evidence.

Step 4: Assess the needs of each party. Conflicts arise when the needs of a person are not met. Each party should define his or her needs without taking positions.

Considering the issue of conducting MURs, Max, the pharmacist, may state that he has to conduct them to meet the targets of the company. On the other hand, Pat, the team member who raised the issue, may insist that MURs must not be conducted during busy periods. In this instance, both Max and Pat have taken positions.

When positions are taken, resolution is difficult.

A positive approach is to state the needs, for example, as follows:

Pat: I need to dispense scripts without much delay. I have to dispense without making mistakes. Interruptions can cause mistakes.

Max: I can *understand* how you feel, but I have to conduct MURs, whenever possible, to meet the targets. I question when I need clarification, and that's not a judgment of your skills. I'm sorry you feel that way. That's not my intention.

The manager wants further information regarding waiting times.

Manager: Pat, you're saying that the waiting time is now longer. How did you arrive at this conclusion?

Pat: Well, it's my observation.

Manager: Pat, in fairness to Max, we need more data. At the moment I don't see much information to go by.

Max has shown empathy by understanding Pat's position, and he has defused a potentially explosive situation. Therefore, Pat is willing to arrive at a compromise. It is clear that the needs are *different* but not *opposite,* and a resolution is possible. These are summarized in Table 7.1. Max needs to conduct MURs, and Pat needs to dispense to prevent a backlog. The next stage is to determine the common needs. The facilitator or the manager has to establish the common needs in consultation with the two parties. Both Max and Pat have needs that are important and some that are less important. The needs that are not important can be given up. Table 7.2 shows which can be given up to arrive at a just resolution for a win-win situation. The common needs are as follows:

- MURs are essential as a source of income for the company.
- Dispensing must be done effectively to satisfy the needs of the patients and to prevent a backlog.
- Accuracy is essential when prescriptions are dispensed.
- Both Max and Pat have to work together for the progress of the company.

Table 7.1 Defining the Needs

Issue	*Max's Needs*	*Pat's Needs*
MURs	Conduct MURs to meet the target	Dispense scripts without delay
Questioning	Clarify issues	Dispense without interruptions
Waiting time	Need to counsel, conduct MURs, answer patient's queries, check prescriptions	No data presented

Table 7.2 Needs That Can Be Given Up

	Needs Not Important to:	
Issue	*Max*	*Pat*
MURs	Conducting MURs during busy times	Interrupting when pharmacy is not busy
Questioning	Clarifying when Pat is busy	Disturbing when Pat is not dispensing

Step 5: Generate options. At this stage, no option is ruled out, however untenable it is. Both parties must be heard without interruption. The facilitator's role is to listen to both sides, clarify statements, when necessary, and avoid offering answers.

Max and Pat arrive at the following options:

1. Maintain status quo.
2. Stop conducing MURs.
3. Refer to British National Formulary (BNF) for clarification before questioning Pat.
4. Ask questions when Pat is not dispensing.
5. Determine reasonable waiting times without compromising patient safety.
6. Conduct MURs when patients are not waiting for their prescriptions.

Step 6: Select the best option(s). Consider the issues again and assess how each option will impact the issue. Other considerations are the effect of the option(s) on individual team members and their support.

In the scenario cited above, options 1 and 2 are not acceptable. Other options are workable.

Step 7: Implement the options and refine, if necessary. An action plan can now be generated for each of the options selected for implementation. If the option or options do not work, determine the root cause and review the options.

7.8 Strategies for Managing Conflict

The purpose of any conflict management program is to defuse the conflict at the earliest opportunity. Therefore, senior executives must embrace conflict, accept its challenges, and put in place mechanisms to manage it. Two strategies can be used for managing conflict constructively (Weiss and Hughes, 2005): (1) strategies for managing disagreement at the point of conflict and (2) strategies for managing conflict upon escalation to higher authorities.

7.8.1 Strategies for Managing Disagreement at the Point of Conflict

1. Create and implement a common structured method of resolving conflict. An effective conflict resolution method offers a clear, stepwise procedure (see Section 7.7) for parties to follow. It should be an integral component of existing business practices, such as accounting, sourcing, budgeting, R&D, and human resources. A well-defined company-wide conflict resolution method will minimize wasted time and growth of ill will associated with attempts to resolve the dispute.

   Intel has introduced a common method and language for decision making and conflict resolution (Weiss and Hughes, 2005). The staff undergo training and use a variety of tools for managing disagreements. The training makes the top management realize the inevitability of conflict and provides a framework for early resolution. Intel's systematic process of resolving differences has helped sustain its leadership qualities in innovation, operational effectiveness, and the ability to make difficult decisions on complex issues.

2. Provide people with criteria for making trade-offs. In the pharmacy sector, where a multitude of services are

offered by pharmacists, dispensers, healthcare assistants, and the manager, differences of opinion exist on how best to provide excellent patient care. Therefore, employees often have to make trade-offs between competing priorities. A pharmacist may be compelled to meet MUR targets because doing so provides extra profit to the company. In such instances, the pharmacist has to balance ethical considerations against generating profit for the organization. Unless clear guidelines are established, such conflicts will continue to occur.

Top management should establish the company's strategy to clearly define trade-offs. Employees then will be in a better position to choose the needs and priorities when different parts of a business conflict. Although it may seem difficult to establish such priorities, it provides a platform to foster productive dialogue.

Blue Cross and Blue Shield of Florida has established a common set of trade-off criteria to enable the employees to analyze the trade-offs associated with various options (Weiss and Hughes, 2005). They use a table format that makes it easier to compare selection criteria and trade-offs. Visual display of individual's choices and discussions help participants realize that access to information or different prioritizing criteria is the real issue. In response to new information, individuals can change their position in the table grid. Eventually, a consensus is reached based on the maximum number of positions in the grid.

3. When conflicts escalate to higher management, use them as an opportunity for coaching. Managers who are involved in managing escalated conflicts have less time on their hands to engage in business activities. Often, senior managers are guilty of continuing the practice, and it encourages the staff to push issues upward at the first sign of conflict. It is more beneficial for senior manag-

ers to use escalations as opportunities for employees to resolve conflicts.

At KLA-Tenor, a major semiconductor product manufacturer, conflicts often arose over the delivery terms for components supplied to two or more divisions under the same contract. In order to address such conflicts, the buyer was asked to consider the requirements of other divisions, alternatives, and standards to be applied in evaluating trade-offs between alternatives (Weiss and Hughes, 2005). This approach resulted in fewer disputes escalating to higher authorities, quicker contract negotiations, and improved contract terms.

In the absence of clear criteria for escalation of conflicts, pharmacy managers in community pharmacies often push up issues to the area manager, who in turn has to intervene to settle disputes such as overtime, staff conflicts, etc. Sometimes, area managers too are guilty of encouraging such practices.

7.8.2 Strategies for Managing Conflict upon Escalation

1. The most effective way to escalate a conflict to senior managers is to present the disagreement jointly to the supervisor. This will ensure that the senior manager has access to all relevant information, various perspectives, its causes, and different ways of resolving it. With this approach, employees take responsibility for the escalation of conflict and are accountable for their decisions. Thus, there is a reduction of problems pushed up the ladder.

    A few years ago, Canadian Telecom Company became a much larger and more complex organization following a merger (Weiss and Hughes, 2005). Senior managers could not cope with the large number of unilateral escalations. Ultimately, the senior managers decided not to respond to unilateral escalation. During a conflict, managers were required to jointly describe the problem, actions taken so far to resolve the issue, and possible solutions. These details had to be presented in writing to their bosses. They appeared together to respond to any questions. In most cases, conflicts were resolved at this stage without having to be pushed up further. This approach resulted in resolving hundreds of unresolved issues.

2. Ensure that managers resolve escalated conflicts directly with their counterparts. Escalation of conflicts up the ladder of hierarchy results in the most senior manager making unilateral decisions. Such poor decisions without having access to all the information lead to inefficiency and ill feelings among the staff. Addressing conflicts directly with counterparts is more efficient than escalating upward for a resolution. Issues can thus be addressed at the earliest opportunity.

    In the 1990s, IBM created a forum called the Market Growth Workshop to resolve cross-unit conflicts (Weiss and Hughes, 2005). The managers, sales force, and product specialists participated in monthly forums. Those involved with disputes analyzed and documented the issue before the conference call. As complex issues were resolved in this manner, participants realized the benefits of these conference calls.

3. Make the process for escalated conflict resolution transparent. Communication is an integral part following the resolution of a conflict. Transparency enhances the willingness and ability to implement decisions relating to conflict. Management must take time to explain how the decisions were reached, the factors that were considered, and trade-offs involved in the decision. Experience thus forms a basis to resolve similar conflicts in the future.

7.9 Prevention of Conflict

The aim of all managers is to ensure that disagreements do not escalate to conflicts. By taking some simple preventive measures, harmony can be established among the team members. Some of these measures are

- Discuss issues openly before they become problems.
- Be aware of triggers that may cause conflicts and respond at the earliest opportunity.
- Have a process of resolving differences among team members.
- Make sure that all team members are aware of their expectations, company goals, responsibilities, and authority.
- Develop conflict resolution skills among the staff.
- Be consistent in performance reviews.
- Do not put down people, and avoid gossip.

A harmonious work environment can be created by being fair to all employees and consistent in all decisions.

7.10 Revisiting the Scenario

The scenario cited above demonstrates how the issues have escalated to a conflict. Clearly, Dianne had no conflict resolution skills and has violated company procedures by not giving an opportunity to Max to respond before bringing them to the attention of the area manager. In this episode, there were a series of failures on the part of management. There may have been some real issues that could have been resolved between Dianne and Max. Dianne lost this opportunity because of a lack of management skills. A discussion about the scenario is described in Section 7.7.

References

Bulleit, B. (2006). White paper: Effectively managing team conflict. Retrieved July 27, 2010, from http://gclearningservices.com/assets/Managing_Conflict.pdf

Dana, D. (2001). *Conflict resolution*. Madison, WI: McGraw-Hill.

Holmes, S. (2010). Types of conflict in the workplace. Retrieved July 10, 2010, from http://www.thecorporatetoolbox.com/articles/118

Patten, J. (2009). Negotiating for excellent results. Retrieved July 22, 2010, from http://www.human-law.co.uk/Resource-Articles/Negotiating-for-Results-White-Paper.aspx

Peterson, A.M. (2004). *Managing pharmacy practice*. New York: CRC Press.

Plunkett, G. (2003). *Supervision* (10th ed.). New York: Prentice Hall.

Ramsey, R.D. (1996). Conflict resolution skills for supervisors. *Supervision*, 57(8), 9–11.

Segal, J., Smith, M., and Jaffe, J. (2009, September). *Conflict resolution skills: Help guide*. Retrieved January 23, 2013, from http://helpguide.org/mental/eq8_conflict_resolution.htm.

Weeks, D. (1992). *The eight essential steps to conflict resolution*. New York: Penguin Putman.

Weiss, J., and Hughes, J. (2005). Want collaboration? *Harvard Business Review*, 83(3), 92–101.

Chapter 8

Managing Stress at Work

Stress is not what happens to us. It's our response to what happens. And response is something we can choose.

**—Maureen Killoran,
creator of Successful Mind Training**

8.1 Scenario

Max Fisher joined Community Pharmacy Limited about two years ago. Recently, one of the experienced dispensers went on sick leave for an operation and another has been away for two weeks on stress leave. Max was left with only one dispenser to help him do all the work. The volume of prescriptions has been increasing constantly, and as result, a backlog has occurred. His main task is checking prescriptions, and he has no time to devote to other tasks of patient counseling and management duties for which he is well qualified. Max's work is constantly interrupted by questions from other healthcare staff. Daily he is harassed by the manager, Dianne, to perform more medicine use reviews (MURs) and reduce the waiting times. He realizes that the targets for MURs and waiting times are unrealistic. When he tried to explain the difficulties, both Dianne and the area manager were not supportive. Now he feels that he is not doing a good job and is emotionally distressed. He experiences constant band-like headaches across the forehead.

8.2 Introduction

The scenario described above is common among pharmacists working as retail chain chemists. In 2009, the Royal Pharmaceutical Society of Great Britain (RPSGB) launched the Workplace Pressure initiative (RPSGB, 2009a, 2009b). The survey has shown that about 48.2% of those who responded claimed that they are constantly under stress, and 74.3% felt that the increasing number of prescriptions dispensed was a key issue. The survey also revealed that 73.2% of the respondents were not able to delegate work due to staff shortages. Lack of rest breaks experienced by 70.3% of respondents was also an issue (RPSGB, 2009c). In 2010–2011, 10.8 million working days were lost due to stress, and it had a ripple effect by increasing the workload of others, creating further stress at the workplace. During the same period, the Health and Safety Executive (2011) reported that 400,000 people were affected by stress, out of a total of 1,152,000 work-related illnesses. According to well-known stress researcher Kenneth Pelletier, 80 to 90% of all illnesses are stress related, and 75 to 90% of all visits to the doctor are conditions associated with stress and anxiety (Leyden-Rubenstein, 1998).

In the United States, more surveys have been conducted to determine job satisfaction than work-related stress among pharmacists. In 2004, a cross-sectional study using a mail survey was carried out among 1,263 pharmacists. In this survey, 15% of the respondents declared their intention to leave their current employer the following year (Gaither et al., 2007). The most common reasons for leaving were a desire for change and stress or workload issues.

Another cross-sectional study involving all members of the American Society of Consultant Pharmacists as of March 2005 using the Health Professional Stress Inventory has shown that 90% of the pharmacists were satisfied in their jobs (Lapane and Hughes, 2006). However, the most frequently reported source of stress was staff shortage affecting their ability to perform their duties. This survey also revealed that more than one-third of the dispensing pharmacists were stressed due to the need to keep up with professional development activities.

A further study using a cross-sectional Web-based questionnaire to determine the level of job satisfaction among 373 practicing pharmacists has found that 80% of the pharmacists in independent pharmacies were satisfied in their jobs, in contrast to 78% in independent inpatient hospital settings (Maio et al., 2004). However, 53% of pharmacists in chain pharmacies were less satisfied in their jobs.

8.3 Definitions

Stress: The word *stress* was virtually unknown before the 1960s. It is now a common term among families and at work. Richard Lazarus defined *stress* as a condition or feeling experienced when a person perceives that the demands exceed the ability to cope with them. The holistic medicines approach modifies this definition (Seaward, 2006) as:

> The experience of a perceived threat (real or imaginary) to one's mental, physical or spiritual well-being, resulting from a series of psychological responses and adaptations.

Stressors: A stressor is a physical, psychological, or social factor(s) that produces real or perceived demands in the body, emotions, mind, or spirit of an individual. There are several types of stressors (Whetten et al., 2000):

1. Time stressors: Caused by a situation where an individual has too much to do in too little time.
2. Encounter stressors: Caused by poor interpersonal relationships such as conflicts and lack of trust.
3. Situational stressors: Arise due to poor working conditions, such as long hours and shortage of support staff.
4. Anticipatory stressors: Arise when an individual anticipates a stressful situation that has not yet happened.

Stress management: Stress management refers to the identification and management of factors associated with stress and the application of a variety of therapeutic measures to change either the origin of stress or the experience of stress (Cotton, 1990).

8.4 Measurement of Stress Levels among Pharmacists

Numerous studies have been carried out to determine the stress at work in both the United States and the United Kingdom. In 1985, Wolfgang et al.[*] identified the 15 most stressful job situations for pharmacists. They include interruptions at work, staff shortages, issues with policies and procedures, inability to participate in decision making, and lack of job advancement.

Causes of stress among pharmacists have been well documented. A study of stress among 573 pharmacists[†] has shown that job conflicts, patient care responsibility, lack of professional recognition, and professional uncertainty were the

---

[*] A.P. Wolfgang, K.W. Kirk, and M.D. Shepard, *American Pharmacy*, NS25: 46, 1985.

[†] G.V. Gupchup, Job Stress as a Transaction and a Process, Ph.D. dissertation, Purdue University, Indiana, 1996.

most stressful situations. The Royal Pharmaceutical Society's Workplace Survey in 2009 (RPSGB, 2009c) has shown that number of scripts to be dispensed and inadequate staff and rest breaks were some of the causes of stress among pharmacists. Professor David Guest, in his report on causes and consequences of stress among pharmacists (Guest, 2009), finds a causative relationship between workload and stress.

The Department of Health and Human Services (DHHS) in the United States quoted the results of three surveys on stress at work (DHHS, 1999). Northwestern National Life reported that 40% of the workers found the job to be "very" or "excessively" stressful, and 26% of the workers who participated in the Families and Work Institute found themselves to be "often or very often burned out or stressed." According to the Yale University survey, 29% of the workers were "quite a bit or extremely stressed."

However, these job situations did not include patient care. Therefore, the list was expanded to 30 job situations and was called the Health Professions Stress Inventory (HPSI). In this list (Gupchup and Worley-Louis, 2005), four types of pharmacists' stress were identified: (1) professional recognition, (2) patient care responsibility, (3) job conflict, and (4) professional uncertainty. They were scored on a scale of 1 to 5, with 1 being "never stressed" and 5 being "frequently stressed."

A study of job satisfaction and stress (Lapane and Hughes, 2004) among 18 consultant pharmacists, 18 dispensing pharmacists, and 60 technicians in the United States using HPSI as one of the criteria has shown that 12% of the dispensing pharmacists were stressed because of patient outcome, 35% for fear of making mistakes, 47% because of family commitments, 76% because of interruptions, and 53% due to staff shortage.

A study of job-related stress among the pharmacists in Ireland using the HPSI model (McCann and Hughes, 2009) has revealed that the mean score of the stresses, patient care responsibility, job conflict, professional recognition, managing workload, and professional uncertainty was 94.66

for community pharmacists and 89.63 for hospital pharmacists, out of a maximum of 165.

The 2009 C+D and Pharmacy Defence Association (PDA) salary survey (PDA, 2010) has shown that 85% of pharmacists experienced stress during the previous year. In addition, 71% were subjected to pressure from management, and 44% suffered intimidation from customers. Insomnia (51%) and suicidal thoughts (4%) were also some of the effects of stress experienced by pharmacists, and 84% of respondents reported lack of support from management.

According to a government report, 41% of health-related problems of pharmacists during the previous five years were due to stress. The RPSGB launched a Workplace Pressure campaign in 2009 (RPSGB, 2009d) to determine the discontent and frustration within the pharmacy profession. Over 600 participated in the survey, and the results showed that 48.2% considered their working days to be "constantly stressful." A further quarter reported their jobs to be "extremely stressful." Only 4.9% of the respondents experienced "occasional stress" (RPSGB, 2009c).

8.5 Impact of Stress

Stress at work is widespread across the globe, and it has an impact on the individual as well as on the organization. According to an International Labour Organization report,[*] stress is rapidly increasing in the world, and in the United States, $200 million is lost annually through reduced productivity, absenteeism, insurance claims and compensation, and medical expenses. In Great Britain, the Health and Safety Commission (HSC) report indicates that stress cost in excess of £530 million in 2006, with a loss of 14 million working

---

[*] C.R. Greer and W.R. Plunkett, *Supervision: Diversity and Teams in the Workplace* (10th ed.) (Englewood Cliffs, NJ: Prentice Hall, 2007).

days due to work-related stress, depression, and anxiety (HSC, 2007).

Stress at work affects the performance of the individual and his or her health. Among pharmacists, stress causes job dissatisfaction, lower commitment to work, higher job turnover, lower commitment to the profession, the potential for substance abuse, and burnout (Gupchup and Worley-Louis, 2005). The symptoms associated with occupational stress are well documented and include (1) psychological symptoms, (2) physical symptoms, (3) emotional symptoms, and (4) behavior symptoms (Donyai and Denicolo, 2009; Health and Safety Executive, n.d. a, n.d. b; Ireland, 2005). These are summarized in Table 8.1.

8.6 Response to Stress

In 1914, Harvard physiologist Walter Cannon first described the flight-or-fight response to stress. According to this response, the body reacts to defend or protect its comfort zone. When a threat or harm is perceived, the body prepares itself to defend by attacking or fighting, or escaping and running to avoid the threat (Figure 8.1). The fight response is triggered by anger or aggression, and the flight response is induced by fear. There are four stages to this response (Seaward, 2006):

1. Brain receives the stimuli from sensors.
2. Brain decodes the message as a threat or no threat. If it is a threat, brain activates the defense mechanism to fight or escape.
3. State of activation until the threat is resolved.
4. Brain returns to the normal state.

Table 8.1 Signs of Stress in Individuals

Emotional Symptoms	Mental Symptoms	Behavior Symptoms	Physical Symptoms
Depression	Confusion, indecision	Change in eating habits	Tiredness and fatigue
Feeling of disappointment with oneself	Inability to concentrate	Smoking, drug abuse, and drinking	Muscle tension
Increased emotional response	Poor memory	Insomnia	Cardiovascular diseases
Loneliness	Job dissatisfaction	Nervous behavior	Asthma
Lack of motivation	Low self-esteem	Lack of interest in work	Cancer
Mood swings	Low morale	Sexual problems	Headaches
		Avoiding friends and family members	Inflammatory bowel disease
			Diabetes
			Sweating
			Fainting

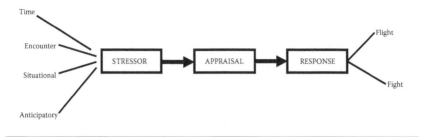

Figure 8.1   Stress response.

8.7 Models of Stress

Several models have been proposed to explain the mechanism
of stress from different perspectives. Commonly used models
are the (1) cognitive appraisal model, (2) transactional model,
and (3) health realization/health innate model.

8.7.1 Cognitive Appraisal Model

The cognitive appraisal model is the most coherent model
based on psychological mechanisms. In this model, a situation
is appraised (primary appraisal) as threatening, causing a loss
or harm, a challenge, or benign (Ireland, 2005). The primary
appraisal considers both personal and environmental factors.
Coping strategies come into force. Problem-focused coping is
aimed at resolving the problem, and emotion-focused coping
manages the emotions. Secondary appraisal comes into effect
to determine whether one has the necessary resources to cope
with the situation. Lack of resources to cope with the situation
leads to stress. This model explains how some people find
some situations to be stressful while others do not. The cognitive appraisal model also explains the different levels of stress
experienced by people exposed to the same situation.

8.7.2 Transactional Model

The transactional model is based on a two-way interaction between the person and the environment (Donyai and Denicolo, 2009). If the person does not appraise the situation as stressful or has sufficient resources to cope, the stress is eliminated. By changing one's perspective, stress can be minimized.

8.7.3 Health Realization/Innate Health Model

The primary focus of the health realization/innate health model (Sedgeman, 2005) is that it is the nature of one's thought that determines whether a situation is stressful or not. This model does not question the existence of stressors. But it is possible to disengage from stress by dismissing negative thoughts and insecure feelings, thus the mind acting as a "mental filter." By understanding the nature of the mind, thought, and consciousness, one can promote a feeling of well-being rather than stress.

8.8 Management of Stress

The aim of stress management programs is to identify the optimal level of stress that motivates the employee and then implement strategies to minimize the level of physical response. Two types of strategies (DHHS, 1999) are employed to manage stress at work: (1) individual stress management and employee assistance programs and (2) organizational changes.

8.8.1 Individual Stress Management Programs (ISMPs)

These programs provide the skills to cope with stressful situations. The scope of ISMPs describes the nature and sources of stress, effects of stress on health and well-being, and personal skills such as time management and relaxation techniques to minimize stress. The strategies (Gupchup and Worley-Louis, 2005) include

Coping techniques: Problem-focused coping involves attempts to resolve the problem that causes the stress and has been found to be most effective in reducing the stress. On the other hand, emotion-focused coping that distances oneself from the problem has not been as successful. Gupchup (1996),[*] in his study, found problem-focused coping to be very effective in managing the four types of stress described in this chapter.

Meditation and relaxation techniques: Mental relaxation is closely associated with physical relaxation. The most commonly used techniques are (1) transcendental meditation, (2) breathing techniques, (3) Benson technique, and (4) progressive relaxation.

Biofeedback: This involves the use of instruments to detect abnormal body functions due to stress and methods to address the abnormalities. For example, an increase in blood pressure is caused by stress, and using methods to control blood pressure is biofeedback.

Physical exercise: The ability to reduce stress and health problems associated with stress through physical exercise is well known. Engaging in daily exercises such as walking, jogging, workouts, and games for at least 30 minutes is effective in reducing stress.

The advantages of ISMPs are that they (1) reduce anxiety and sleep disturbances associated with stress, (2) are inexpensive, and (c) are easy to implement. However, the benefits of ISMPs are short-lived, and the programs do not address the root causes of stress and the focus is on the employee rather than on the environment.

---

[*] Gupchup, G. V. (1996). Pharmacists' job stress as a transaction and a process. PhD Dissertation, Purdue University, Indiana.

8.8.2 *Organizational Changes*

Organizational changes involve the identification of the stressful aspects of the job and designing strategies to minimize or eliminate stressful situations. Prior to making changes, stressors must be identified using tools such as HPSI, as described earlier, intervention strategies implemented, and interventions evaluated constantly. A healthy working environment can only be created by constantly evaluating these three steps.

8.8.3 *Prevention of Stress*

The most effective way to manage stress is to combine ISMP and organizational changes with preventive measures (DHHS, 1999) that focus on the environment and include

1. Reasonable workload that employees can cope with.
2. Redesigning jobs to stimulate and motivate employees to match their skills.
3. Clearly defining roles, responsibilities, and authority. Responsibility without authority is a poor management technique.
4. Allowing employees to participate in decision-making processes.
5. Providing opportunities for advancement.
6. Enhancing social interactions.
7. Balancing work schedules with family situations.

8.9 Revisiting the Scenario

In the scenario described in Section 8.1, first Max can benefit from an ISMP. Working conditions also must be improved. When dispensers were on sick leave, sick cover should have been arranged. Obviously, targets for MURs and waiting times are unrealistic. Problem-solving exercises should be carried out to determine realistic targets, identify areas that can be improved, and minimize interruptions. All members of the dispensing team need to participate in these discussions. Lack of motivation is another factor that contributes to Max's stress. The manager has to take leadership and redesign roles and responsibilities that take into account his talents and skills. In addition, Max has to see some prospects of advancement in his job.

References

Cotton, D.H.G. (1990). *Stress management: An integral approach to therapy*. New York: Brunner/Mazel.

Department of Health and Human Services. (1999). *Stress at work* (Publication 99-100). National Institute for Occupational Safety and Health. Retrieved December 29, 2010, from http://www.cdc.gov/niosh/docs/99-101/

Donyai, P., and Denicolo, P.M. (2009). Understanding and dealing with stress and pressure in the workplace. *Pharmaceutical Journal*, 282, 643–645.

Gaither, C.A., Nadkarni, A., Mott, D.A., Schommer, J.C., Doucette, W.R., Kreling, D.H., and Pedersen, C.A. (2007). Should I stay or should I go? The influence of individual and organisational factors on pharmacists' future work plans. *Journal of the American Pharmacists Association*, 47, 165–173.

Guest, D. (2009). Causes and consequences of stress amongst pharmacists. In *Work Load Pressure and the Pharmacy Work Force: Joint Royal Pharmaceutical Society of Great Britain and Primary Practice Research Trust Symposium* (p. 4).

Gupchup, G.V., and Worley-Louis, M.M. (2005). Understanding and managing stress among pharmacists. In S.P. Desselle and D.P. Zgarrick (Eds.), *Pharmacy management: Essentials for all practice settings* (pp. 51–62). New York: McGraw-Hill.

Health and Safety Commission. (2007). Workplace stress costs Great Britain in excess of £530 million. Retrieved December 29, 2010, from http://www.hse.gov.uk/press/2007/c07021.htm

Health and Safety Executive. (2011). Stress and psychological disorders. Retrieved February 10, 2011, from http://www.hse.gov.uk/statistics/causdis/stress/stress.pdf

Health and Safety Executive. (n.d. a). Work related stress. Retrieved December 29, 2010, from http://www.hse.gov.uk/stress/further-advice/wrs.htm

Health and Safety Executive. (n.d. b). Work related stress: Signs and symptoms. Retrieved January 1, 2011, from http://www.hse.gov.uk/stress/furtheradvice/signsandsymptoms.htm

Ireland, J. (2005, July). Stress: The enemy inside. *Pharmacy Today*, 33–35.

Lapane, K. L., and Hughes, C. M. (2006). Job satisfaction and stress among pharmacists in the long-term care sector. *Consultant Pharmacist*, 21(4), 287–292.

Lapane, K., and Hughes, C.M. (2004). Baseline job satisfaction and stress among pharmacists and pharmacy technicians participating in the Fleetwood Phase III study. *Consultant Pharmacist*, 19(11), 1027–1037.

Leyden-Rubenstein, L.A. (1998). *The stress management handbook*. New Canaan, CT: Keats Publishing.

Maio, V., Goldfarb, N.I., and Hartmann, W. (2004). Pharmacists' job satisfaction: Variation by practice setting. *Pharmacy and Therapeutics*, 29, 184–190.

McCann, L., and Hughes, C.M. (2009). Assessing job satisfaction and stress among pharmacists in Northern Ireland. *Pharmacy World and Science*, 31, 188–194.

Pharmacy Defence Association. (2010, Summer). Workplace pressure campaign. Is the RPSGB the solution or part of the problem? *Insight*, 17.

Royal Pharmaceutical Society of Great Britain. (2009a). Is workplace pressure affecting you? *Pharmaceutical Journal*, 282, 103.

Royal Pharmaceutical Society of Great Britain. (2009b). Long hours put you (and others) at risk. *Pharmaceutical Journal*, 282, 706.

Royal Pharmaceutical Society of Great Britain. (2009c). Half of all pharmacists are "constantly stressed." *Pharmaceutical Journal*, 282, 706.

Royal Pharmaceutical Society of Great Britain. (2009d). Stress accounts for 41 percent of pharmacists' health problems. *Pharmaceutical Journal*, 284, 258.

Seaward, B.L. (2006). *Managing stress: Principles and strategies for health and wellbeing*. Burlington, MA: Jones and Bartlett.

Sedgeman, J.A. (2005). Health realisation/innate health: Can a quiet mind and a positive feeling state be accessible over the life-span without stress-relief techniques? *Medical Science Monitor,* 11(12), 47–52.

Whetten, D.A., Cameron, K.S., and Woods, M. (2000). *Developing management skills for Europe.* Essex, England: Pearson Education.

Chapter 9

Team Building

Coming together is a beginning. Keeping together is progress. Working together is success.

—Henry Ford

9.1 Scenario

Dianne recruited a new dispenser, Clare, to the team. Since her appointment, Dianne has openly commented how skilled and talented she is. Most projects that were considered important were taken from the other staff and given to Clare without any consultation. Other staff were disappointed, and soon communication broke down among the team. In utter exasperation, Dianne brought the issue to the attention of the area manager.

9.2 Introduction

All patients have high expectations from a pharmacy, whether it is a community pharmacy or a hospital pharmacy. To deliver the services required by the patients and meet the overall goals of the organization, the pharmacy staff have to work together as a team. Teamwork has been considered such an essential feature of pharmacy practice that its necessity has been included in the *Standards of Conduct, Ethics and Performance* that all pharmacists have to comply with (General Pharmaceutical Council, 2010). Principle 7 in the standards states:

> Working in a team is an important part of professional practice and relies on respect, co-operation and communication between colleagues from your own and other professions. When you work as part of a team you are accountable for your own decisions and behaviour and any work you supervise.

9.3 Groups and Teams

Groups representing task forces, committees, and councils are not teams. Even the workforces in a large organization that work together cannot be considered teams. A group can be defined as (Mackin, 2007):

> A small group of people with complementary skills and abilities who are committed to a leader's goal and approach and are willing to be held accountable by the leader.

According to Katzenbach and Smith (2005), a team "is a small number of people with complementary skills who are committed to a common purpose, set of performance goals and approach for which they hold themselves mutually accountable."

The distinction between teams and groups is based on performance results. A working group's performance depends on what members in the group do as individuals. Essential

Table 9.1 Differences between Groups and Teams

	Group	Team
1	Leadership clearly focused	Leadership changes among members
2	Individual members are accountable	Both individuals and team are accountable
3	Organizational mission drives the purpose	Team delivers its specific purpose
4	Focus on individual goals	Focus on team goals
5	Produce individual work products	Produce collective work products
6	Members have individual roles, responsibilities, and tasks	Members have individual roles, responsibilities, and tasks to work as a team
7	Concern with individual outcomes and challenges	Concern with collective outcome and challenges
8	Manager defines the goals and approaches to work	Team leader with team members defines goals and approaches to work
9	Comes together to run efficient meetings for discussions, decisions, and delegation	Open-ended discussions and problem-solving sessions for discussions, decisions, and working together

differences between groups and teams are summarized in Table 9.1 (Katzenbach and Smith, 2005).

9.4 Benefits of Team Approach

Teamwork has been found to have a strong influence on the performance of the organization. Although organizations have teams that are supported by the management to achieve excellent results, there are occasions where teams have not succeeded all the time. Therefore, managers must decide when teams should be formed. However, teamwork has the following benefits (Whetten et al., 2000):

1. Teams produce a wealth of ideas and information to enable decision making and solutions to problems to be carried out effectively.
2. Participation of all the members of the team improves understanding and acceptance among the members of the team involved in decision making and problem solving.
3. Social facilitation among the members leads to higher motivation and performance levels.
4. Members of teams overcome inhibitions that prevent participation in discussions and promote contribution to teamwork.
5. Teams are more likely to produce novel and creative ideas.
6. There is greater cohesion among team members.

9.5 Types of Teams

Teams can be classified in several ways depending upon the objectives of the team. The best classification is the one proposed by Katzenbach and Smith (2005). According to these authors, teams can be classified as (1) teams that recommend things, (2) teams that make or do things, and (3) teams that run things.

9.5.1 Teams That Recommend Things

These teams have been formed to study or solve particular problems and include teams such as task teams, quality teams, audit teams, and project teams. They have been assigned completion dates to achieve their goals. Teams that recommend things have to commence their tasks without delay and address the manner of implementing their recommendations. In order to achieve their objectives within the specified period, the team members need to know why their efforts are important, who the participating members are, and the expected completion date. The management has to select the team members with appropriate skills. The people who have been instructed to implement the recommendations must have had an early briefing. It is also important to include some members of the team who were responsible for the recommendations.

In a community pharmacy, the manager may appoint a team to reduce the waiting time for dispensing prescriptions for patients. It is essential to include counter staff as well as dispensary staff because the first contact with the patient is with the counter staff.

9.5.2 Teams That Make or Do Things

The activities of teams that make or do things are ongoing and are generally value adding. These teams include manufacturing, operations, sales, marketing, etc. New product development teams or new design teams are also included in this category, and apart from these two categories, the teams that make or do things do not have set completion dates. The appointment of members with appropriate skills is crucial to the success of the team's performance. Team performance has the greatest impact on critical delivery points, and therefore the management must focus on points where accounts are managed, customer services are performed, products are designed, and production efficiency is monitored.

Reducing dispensing errors in a pharmacy is an ongoing activity. The appointed team has to look at how the service can be delivered to the patient without compromising the health and safety of the patient.

9.5.3 Teams That Run Things

A group that oversees some business activity, ongoing program, or a significant functional activity is a team that runs things. Some groups that run things can be more beneficial than teams. Therefore, top management must decide whether the group structure or the team structure is better for the task at hand. Group structure has several advantages over team structure: it has fewer risks, needs less time to construct the purpose, facilitates more efficient meetings, can implement decisions through individual assignments, and has accountability.

However, organizations may prefer a team approach for satisfying performance needs. The team approach is particularly useful when organizations go through major changes. For a team that runs things to be effective, the top management has to define specific goals for the team to meet, which should not be confused with the organization's mission. Although the teams at the top are more powerful, long-term challenges are more complex and incur heavy demands of executive time. Furthermore, individualism can dominate, leading to an ineffective team approach.

For example, the hospital board may appoint a team to address the issues raised at the previous external audit.

9.6 Skill Requirements

For the team to be effective, the team must be of the right size and have a mix of complementary skills needed for the team's job. There are three categories of skill requirements (Katzenbach and Smith, 2005): (1) technical or functional skills, (2) problem-solving and decision-making skills, and (3) interpersonal skills.

1. Technical or functional skills: Teams that include members having complementary skills are more likely to succeed than groups consisting of individual skills. For example, quality improvement groups that include quality professionals and managers are less likely to succeed than those with complementary skills of both. Pharmacists with management skills can make a better contribution to team efforts than pharmacists without them.

2. Problem-solving and decision-making skills: The team must be able to identify and analyze the problems without jumping into solutions, evaluate various options, and decide on the best options for implementation. Most teams need a few members with these skills initially, but others can acquire them on the job.

3. Interpersonal skills: The team must have a common understanding and purpose that can only be achieved with communication skills and proper management of conflict. These depend on interpersonal skills. Other essential interpersonal skills for teamwork are ability to take risks, offer constructive criticism, listen actively, appreciate the viewpoints of others, acknowledge the achievement and interests of others, give benefit of the doubt, and behave impartially.

9.7 Why Teams Are Necessary

Teams are much more than individual contributions. The leader gains a new perspective with team building. His or her confidence grows, and each member of the team values his or her individual contributions. The members are able to overcome inhibitions that prevent them from participating in discussions. The following are the reasons why teams are necessary (Barrett, 1992):

- Recognition and acknowledgment of mutual responsibility in achieving common objectives
- Overcome barriers such as rivalry and jealousy, which are common among group structures
- A harmonious environment for discussion of important issues
- Create a climate where individuals can contribute and participate in discussions and mutually support each other
- Greater confidence to express one's opinion
- Increasing awareness of other members' pressures and problems

9.8 How to Build a Successful Team

In a team-oriented environment, the team members contribute toward the success of the organization. However, to build a successful team to accomplish specific goals, special attention is required to the following factors (Heathfield, 2011):

1. Clearly communicate the purpose of creating the team to all the members.
2. Explain how the team can help achieve goals and where it fits in with the organization's overall goals, purpose, values, and vision.
3. Explain the need for commitment to the vision of the team.
4. Select members with appropriate knowledge, skills, capabilities, and having the ability to address issues. The leader must provide access to necessary resources to the team.
5. The team needs to accept its area of responsibility. It must create its own mission, vision, and strategies that fit in with the overall mission of the organization. The team must communicate the goals to all. The process of accomplishing the tasks and how the outcome is measured must be clearly defined.

6. The team must have the freedom and empowerment to take ownership for its actions. All limitations must be clearly specified. All team members must understand the authority and accountability for the results.

7. Problem solving, process improvement, goal setting and measurement, conflict resolution, and consensus decision making require collaboration.

8. Team members must clearly understand the context for their formation. The leader must communicate the tasks and their priorities and relevant business information. A method must be established to give and receive feedback.

9. The organization must promote creative innovation, new ideas, and unique solutions. Accomplishments must be rewarded, and the organization must provide training and education as necessary for the team to perform.

10. All team members must be held responsible and accountable for their achievements. The organization must create a "no blame" culture without reprisals. The team's performance can increase, if the members feel that their achievements have an impact on the success of the organization.

11. For success of the team, a central leadership team must coordinate the team. This will enable cross-functional and multifunctional teams to work together effectively. All team members must understand the concept of internal customer and a customer-focused, process-oriented approach.

12. Building an effective team requires a culture change. A team-based, collaborative, empowering, and enabling organization culture must be created. Organization plans to change the reward system, recognition, appraisal, hiring, developing plans, motivation, and managing people have an impact on the success of the organization.

9.9 Stages in Developing Teams

Leadership is essential to make an efficient and effective team. Talents should be managed to guide the team through the various stages of development. The leader should harness the full potential of the team at every stage of team development. The five sequential stages in team development are (Asopa and Beye, 1997):

1. Forming—awareness: Team members are oriented and commit themselves to the purpose, goals, and programs.
2. Storming—resolution and development of a sense of belonging.
3. Norming—cooperation, collaboration, and communication are promoted among the team members, which results in a feeling of enticement and support.
4. Performing—productivity: This is the stage of activity where problems are solved and interdependence fostered.
5. Adjourning—separation: The activities are completed without encountering problems. This stage occurs only if the other stages have been successfully completed.

9.10 Enhancing Team Performance

There is no magic rule for enhancing team performance. However, many successful teams share the following approaches (Katzenbach and Smith, 2005):

1. Establish urgency and give clear directions for performance. The team should be aware of the urgency, purpose of forming the team, and expectations of the

organization. Teams work best in a compelling situation. It is known that organizations with strong performance ethics form teams readily.

2. Selection of the team should be based on skills and skill potential. A skilled manager selects the team members for their existing skills, and the potential to improve their existing skills and learn new ones.

3. The first meeting and early actions are important. Attention should be paid to those in authority.

4. Establish clear rules of behavior. At the earliest stage, the importance of attendance, participating in discussions, confidentiality, analytical approach, outcome orientation, constructive conflict, and contribution should be emphasized.

5. Focus on a few immediate performance-oriented tasks and goals. Establish challenging goals that can be achieved early. The results are important, and the sooner they are shown, the sooner the team becomes cohesive.

6. Update relevant information and facts so that the team can redefine and enrich their understanding of performance criteria. Always remember that all the information does not exist with the team.

7. Spend more time together. Personal bonding is important for the team's performance, and impromptu and casual meetings and get-togethers should be encouraged, especially in the beginning.

8. Offer positive feedback, rewards, and recognition. Positive reinforcement is a powerful tool to encourage contribution by the members. Awards for recognizing the contributions are essential to keep the momentum of the group. However, the team gets most satisfaction from completing the task successfully.

9.11 Indications of a Winning Team

The following criteria enable a leader to identify a winning team (Barrett, 1992):

- Fully aware of its direction and progress
- Sets realistic and achievable targets
- Utilizes all the resources in energetic and innovative ways
- Develops a wide range of options for action
- Initiates coping strategies when necessary
- Regularly monitors the progress of tasks
- Confidence in members to follow their contribution to the common goal
- Has a positive and realistic self-image
- Handles external relationships with sensitivity and assertiveness

9.12 Team Building Exercises

Team building exercises have been used extensively to foster communication among the members of a team. Appropriate exercises can improve morale, promote cohesion, enhance motivation, and create a clear focus on a team problem. However, they must be used wisely in tough economic times (Olsen, 2009). In selecting exercises for team building, considerations should be given to the following:

1. Present a real-world problem: Identify a problem that the staff are familiar and comfortable with. Such a problem enables the staff to make a vital contribution to the discussion on familiar grounds. The outcome can be directly applied when they return to work.
2. Account for different styles and personalities: Some exercises and games are not appreciated by everyone on the team. People are generally more comfortable with what

they know. To appreciate the differences in styles and personalities, design an exercise that involves different roles to choose from in order to accommodate everyone on the team.

3. Choose a facilitator who will introduce the program: The selection of a facilitator is crucial to the success of the project. A facilitator will work on what the organization wants to accomplish, rather than a ready-made program. The organization should ensure that the program offered by the facilitator fits in with the culture of the organization.

9.13 Teams in Large Organizations and Business Units

In pharmacies with few employees, cross-functional teams are inconceivable. However, in larger units and business corporations, teams are sometimes essential to implement their strategic plans. Although cross-functional teams do not resolve all problems in the corporate world, some companies have created and successfully managed such teams to achieve their business goals (Mankins and Steele, 2005).

In 2002, Tyco, with 42 business units and several hundred profit centers, was a struggling company. The CEO then assigned cross-functional teams at each business unit to continuously analyze their business indicators, such as market profitability and their offerings, cost, and price positioning in the market relative to competitors. Biweekly meetings were held with corporate executives to review and discuss the findings of each team. The focus of each unit was the assumptions that would lead to their individual long-term financial performance and not to the financial forecasts. These discussions promoted the trust between the cross-functional team and the unit. The cross-functional teams' concept and their performance contributed to Tyco's revival (Mankins and Steele, 2005).

Cisco Systems utilized cross-functional teams to review the level and timing of resource deployment early in the planning stage. The teams regularly met with the CEO and the executive team to discuss their findings and recommendations. When agreement on resource allocation and timing at the unit level was reached, those elements were incorporated into their two-year plan. Each unit's resource deployments were monitored monthly to ensure that plans were being followed and were achieving expected results (Mankins and Steele, 2005).

9.14 Revisiting the Scenario

Leadership skills are essential to create a winning team. Pharmacy practice involves teamwork with colleagues and external healthcare professionals. As a result of unilateral action by the manager, conflicts and interpersonal relationships issues have arisen. Dianne should have first identified the issues to be resolved by a team. She also should have identified skills of the members of the team. The stage is now set for the team to develop and commit themselves to the purpose, goals, and programs. Working as a team, individual skills will be appreciated, thus eliminating friction among members and promoting cohesion. The team makes the decisions and is accountable to deliver the expectations of the manager.

References

Asopa, V.N., and Beye, G. (1997). *Management of agricultural research: A training manual. Module 4: Leadership, motivation, building and conflict management.* Research and Technology Development Service Research Extension and Training Division, Food and Agriculture Organisation. Retrieved November 12, 2011, from http://www.fao.org/docrep/w7504e/w7504e00.htm#Contents

Barrett, P. (1992). Team building. In D.M. Stewart (Ed.), *Handbook of management skills* (pp. 252–268). London: BCA.

General Pharmaceutical Council. (2010). *Standards of conduct, ethics and performance.* London: General Pharmaceutical Council.

Heathfield, S.M. (2011). Twelve tips for team building: How to build successful work teams. About.com. Retrieved November 12, 2011, from http://humanresources.about.com/od/involvementteams/a/twelve_tip_team.htm

Katzenbach, J.R., and Smith, D.K. (2005). Discipline of teams. *Harvard Business Review*, 83(9), 162–171.

Mackin, D. (2007). The difference between a team and a group. *The Side Road*. Retrieved November 2, 2011, from http://www.sideroad.com/Team_Building/difference-between-team-and-group.html

Mankins, M.C., and Steele, R. (2005). Turning great strategy into great performance. *Harvard Business Review*, 83(3), 64–72.

Olsen, P. (2009). Team building exercises for tough times. HBR Blog Network. Retrieved November 12, 2011, from http://blogs.hbr.org/hmu/2009/03/teambuilding-exercises-for-tou.html

Whetten, D., Cameron, K., and Woods, M. (2000). *Developing management skills for Europe.* Essex, England: Pearson Education.

Chapter 10

Effective Communication

To effectively communicate, we must realize that we are different in the way we perceive the world and use this understanding as a guide to communication with others.

—Anthony Robbins

10.1 Scenario

When the pharmacy manager handed over the medication to a patient following a brief counseling session with the pharmacist, the pharmacy manager informed the patient that the balance of the medication in the prescription would be ordered and ready in two days. This time frame was important to the patient, as she was going overseas. The pharmacy manager instructed the dispenser to order the remaining items. The dispenser ordered the items, but some of them would not be available for another week. The pharmacy manager did not explain the urgency to the dispenser because she wanted to handle the matter herself, but she was sick and was not available during the next few days. When the patient returned to collect the balance, it was not ready. She was became angry.

10.2 Introduction

Communication is an essential part of everyday life. Whether it is in business or in family, human-to-human interaction is inevitable. It is frequently taken for granted. It can be a critical issue in an organization's ability to achieve its objectives. Unless a manager can effectively communicate what, how, by whom, and when it is to be done, the chance of objectives being completed as expected is greatly reduced (Ehlert, 2004).

Communication in the healthcare sector is a complex process involving multidirectional movement, upward, downward, and in all directions (Longest, 1984). The pharmacy practice essentially involves teamwork, and effective communication permits the team to influence and react to each other.

The pharmacy staff at Milton Keynes Hospital NHS Foundation Trust have evolved a novel approach to leadership and communication that has allowed the pharmacy department to deliver a wide range of more effective services (Pringle, 2011). All prescribers have been asked to visit the pharmacy and talk to the staff to pick up their copy of the British National Formulary (BNF), thus improving the communication between the pharmacy staff and the prescribers. Ward staff have been encouraged to raise medicine-related questions with the pharmacy staff. Training and educating other health professionals in the hospital has also been a key function. Newly qualified doctors have to undertake a pharmacy assessment before prescribing. These steps have enormously improved communication between the pharmacy staff and other staff in the hospital.

10.3 Communication Needs of Health Professionals

Communication skills in a healthcare pharmacy setting involve (OSCE, 2004–2009; Maguire, 2002)

- Explaining to the patient what the medication is for
- Involving the patient in decision making and seeking informed consent
- Communicating with relatives and other healthcare professionals
- Giving advice on lifestyle measures, health promotions, and risk factors
- Eliciting the patient's main problems
- Communicating what the patient wants to know, checking his or her understanding of the information, and eliciting the patient's response
- Ensuring that the patient will follow agreed-upon decisions about treatment and advice on lifestyle measures

10.4 Benefits of Effective Communication

Effective communication involves the individual, the future, and the tasks. Interchange of an effective communication enhances the relationship between the two parties. Organizations that promote effective communication enjoy the following benefits (Whetten et al., 2000; Hargie et al., 2004):

- Higher productivity
- Faster problem solving
- Improved quality of services and products
- Reduced conflict
- Better understanding of what must be achieved
- Better performance by the staff
- More staff suggestions
- Higher level of creativity
- Greater job satisfaction
- Reduced staff turnover and decreased absenteeism

10.5 Communication Process

Longest (1984) defines communication as "the passing of information and understanding from a sender to a receiver." The definition does not restrict the mode of conveying the message to written or spoken words. It includes all methods by which the message is conveyed from one person to another. Even silence can be considered a part of the communication process.

Although in the business environment communication is often formal, an informal channel of communication, called a grapevine, also exists. The term *grapevine* was coined during the Civil War when telegraph lines were attached to trees much like a grapevine. The messages transmitted through these lines were often unclear and distorted. As a result, any rumor that is circulating in the organizations is said to come from the grapevine.

Traditionally, communication is used to (1) convey our inner purpose, feelings, and attitudes; (2) describe events and objects in the external environment; and (3) share the information between the sender and the recipient. Since the 1940s, several models have been proposed to describe the concept of communication. Narula (2006) has published an excellent review of these models. However, the basic model is presented here (Figure 10.1).

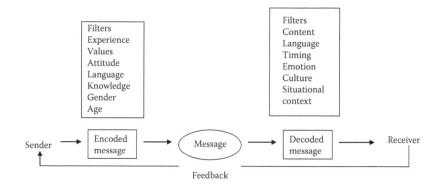

Figure 10.1   Communication process.

The sender develops or encodes the message based on his experience, values, attitudes, etc. These are the filters in encoding and are often unconscious influences in the manner we say or write things (Ellis, 2005). The receiver sees or hears the message and interprets the message using the filters from the receiver's own perspective. For the communication loop to be completed, the receiver sends his or her feedback based on his or her understanding of the message:

> I was the charge pharmacist in Gore, a remote hospital in the south island of New Zealand. I did not have any assistants, and the patients did not have any previous experience in dealing with foreign pharmacists. One day, a patient visited the pharmacy with a prescription. I extended my hand through the hatch to retrieve the prescription. The patient, having noticed me, withdrew the prescription. I tried to recall the patient, but he was gone. The next day the patient returned with the prescription, having spoken to other staff in the hospital, and told me that he did not imagine that I could read the doctor's handwriting!

The case cited above clearly indicates that the message given by the pharmacist could not be received by the patient. The patient filtered the information based on his previous experiences and prejudices.

10.6 Communication Components and Methods

Communication takes place all the time between individuals or groups. The three components of communication are (Ellis, 2005):

1. Verbal: The words chosen for communication.
2. Vocal: The way we say the words—tone, pitch, and volume.

3. Visual: Nonverbal communication, such as facial expression, eye movement, and gesturing.

There are three basic methods of communicating:

1. Person to another person, a group, or a large gathering (public speaking). In this method of communication, all three components are used to convey the message.
2. Voice only. Voice-only communication takes place via telephone, voicemail, or recorded message. This method of communication is devoid of the visual component of communication. It can be an effective method for some messages.
3. Written. The written method of communication involves memos, letters, instructions, standard operating procedures (SOPs), and email. Without the vocal and visible components of communication, the receiver interprets the message using his or her filters. Hence, written messages are most likely to be misinterpreted.

10.7 Nonverbal Communication

Communication involves both verbal and nonverbal expression. Words are used to express ideas of the sender, whereas nonverbal communication relays attitudes and emotions. The dress, facial expression, body movement, and other aspects of behavior and appearance convey messages to the receiver.

Nonverbal communication has three characteristics: (1) it conveys innermost thoughts and feelings, (2) it is difficult and happens unconsciously, and (3) when the nonverbal message is not congruent with the verbal message, interpersonal communication between the sender and the receiver fails. Nonverbal communications must be interpreted with care because often they are based on different social, psychological, cultural, and other background variables (Beardsley et al., 2007).

10.8 Communication Skills

The skills necessary for effective communication have been described by many authors, but most of the skills presented in the literature refer to the description of the process of communication, such as compiling the message, encoding, etc. Maguire (2002) describes four essential skills necessary for effective communication in the healthcare sector:

1. Ability to identify patient's problems and concerns
2. Competency to provide information to the patient
3. Having knowledge to discuss treatment options
4. Demonstrating empathy

Although these skills have been described to enhance communication between medical professionals and the patient, they are directly applicable to the pharmacy practice environment too.

Communication skills can be classified into three categories: expressive skills, listening skills, and skills for managing the overall process (Dick, 1997):

Expressive skills: Used to convey the information to another person by getting the other person's attention, conveying the information, and checking the recipient's understanding.

Listening skills: Needed to help the other person make a clear statement of his or her understanding, giving every opportunity for him or her to express his or her opinion without interruption.

Managing the overall process: Skills needed to decide whose concerns to work on and what sort of information to convey.

Nine core competencies have been described by Hargie et al. (2004). These competencies can be classified as shown in Table 10.1 under the categories described earlier.

Table 10.1   Communication Skills

Dick (1997)	Hargie et al. (2004)	Description
Expressive skills	Nonverbal communication	Section 10.7
	Explaining	Clarifying points
	Self-disclosure	Information about the sender
	Humor and laughter	Clues for better reception
	Persuasion	Motivates the recipient to some action or for response
	Reinforcement	Emphasizes key points to promote understanding
Listening skills	Active listening	Gives the speaker time and space after talking
		Restates the key points according to the understanding by the recipient
		Asks questions in a positive, nonthreatening manner
	Questioning	Should relate to the discussion
		Should make a positive contribution to the discussion
	Reflection	Clarify and restate what the sender conveyed
Managing the process	Empathy	Be supportive and demonstrate empathy
		Show understanding

10.9 Managing Communication

Useful guidelines for managing communication in the workplace are expressed as the following (Weinstein, 1992):

1. **Who** you are communicating with? The type of communication and the method of conveying the information depend on the person with whom communication takes place. The information must be relevant and should be translated to match his or her needs.

2. **Why** are we communicating? There is a purpose for communicating and an intended outcome. The prompt for communicating and the intended outcome lead to the task of communication.

3. **Where** will you communicate? This denotes the place where communication occurs and whether it is formal or informal.

4. **When** will you communicate? Rumor and grapevine travel very fast in all levels of the organization, and therefore the managers have to provide the necessary information to the staff without delay.

5. **What** am I communicating? The information must be tailored to the needs of the recipient.

6. **How** shall I communicate? The most appropriate method depends upon the complexity or simplicity of the information that must be conveyed. If a response is needed, communication should be two-way.

10.10 How to Improve the Effectiveness of Communication

There is no magic formula to improve communication and guarantee success. However, some principles can be formulated that will provide the communication strategy of the organization a greater chance of success (Ehlert, 2004):

1. Gain confidence of the employees. This is achieved by being impartial and consistent, fulfilling obligations and commitments, addressing any issues that affect the staff, and representing the interests of the staff.
2. Gain respect of the employees. Demonstrate a sincere interest in issues that are important to employees, show consideration, and be supportive and display interest in their progress.
3. Promote upward and downward communication. Up-and-down communication is essential to get commitment from the staff to achieve an organization's goals. Listening, talking, and selling skills are important. Decisions that affect the employees in the pharmacy must be communicated by the top management, and they must also be prepared to listen to them and address any issues.
4. Develop active listening skills. Listen carefully without interruption, ask questions to clarify the information in a nonthreatening manner, take action based on the understanding, and communicate the results of such action. A person listens at the rate of 500 words per minute and speaks at a normal rate of 125 to 250 words per minute. Therefore, the recipient's mind can wander onto other things half the time.

Other principles that improve communication are (Barker, 2010; Whetten et al., 2000):

1. Clarify your objectives. The purpose of communicating what information should be communicated, and the expected outcome, should be clear to both the sender and the receiver.
2. Structure your thinking. Communicate the information in a logical manner to promote understanding. Unstructured information confuses the receiver and fails to achieve the object of communicating. The communication skill that

needs greatest improvement is the ability of the sender to transmit a clear, precise message accurately. Inaccurate information can lead to disastrous results.

A pharmacy inserted a flyer promoting the medicine use reviews (MURs) in the medicine bags if patients. The flyer avoided the acronym *MURs* and instead stated, "Speak to the pharmacist about your MOT (Ministry of Transport test) when you collect medicines next time." An elderly patient who read this flyer approached the pharmacy to get the MOT for his vehicle done in the pharmacy! The flyer was then withdrawn.

3. Manage your time and the recipient's time. Choose a time and place convenient to both parties and be prepared to postpone, if the time and place are unsuitable.

4. Establish common ground. In order to convey the message, it is important to identify common ground, such as interests, issues, the "language" to be used, etc. Check basic facts before any communication. The recipient should be the right person to receive the message, and it may be necessary to inform the person in advance.

5. Avoid argument and be honest. When communicating, arguments affect the understanding and delivery of the message. The best relationships are based on matching the communication verbally and nonverbally. Genuine honest statements without hidden agendas are always better than artificial or dishonest statements.

A pharmacist who was keen to meet financial targets for the MUR (the targets are often unrealistic and decided by top management without any consultation) approached a patient while handing over the medications and informed the patient that he wanted to talk to the patient about the medicines. The patient assumed that the pharmacist wanted to inform the patient about some issues with the medicines in the bag. In the consulting room, the pharmacist started a discussion about all the drugs the patient is taking and the clinical history. The patient was angry and told the pharmacist that he thought there were some issues with the medicines in the bag. The pharmacist informed him that he was conducting an MUR, and the unhappy patient walked out of the room.

In this case, the patient was coerced into an MUR session, which is unethical, dishonest, and violates the code of ethics. Patients who are invited must be given the necessary information on MUR service before the session is conducted.

6. Establish empathy. Each individual has a unique perspective that should be valued. Empathy is about understanding and listening to another person's point of view. Be prepared to disclose your feelings and beliefs so that others are encouraged to do so.
7. Summarize often.
8. Use visuals.

10.11 Improving Communication between Pharmacist and Patient

Community pharmacies and hospital pharmacies offer numerous services to patients, and therefore the communication between the patient and the pharmacist must be effective in order to promote a patient's understanding of his or her medication. Health literacy skills (HLS) and general literacy skills (GLS) of patients are important considerations in the communication process. According to the data from the U.S. Department of Education 2003 National Assessment of Adult Literacy study, nearly 36% of the adult population have limited abilities to read and understand health information (Kutner et al., 2006). These skills have not changed during the past decade. Limited HLS have been associated with medication nonadherence and other health issues of patients. Furthermore, limited literacy skills (LTSs) are associated with the inability to understand written and oral communication (Ngoh, 2009).

Therefore, effective communication between the pharmacist and the patients whenever medicines are delivered can make a critical difference. Patients with low HLS generally depend on oral communication. Pharmacists have an important role to play in identifying patients with low HLS and developing strategies that promote understanding and adherence. Many resources are available in the United States to enhance communication with patients (Health Resources and Service Administration, 2009).

Another cause of nonadherence is the complexity of the health information provided to the patient as oral and written information. According to a study that examined the distribution and quality of patient information leaflets (PILs) provided in U.S. pharmacies, 36% of the PILs could not be understood.[*]

Therefore, pharmacists have to use the following strategies to promote the understanding of medical information and adherence (Ngoh, 2009):

■ Speak clearly and slowly.
■ Use appropriate vocabulary and avoid jargon.
■ Explain the specific steps of the regimen.
■ Review the most important actions of the medication.
■ Encourage patients to ask questions.
■ Use simple written instructions or visual aids.
■ Demonstrate the use of devices such as inhalers.
■ Assess patient's HLS.
■ Be respectful, caring, and sensitive so that the patient can be empowered to promote self-care.
■ Confirm patient's understanding of the information provided.

---

[*] M.M. Koo, I. Krass, and P. Aslani, Patient characteristics influencing evaluation of written medicine information: Lessons for patient education, *Annals of Pharmacotherapy*, 39: 1434–1440, 2005.

10.12 Communication Barriers

Communication is a two-way process. When there is effective feedback, mutual understanding is greatly enhanced. According to Rogers and Roethlisberger (1991), the greatest obstacle to communicating effectively is people's tendency to evaluate. The natural tendency is to judge, evaluate, approve, or disapprove another person's statement.

Since the 1990s, barriers to communication have been discussed in detail by many authors. It is convenient to classify these barriers into five categories (Sreenath, 2011; Stanton, 2009):

■ Physical
■ Semantic
■ Organizational
■ Psychological
■ Cultural

Physical barriers are easy to control, and they include poor modes of communication, time constraints, interruptions from the external environment, failure of equipment, etc.

Semantic barriers refer to difficulties associated with conveying the message and include lack of knowledge of the subject matter, lack of clarity in the presentation, use of jargon, lack of common language, lack of interest, poor grammar and punctuation, difficulties of expression, and verbiage.

Organizational barriers to communication reflect the organization's issues. Every organization has its own structure and communication technology. Barriers are due to complexity of the organization, one's own position and status in the organization, policies, rules, and regulations that employees have to comply with, wrong choice of medium, communication overload, and fear of one's superiors.

Psychological barriers are more complex and difficult to deal with. These barriers distort the message given by the sender. They are often associated with mental attitudes and values. People see the world in different ways, and this can distort the message. Other psychological barriers are emotions, clash of personalities, past experiences, resistance to change, and abstraction.

Cultural barriers are due to individual and cultural differences and diversity issues. One of the major problems in communication is stereotyping, and this is often associated with previous experiences. There is no universal interpretation of body language. For example, in Western society, pointing fingers and the use of hands in expression are considered rude. But people from Asian countries often use gestures with fingers and hands for expression, which is normal.

Most of the corner shops in New Zealand are owned by the Indian community. One day an Asian pharmacist, during his day off, was painting the fence. A neighbor who moved to the locality recently saw the pharmacist and asked him whether he closed his corner shop early!

10.13 How to Overcome Communication Barriers

Communication is the key to strong and effective business relationships, which can be between the organization and the customer or between the employees in the same organization. In a workplace, there are many opportunities for poor and ineffective communication. The organization must make a genuine effort to overcome the issues surrounding the barriers to communication. Table 10.2 shows some methods to overcome various barriers discussed earlier.

Table 10.2 Methods to Overcome Communication Barriers

Communication Barriers	How to Overcome
Physical	Select an appropriate location, minimize distractions, ensure audibility and visibility, choose a mode of communication that satisfies both parties
Semantic	Improve communication skills, use simple language, improve listening skills, avoid jargon, use a common language, be competent about the topic
Organizational	Provide opportunities for communicating upward, downward, and laterally, employing techniques such as employee surveys, open-door policies, company newsletters, memos, and minutes of group meetings Promote two-way communication to enhance communication between departments
Psychological	Plan and clarify ideas and opinions, collate ideas from other employees, motivate the listener, avoid prejudices and assumptions, have an open attitude toward others
Cultural	Demonstrate empathy, avoid imposing your own background and culture on others, develop your own understanding and background of others, their perceptions, and scope of knowledge Do not assume generalized behavior

10.14 Revisiting the Scenario

In a community or hospital pharmacy, communication takes place at all levels among the staff, patients, prescribers, other healthcare professionals, and suppliers. Delivery of services takes priority among all other tasks. Unless messages are written down, especially when the pharmacy is busy, they can easily get lost. In the scenario described earlier, satisfying the patient's request would not have been a problem under normal circumstances. However, the pharmacy manager's sudden illness complicated the issue. If the message was written down, the staff could have followed up the request to provide the service required by the patient. A simple procedure to record the message is always a good practice.

References

Barker, A. (2010). *Improve your communication skills* (rev. 2nd ed.). London: Kogan Page.

Beardsley, R.S., Kimberlin, C.L., and Tindall, W. (2007). *Communication skills in pharmacy practice.* Baltimore: Lippincott William & Wilkins.

Dick, B. (1997). Communication. Action research. Retrieved September 28, 2012, from http://www.aral.com.au/resources/communicn.html

Ehlert, D.A. (2004). Managing professionals. In A.A. Peterson (Ed.), *Managing pharmacy practice* (pp. 39–55). Boca Raton, FL: CRC Press.

Ellis, C.W. (2005). *Management skills for new managers.* New York: Amacom.

Hargie, O., Dickson, D., and Tourish, D. (2004). *Communication skills for effective management.* New York: Palgrave Macmillan.

Health Resources and Service Administration. (2009). *Unified health communication.* U.S. Department of Health and Human Services. Retrieved August 28, 2012, from ftp://ftp.hrsa.gov/healthliteracy/training.pdf

Kutner, M., Greenburg, E., Jin, Y., and Paulsen, C. (2006). *The health literacy of American adults: Results from the 2003 National Assessment of Adult Literacy (NCES 2006-483).* Washington, DC: U.S. Department of Education, National Center for Education Statistics.

Longest, B.B. (1984). *Managing practices for the health professional* (3rd ed.). Reston, VA: Reston Publishing.

Maguire, P. (2002). Key communication skills and how to acquire them. *British Medical Journal*, 325, 697–700.

Narula, U. (2006). *Communication models*. New Delhi: Atlantic Publishers.

Ngoh, L.N. (2009). Health literacy: A barrier to pharmacist-patient communication and medication adherence. *Pharmacy Today*, 15(8), 45–57.

OSCE. (2004–2009). *Communication skills for healthcare professionals*. Retrieved November 15, 2011, from http://www.oscehome.com/Communication-Skills.html

Pringle, C. (2011). Communication is the key to building strong interprofessional relationships. *Pharmaceutical Journal*, 287, 359.

Rogers, C.R., and Roethlisberger, F.J. (1991). Barriers and gateways to communication. *Harvard Business Review*, 69(9), 105–111.

Sreenath, S. (2011). Communication barriers. Slideshare. Retrieved November 25, 2011, from http://www.slideshare.net/sreenath.s/communication-barriers

Stanton, V. (2009). *Mastering communication* (5th ed.). Basingstoke: Palgrave Macmillan.

Weinstein, K. (1992). Managing communication. In D.M. Stewart (Ed.), *Handbook of management skills* (2nd ed., pp. 275–292). Worcester: BCA.

Whetten, D., Cameron, K., and Woods, M. (2000). *Developing management skills for Europe*. Essex, England: Pearson Education.

Chapter 11

Leadership

The task of the leader is to get his people from
where they are to where they have not been.

—Henry Kissinger

11.1 Scenario

The area manager, Jeremy White, of Community Pharmacy
Limited instructed the pharmacy manager, Dianne, to cut
overtime altogether, as the pharmacy had exceeded the overtime budget. Overtime was spent mainly on dispensary staff
who were trying to cope with a huge increase in prescriptions from the medical center, which has extended its opening
hours. Because it was a dispensary issue, Naomi, the regular
pharmacist, accepted the challenge to resolve the issue.

11.2 Introduction

A high-performance community pharmacy aspires to enhance
its contribution to the care of patients it serves and improve

its financial position by performing at the highest level of effectiveness and efficiency (Zilz et al., 2004). The leaders of the organization have to demonstrate their commitment to the future vision of excellent practice. Effective pharmacy leaders use recognized benchmark practices to continuously develop the team's commitment to the vision and extend the pharmacy's influence across the entire healthcare system.

11.3 Leadership and Management

Leadership and management are complementary. Leadership in pharmacy practice is about the ability to create a vision for the future of pharmacy and mentor future managers to establish an innovative environment (American College of Clinical Pharmacy, 2000). Effective leaders set strategy and motivate the staff to create a clear vision for the future and a new culture (Goleman, 2000). They do so by getting the people to do the right thing by motivating them (Gaither, 2005; Kotter, 2001). Table 11.1 summarizes the essential differences between managerial and leadership activities.

Over the past few decades, organizations have become more complex, and managers therefore need to develop skills to manage the complexities of organizations. Lack of good management skills leads to chaotic organizations. Good product quality and profitability can be achieved through order and consistency, which are key features of good management. The business environment is more competitive and more volatile than ever before, and good leaders have to develop new skills to manage and cope with change due to both internal and external factors.

11.4 Visionary Leadership in Pharmacy Practice

In order to provide more efficient patient care, the leaders have to understand the demography of the population and the

Table 11.1 Activities of Management and Leadership

Management			Leadership		
Managing complexity	Planning and budgeting	Establish long-term and short-term goals Plan the steps to achieve the goals Allocate resources	Managing change	Setting direction for the future	Develop a vision for the future Make changes to achieve the change
Develop the capacity to achieve the plan	Organizing and staffing	Create the organizing structure Identify job descriptions Communicate the goals to the team Delegate responsibility Set controls to monitor implementation	Developing the capacity to achieve the vision	Aligning people	Communicate the vision to those who are committed and those who value the vision
Accomplish the plan	Controlling and problem solving	Measure performance against standards Identify deviations from the plan Solve problems and correct deviations	Achieving the vision	Motivating and inspiring the team	Overcome obstacles Guide the team Focus on needs, values, and emotions of the team

community they serve and their needs. The pharmacy leaders should focus on a triple aim: improve the health of the population, best possible care, and better value for all (Boudreau, 2011). This aim can only be achieved by providing an innovative working environment through a unified vision for the pharmacy profession and mentoring the entire pharmacy team. Visionary leadership requires attention to eight critical processes (Maddux et al., 2000):

1. Identify and seize major opportunities for the progress of the profession with a sense of urgency.
2. Be prepared to lead the change.
3. Establish a vision and implement strategies to achieve it.
4. Communicate the vision to the team.
5. Empower the team to realize the vision by removing roadblocks, encouraging risk taking and new ideas, and modifying the system to overcome resistance.
6. Develop short-term goals and reward those who achieve them.
7. Consolidate improvements and make further changes.
8. Encourage new behavior that promotes progress and harmony.

11.5 Pharmacy Leadership in High-Performance Pharmacy Practice

Pharmacy leaders are essential to achieve a high-performance pharmacy practice (HPPP). HPPP is a pharmacy environment that is able to make a maximum contribution to the clinical outcome of patients and functions efficiently and effectively as a financial unit. These pharmacy leaders must demonstrate their commitment to the vision, employing best practices that enhance patient care (Zilz et al., 2004). Pharmacy leaders must

- Possess pharmacy-specific knowledge and skills
- Ensure credibility within and outside the profession
- Be able to recruit and retain suitable team members
- Extend the team's values beyond traditional roles
- Become an influential player within the healthcare team
- Identify challenges and opportunities as they arise
- Embrace change
- Make difficult decisions when required

Current and former directors of pharmacy in the United States, with a combined total of over 140 years of experience, have presented an excellent discussion on pharmacy leadership (Zilz et al., 2004). They identify five critical components of leadership:

1. Core self: Each individual's core self comprises values and beliefs acquired during his or her childhood and his or her professional outer layer closely linked to the commitment for patient care, humanity, and professional ethics and integrity.
2. Vision: The vision involves identifying opportunities in the healthcare system, such as the importance of medicine in people's health, financial outlook of the organization, and the safety of medicines. Pharmacy leaders are also able to identify opportunities to contribute toward safe medicine management systems and cost-effective procedures.
3. Relationships: Pharmacy leaders are able to communicate the vision through relationships with other healthcare providers, such as the pharmacy team, health system administrators, medical and nursing professionals, peer groups in other departments, and the wider community.
4. Learning: Pharmacy leaders are able to develop their professional skills through a continuous learning process, analysis, questioning, and taking appropriate action. It enables the pharmacy leaders to support the practice environment.

5. Mentoring: A critical component of leadership is mentoring that leads to succession planning. It enables an organization to maintain and enhance the level of service and influence within the organization upon retirement of current leaders. Mentors demonstrate a caring attitude to communicate what they need to hear and not necessarily what they want to hear.

These five critical components form the basis needed to sustain an HPPP.

11.6 Leadership Theories

Early leadership theories focused on qualities that distinguish leaders from followers. Subsequent theories emphasized situational factors such as skills. Although many theories have been proposed, all theories can be classified into eight types (Cherry, 2011):

1. **"Great man" theories.** Great man theories emerged during the nineteenth century. According to those, great leaders are born and not made. The support for these theories comes from leaders such as Abraham Lincoln, Mahatma Gandhi, and Alexander the Great, who emerged when needed.
2. **Trait theories.** Similar to great man theories, trait theories propose that some people inherit certain qualities that make them leaders. Qualities such as intelligence, self-confidence, high energy levels, and technical knowledge were identified as leadership traits that distinguished leaders from nonleaders (Gaither, 2005). However, the trait theories cannot explain why some people who possess these traits are not leaders.
3. **Contingency theories.** Contingency theories are based on variables related to the environment that determine the type of leadership style best suited for the situation.

There is no universal leadership style that suits every situation. Success depends on several variables, such as the leadership style, the type of followers, and aspects of the environment or situation.

4. **Situational theories.** Situational theories propose that leaders make decisions and choose the best course of action depending upon the situation.

5. **Behavioral theories.** Behavioral theories are based on behavioral attitudes of leaders toward the followers (Gaither, 2005). Autocratic leaders do not seek input from their followers and make all the decisions. Democratic leaders allow input from the team in decision making. Laissez-faire leaders allow employees to set their own goals and expect them to work toward them without any interference. A pharmacy manager may want to introduce a program of home delivery of medicines. An autocratic leader would prepare the program and then instruct the staff to implement the program. A democratic leader would present the issue to the staff, receive suggestions for a plan, and take into consideration their ideas in the final program. A laissez-faire leader would give complete autonomy to identify an issue, come up with a program, and implement it.

6. **Participative theories.** Participative theories allow input from subordinates. The level of participation depends upon the situation. In these models, the leader retains the right to allow participation. The leader-participation model assumes five types of behavior (Gaither, 2005). The leader may (a) solve the problem with the information available to him or her; (b) obtain information from the team and decide on a course of action; (c) discuss the problem with the subordinates individually, gather all the information, and make the decision; (d) discuss the problem with the subordinates as a group, obtain all the necessary information, and make the decision, which may or may not reflect the views of the subordinates; and (e) share the

problem with the group and with the available information generate options and attempt to reach consensus. Organizing healthcare requires new leadership models, and these models are beneficial in a pharmacy environment. Leadership in pharmacy requires a high regard for people and production, with emphasis on shared responsibility, involvement of the team, total commitment to the vision, and mutual support.

7. **Transactional theories.** Transactional theories focus on supervision, chain of command, and performance. These theories are based on assumptions that people (a) perform best when the chain of command is clearly defined, (b) are motivated by reward and punishment, (c) are willing to follow the leader's instructions, and (d) must be closely supervised.

8. **Transformational theories.** Transformational theories are based on the relationship between the leader and the subordinates. Transformational leaders are able to motivate and inspire the subordinates and convince them of the importance and benefits of the task. According to transformational theories, group performance and the attainment of full potential by individuals are both critical. Transformational leaders are bound by high standards of moral and ethical conduct.

11.7 Leadership Skills

Strong management skills are essential to manage a community or a hospital pharmacy. Although they are essential, they are not sufficient to take the pharmacy and its employees to new horizons. They need leadership skills. Leaders have followers who adapt the leader's behavior and inspire people through their own character and charismatic ways. Being people focused, leaders create loyalty among the followers.

The following are essential leadership skills (Thadani, 2008; Siang, 2006; Woodcock, 2011):

1. **Integrity.** Integrity is an essential characteristic for leadership to gain respect from the followers. Leaders who possess this skill are honest and avoid placing blame when things do not work out. They take responsibility for their own actions and those of others and for wrong decisions and mistakes. Mistakes are considered opportunities for learning new ways.

   Referring to winemakers, the CEO of a large winery in New Zealand once remarked, "Winemakers are a special breed. They want all the glory, but when things go wrong it is always somebody else's fault."

   The above remark was made by the CEO when he was so frustrated with the attitude of winemakers who had the habit of blaming the process or the people when mistakes were made.

2. **Motivation.** Effective leaders are able to motivate and direct the team. They have a strong desire to influence and lead the followers, creating enthusiasm among them. Leaders are prepared to praise, reward, and offer feedback. When providing feedback it is important to be specific about the tasks accomplished by the followers. For example, "I really appreciate your effort to minimize stock levels without compromising patients' needs." Followers respect the leader when he or she demonstrates empathy. For example, "I know you have a tight schedule to complete the audits. Is there any way I can help you?"

3. **Intelligence.** A thorough knowledge of work, industry, and technical matters is necessary to lead a team of followers who are focused on technical matters. An in-depth knowledge will lead to informed decision making. A leader's role is to support and guide his or her followers to accomplish the goals. Intelligence also includes the

ability to gather, analyze, and interpret large amounts of information relating to the pharmacy environment.

4. **Vision.** Effective leaders are able to create a vision for the organization and develop strategies to accomplish the vision. They are able to gain commitment from the followers. Leaders are flexible enough to adapt to changes in the internal and external environment.

5. **Problem solving.** Problem-solving ability involves clarifying issues and arriving at logical decisions. The leaders are able to expect and accept advice or ideas from employees at all levels. When leaders appreciate input from the followers, they are willing to contribute toward the big picture.

6. **People skills.** Good leaders possess excellent human resource skills. They listen, support, and offer constructive criticism. Effective leaders train, coach, and teach the followers for better performance. They present a positive personal image.

11.8 Leadership Styles

There are six main leadership styles that executives use, and no single style is appropriate in all situations (Goleman, 2000). Depending on the climate of the working environment, a leader may have to use more than one style of leadership. The climate of the organization can be defined in terms of six parameters:

- Flexibility: Freedom for innovation.
- Responsibility: Responsibility toward the organization.
- Standards: Standards that employees try to achieve.
- Rewards: Feedback accuracy and reward system.
- Clarity: People's vision of the mission and values of the organization.
- Commitment: Level of commitment toward the vision of the organization.

1. **Coercive style.** Coercive leaders demand immediate compliance from their followers. They have to do exactly what the leader tells them to do. Leaders who adopt a coercive style have drive to achieve, initiate, and self-control. This style of leadership is suitable in an emergency situation when a turnaround is necessary to save the organization or for dealing with problem employees. It has a negative impact on the climate of the organization.

2. **Authoritative style.** Authoritative leaders are able to organize the followers toward the vision of the organization and provide the freedom to innovate, experiment, and take calculated risks. The leaders who use this style achieve commitment by rallying around the followers. They set the standards and goals, but allow the followers sufficient freedom to devise their own methods to achieve them. Authoritative leaders demonstrate empathy, self-confidence, and are effective in managing change. Therefore, this style of leadership is appropriate when a change of direction or vision is needed. It has a strong impact on the climate of the organization

3. **Affiliative style.** Affliliative-style leaders focus on people. They demonstrate empathy and are most effective as relationship builders. Affliliative leaders give ample room for their followers to achieve the targets and goals in a manner that they think is most effective. Feedback and rewards are not limited to annual performance reviews. This style of leadership is most suited when there are conflicts in the team or for motivating the followers. It has a very favorable impact on the climate of the organization.

4. **Democratic style.** Democratic leaders focus on consensus of opinion and are most effective in gaining trust, respect, and commitment from their followers. They are good listeners and communicate well with their followers. The followers are realistic about what can and cannot be achieved. The democratic style of leadership is not

appropriate in all situations. It is most effective when a consensus of opinion is deemed necessary or when input is needed from valuable followers. The impact on the climate of the organization is positive.

5. **Pacesetting style.** A pacesetting style of leadership is the least effective of all the leadership styles. Such leaders set very high performance standards and demonstrate commitment to them by their actions. They demand work to be done better and faster, and poor performers are removed. There is little or no feedback, and therefore the followers show no commitment to tasks. A pacesetting style is most suited when results are expected from highly motivated and competent employees, but it has a negative impact on the climate of the organization.

6. **Coaching style.** Leaders who adopt the coaching style are able to identify strengths and weaknesses of the followers and encourage the development of personal aspirations. Coaching leaders support their followers to set goals and achieve them. Challenging assignments are given so that the employees can set their own pace. These leaders develop their followers and show empathy and self-awareness. A coaching style can be employed to improve performance and develop long-term strengths. It has a positive impact on the climate of the organization.

A small manufacturing organization in Auckland, New Zealand, with about 30 workers, employed me as quality control (QC) manager following the resignation of the QC manager, who was responsible for all QC operations. It manufactured a wide spectrum of products, some of them under license, including hair cosmetics, products for the printing industry, sheep drench, and breath fresheners. The previous QC manager left a legacy of many unresolved problems. They were highlighted by the latest good manufacturing practices (GMP) inspection report, which was damaging to the reputation of the organization. But the irony of the situation was that the workers were unaware of what GMP meant and the findings in the report. With so much competition for hair cosmetic products, the general managers were very concerned about the critical situation. The task before me was to turn around the situation.

I commenced by conducting several coaching sessions on GMP activities and explaining to the employees how these affect their work. The findings in the report were discussed with the staff. At the end of the coaching sessions, they realized how serious the situation was. Leading workers approached me and asked, "How can we help you?"

Manuals were prepared and laboratory methods were updated. Tasks that could be handled by the staff were delegated. Gradually, the problems highlighted in the report were addressed. The factory transformed into a clean work environment where the staff enjoyed their work, and the laboratory became a showpiece of the factory. At the GMP inspection, the inspectors were surprised at the transformation. After about two years, I moved on. Unfortunately, owing to the declining economic climate and shrinking market share in the 1970s, the board decided to close the operation in Auckland.

11.9 Leadership Styles in the United States, United Kingdom, and Ireland

In America, the CEOs tend to use one of five leadership styles: directive, participative, empowering, charismatic, and celebrity (Taleghani et al., 2010). Some common leadership tendencies are as follows:

- Treat human beings as either good or bad
- Have noncompulsory thought and rely on performance of work and change rather than on fate

- Dominant in nature
- Inclined to solve problems and focus on the three variables of structure, strategy, and system
- Enjoy personal particulars and success
- Emphasize value on the work, place importance on planning, and decide what needs to be done and when
- Attention to the present and the future

The management styles of Irish and UK managers are very similar to each other. The leaders in the United Kingdom often delegate tasks and responsibilities and seek input and ideas from others. Irish leaders tend to use past experience as a guide to handle current situations, develop technical skills, and place process and structure in place to meet the goals and complete the tasks. Leaders from both countries tend to make independent decisions and are comfortable in managerial roles.

11.10 Emotional Intelligence

Salovey and Mayer (1990) developed the concept of emotional intelligence (EI) as a tool for organization development and developing people. It provides a means of understanding and assessing people's behavior, management styles, attitudes, interpersonal skills, and potential. The principles of EI are important in human resource activities such as recruitment, selection, management development, customer service, etc. It is defined as

> The ability to monitor one's own and others' feelings and emotions, to discriminate among them and to use this information to guide one's thinking and actions.

In 1995, Goleman developed the concept further and postulated that while qualities such as intelligence, toughness, vision, and determination are important for effective leadership, they are not sufficient. Effective leaders also possess a high degree of EI (Goleman, 2004). In his research, he found direct ties between EI qualities (self-awareness, self-regulation, motivation, empathy, and social skills) and measurable business results.

11.10.1 Self-Awareness

Self-awareness is the ability to identify one's emotions, strengths, weaknesses, needs, and drives and their effects on others. People who have developed self-awareness are aware of their values and goals and are self-confident. At performance reviews they have a realistic assessment of themselves.

11.10.2 Self-Regulation

Self-regulation is a necessary quality for effective leadership. People who have cultivated self-regulation are able to create an environment of trust and fairness among the team. Self-regulation enhances integrity. They are not moved by sudden impulses. Instead, there is a tendency for reflection and thoughtfulness. In a competitive business environment, such leaders are comfortable with change.

11.10.3 Motivation

Leaders who are motivated have a strong desire to achieve beyond expectations. They have a passion for work and seek creative challenges. Motivated leaders take pride in their job and are eager to explore new horizons. Those with leadership potential are optimistic and have a strong commitment to the organization.

11.10.4 Empathy

Empathy is the ability to understand the feelings and emotions of other people. Therefore, the leaders who demonstrate empathy are skilled in treating people according to their reactions. They are able to use teams effectively because they understand the viewpoints of others on the team. Increasing globalization leads to diversity, and the leaders who show empathy have a deep understanding of ethnic and cultural differences. Empathy plays a significant role in developing and retaining employees.

11.10.5 Social Skill

Social skill is the ability to manage relationships with others. Leaders who have social skills have a strong network of supporters who can be called upon in times of need. They build, manage, and lead teams effectively. Social skill enables these leaders to persuade others easily.

11.11 Leadership Wisdom

The National Health Service (NHS) contract demands more clinically focused services from community pharmacies. Hospital pharmacies also have to provide clinical services and dispensing to a wide spectrum of the public and are required to run pharmacies in a business-like fashion. Pharmacists working for primary care organizations are involved with the management of medicines within general practitioners (GP) practices and developing pharmacy services in the locality. They run clinics and review medicines in GP practices. Their roles also extend to prisons providing public service and to the pharmaceutical industry. Visionary leaders are needed to meet these current and future challenges. Optimal leadership style may change over time, and developing leadership wisdom enables individuals to appropriately alter their leadership styles to meet the changes in social and healthcare needs, improve the cost-effectiveness of services, and promote innovation. Leadership wisdom is defined as (Adams, 2007):

> Informed values, and principles based decision making, used to do the most appropriate things with and through people, for the greater good in the longer term.

The Royal Pharmaceutical Society of Great Britain and the NHS Institute of Innovation and Improvement aim to achieve leadership wisdom through the Leading Across Boundaries Program (LABP). The program involves the identification of leadership attributes and individual leadership styles and developing appropriate skills for individual leadership style development. The NHS Leadership Qualities Framework (LQF) defines a set of 15 attributes that identifies highly effective leaders (NHS Institute for Innovation and Improvement, 2005). These attributes fall into three categories:

1. Setting direction. Seizing the future, intellectual flexibility, broad scanning, political astuteness, and the drive for results.
2. Delivering the services. Leading change through people, accountability, empowering others, collaborative working, and effective and strategic influencing.
3. Personal qualities. Self-belief, self-awareness, self-management, drive for improvement, and personal integrity.

LQF attributes provide an effective and comprehensive framework to develop leadership skills, and these incorporate the skills described by Thadani (2008), Siang (2006), Woodcock (2011), and Goleman (2004).

Individual leadership styles are identified using the Formula 4 model (Formula 4 Leadership, 2009). This model defines four leadership styles:

1. Directive: The leader makes decisions on his or her ideas.
2. Consultative: The leader makes decisions based on the ideas of the team.
3. Delegative: The team itself makes decisions based on their ideas.
4. Consensual: The leader and the team make decisions based on their ideas.

The Formula 4 model enables leaders to discover their own leadership style and develop individual needs and cross boundary networks based on the LQF.

11.12 Which Style Is Most Suitable?

No one style of leadership is appropriate in all situations. Sometimes, leaders have to use a combination of styles, depending upon the situation. Table 11.2 shows situations where and when the various styles can be used.

11.13 Revisiting the Scenario

In the scenario cited in this chapter, Naomi assumed authoritative leadership. She sought ideas from the pharmacy staff regarding the workload, work schedule, roles of individual staff, and resources needed to meet patients' expectations. By rearranging the work schedule and changing the roles of staff with minimum resource requirements, she produced a plan for implementation. She monitored the new arrangements for one week and made minor changes to the original plan. The new plan was effective, and Naomi was able to turn around the situation.

Table 11.2 Application of Leadership Styles

Leadership Style	Most Appropriate Situation	Examples
Coercive Directive	Situations that demand immediate compliance	Inability to supply medicines as a result of IT failure in the pharmacy Dealing with underperforming employee Only to be applied as a last resort
Authoritative Consultative	When a new vision is needed after a change or when clear directions are necessary to guide the team	Pharmacy has to cut the overtime budget drastically
Affiliative	Resolve conflicts in a team Motivate people in a stressful situation	Stressful situation created by a shortage of pharmacy staff after two members went on stress leave and the remaining staff were harassed to meet financial targets
Democratic Consensual	Situations where consensus or approval of majority is required When input is needed from valuable employees	Need to reduce the waiting time for dispensing prescriptions

(continued)

Table 11.2 Application of Leadership Styles (continued)

Leadership Style	Most Appropriate Situation	Examples
Delegative	Where the staff are skilled and qualified and capable of implementing solutions	Seek pharmacy staff support to implement a new procedure to handle repeat prescriptions
Pacesetting	When a quick solution is required from highly motivated staff	A successful bid to supply medicines to a care home at short notice
Coaching	Help employee improve performance Developing people for promotion	A healthcare assistant has been promoted to the supervisor position

References

Adams, A. (2007). Developing leadership wisdom. *International Journal of Leadership in Public Services*, 3(2), 39–50.

American College of Clinical Pharmacy. (2000). White paper: Vision of pharmacy's future roles, responsibilities and manpower needs in the United States. *Pharmacotherapy*, 20(8), 991–1022.

Boudreau, K.M. (2011). Visionary leadership for enhanced care. *Healthcare Executive*, 26(3), 86–87.

Cherry, K. (2011). Leadership theories: 8 major leadership theories. Retrieved June 30, 2011, from http://psychology.about.com/od/leadership/p/leadtheories.htm

Formula 4 Leadership. (2009). Formula 4 leadership. Retrieved July 15, 2011, from http://www.formula4leadership.com/Models

Gaither, C.A. (2005). Organizational structure and behaviour. In S.P. Deselle and D.P. Zgarrick (Eds.), *Pharmacy management* (pp. 164–170). New York: McGraw-Hill.

Goleman, D. (2000). Leadership that gets results. *Harvard Business Review*, 78(2), 78–90.

Goleman, D. (2004). What makes a leader? *Harvard Business Review*, 82(1), 82–91.

Kotter, J.P. (2001). What leaders really do. *Harvard Business Review*, 79(11), 85–96.

Maddux, M.S., Dong, B.J., Miller, W.A., Nelson, M.K., Raebel, M.A., Raehi, C.L., et al. (2000). A vision of pharmacy's future roles: Responsibilities and manpower needs in the US. *Pharmacotherapy*, 20(8), 991–1022.

NHS Institute for Innovation and Improvement. (2005). NHS leadership quality framework. Retrieved July 15, 2011, from http://www.nhsleadershipqualities.nhs.uk/

Salovey, P., and Mayer, J.D. (1990). Emotional intelligence. *Imagination, Cognition and Personality*, 9(3), 185–211.

Siang, L.Y. (2006). Developing leadership skills for the new in the workplace. Retrieved July 1, 2011, from http://www.career-success-for-newbies.com/developing-leadership-skills.html

Taleghani, G., Salmani, D., and Taatian, A. (2010). Survey leadership styles on different cultures. *Iranian Journal of Management Studies*, 3(3), 91–111.

Thadani, M. (2008, October). Leader vs manager. *Retail Pharmacy*, 29.

Woodcock, B. (2011). How to find out your style of leadership. University of Kent Career Service. Retrieved July 1, 2011, from http://www.kent.ac.uk/careers/sk/leadership.htm

Zilz, D.A., Woodward, B.W., Thielke, T.S., Shane, R.R., and Scott, B. (2004). Leadership skills for a high performance pharmacy practice. *American Journal of Health-System Pharmacy*, 61, 2562–2574.

Chapter 12

Effective Delegation

Never tell people how to do things. Tell them what
to do and they will surprise you with ingenuity.

—General George Smith Patton, Jr.

12.1 Scenario

Since her promotion from the position of supervisor to the
pharmacy manager's role, Dianne has been busy trying to
meet the goals and expectations of the organization. Her role
involves not only financial accountability, but also administrative work that could be easily performed by the supervisor or
some of the other staff. Because she has not prioritized her
work, it has been very difficult for the other staff to accomplish their day-to-day tasks. One of the major problems is preparing and sending the prescriptions at the end of each month
to the pricing bureau. This task involves classifying the prescriptions, endorsing where necessary, preparing the necessary
documents, sending the prescriptions to the pricing bureau,
and finally informing the senior executive. All these activities
are handled by the pharmacy manager, and when she is busy

with these tasks, she is not available for consultation for any problem. As a result, there was dissention among the staff and the morale was very low. The senior executive approached her one day and instructed her to prioritize her work and delegate some of the work to others.

12.2 Introduction

In a complex business environment such as a community pharmacy or a hospital pharmacy, it is impossible for the manager to perform all the work needed to accomplish the organization's mission without effective delegation. Therefore, managers are expected to empower their staff so that they can accomplish the necessary tasks effectively. Without delegation and empowerment, no organization can succeed in the long term. Unwillingness to delegate properly and lack of knowledge of how to achieve it have been recognized as common causes of failure in organizations. Delegating is one of the most important skills demonstrated by the managers of successful organizations, and is often overlooked by unsuccessful and "overworked" managers.

12.3 Definitions

In very broad terms, *delegation* is the transfer of authority by one person to another for an agreed purpose. In business, it refers to the "sharing or transfer of authority and associated responsibility from an employer or 'superior' having the right to delegate to an employee or 'subordinate'" (Serrat, 2010).

Leucke and McIntosh (2009) define delegation as "the process through which managers and supervisors assign formal authority, responsibility, and accountability for work activities to subordinates." This process involves the transfer of three qualities—authority, responsibility, and accountability—from a higher level of hierarchy in the organization to a lower level.

Delegation normally refers to the assignment of a task or an activity, whereas empowerment is related to people's feelings and the way they think about themselves. Delegation can only be effective when people are empowered (Whetten et al., 2000).

12.4 Benefits of Delegation

Effective delegation has benefits to the manager, the organization, and its employees. Some of the benefits are (Harvard Business School, 2008; Whetten et al., 2000)

1. Reduces manager's workload and stress. The manager has fewer tasks to accomplish, and therefore has more time to devote to projects that require his or her skills and responsibilities. In addition, he or she can focus on management activities, such as planning, controlling, coordinating, meeting key business people, etc.
2. Enhances trust between the manager and the subordinates. Employees feel that their skills and competencies are acknowledged, and they learn to achieve goals through teamwork.
3. Offers the opportunity to test the capabilities of the employees. The strengths and weaknesses of a person can be assessed by entrusting tasks to the person. This information is useful when delegating tasks to the employee.
4. Employees benefit from delegating tasks and projects. Delegation offers the employees the opportunity to accept responsibility, plan work, and work in cooperation with others. They can develop managerial skills.
5. Enhances the commitment of individuals receiving work. When employees participate in work that has been delegated to them, they derive enormous satisfaction, commitment, acceptance of change, and the desire for more work.

6. Improves the quality of decision making. Employees have more information and are closer to the problem than the manager. Therefore, they are able to make better decisions.
7. Enhances efficiency. Because the employees have direct access to the information they need, they can retrieve it in less time with fewer resources.
8. Improves coordination and integration of work. Empowering managers avoid cross-purposes in delegating and ensure that different tasks do not produce contradictory results.

12.5 Essential Skills for Delegation

Delegation can only be successful if the person delegating has the necessary skills to do so. Authors often confuse skill requirements with the actual process of delegation. For example, identifying the tasks for delegation is not a skill. The managerial skill associated with identifying tasks is planning and organizing. A manager who is effective in planning and organizing can prioritize the tasks and identify the tasks that could be delegated to the staff. Again, identifying the skills of the staff to whom the tasks are delegated is not a skill. The skill involved with identifying the skills of employees is the ability to assess the competence and skills of subordinates. On this basis a number of managerial skills can be formulated that are essential for delegation (Finch and Maddux, 2006):

1. Planning and organizing skills. Planning and organizing skills in the context of delegation involve the creation of a plan to delegate. Involvement of the staff at this stage will encourage the staff to "buy in."
2. Motivation skills. The manager must be able to motivate the staff for achieving desired results.
3. Training skills. An essential part of delegation is the training necessary to accomplish the tasks. The selection

of a person for delegation depends upon the nature of the project or task and the skill level of the person to whom the task is delegated. Any shortcomings should be addressed before commencement of the project.

4. Leadership skills. Delegation requires leadership skills not only to motivate, train, and develop the staff, but also to monitor the performance and check the progress at predetermined phases. Controls must be exercised to compare results with plans and make changes when results differ from expectations. Often managers have too much control, and as a result they overmanage. The manager has the authority, power, and command to run the organization, and therefore should not have any fear of losing control. Employees have different skill levels, and the amount of control that must be exercised over their performance will differ from person to person. Once this fact is recognized, it is easy to strike a reasonable balance.

5. Negotiation skills. During the development of the plan to delegate, it is necessary to negotiate the tasks that must be delegated. There should be a mutual agreement between the two parties. Employees gladly accept tasks for which they have the necessary skills. As part of the staff development program, support must be given to expand their skills, if necessary.

6. Communication skills. A communication procedure must be established for coordinating and reporting tasks between the employees and the manager.

7. Empowerment. Empowerment is about instilling a sense of power and authority in a person. This skill enables a manager to help people develop a sense of self-worth, self-confidence, take appropriate action, and motivate the people (Whetten et al., 2000). It gives them the authority to make decisions, create opportunities to influence decisions, and the ability to make choices.

12.6 The Process of Delegation

To delegate effectively, it is necessary to select the right tasks, identify the people for delegation, and delegate in the right way. Following are the essential steps for effective delegation (Sykes, 2006; Leucke and McIntosh, 2009; Whetten et al., 2000):

1. Identify the tasks for delegation. Prioritize the tasks and identify those that could be delegated. Delegation must be consistent. A manager who only delegates when he or she is busy or assigns more difficult tasks for delegation will not receive support from subordinates. The steps necessary to complete the assignment must be clarified. This is essentially the planning step of the whole process, and involvement of staff at this stage promotes motivation and a willingness to carry out the task. Empower them to decide what tasks should be delegated and when.

2. Determine when to delegate. Delegation is most appropriate when there are subordinates with the necessary skills and expertise, the tasks provide an opportunity for growth, and the manager has the time and commitment to delegate. Other factors to consider are the time frame within which the tasks must be accomplished, the quality of the outcome, the risk of failure, and the impact of failure on other activities.

3. Determine the person or persons to whom the tasks must be delegated. The relevant factors are the skill base of the individual and the availability of time and resources for training to accomplish the tasks. Ideally, the skill and competence of the individual should match the essential skill requirements for delegation. More often than not, the staff must be given further training. An individual's goals and expectations from the assigned tasks and the current workload of the person also must be considered.

4. How should the delegation be carried out? Communicate clearly the intended outcome and the expected results.

Authorities, responsibilities, accountabilities, and limitations should be clearly defined. Responsibility without adequate authority serves no purpose. However, ultimate accountability rests with the manager. This is not transferable. Delegate to the lowest possible level in the hierarchy. People at this level are closer to the work and work patterns, and therefore they possess detailed knowledge of everyday work. Communication lines should be left open to afford support for those who need. Allow the person to make the decisions, but the manager should focus on the results. One of the failures of delegation is "upward delegation." At all costs, the manager should not allow the subordinate to shift responsibility back to the manager. The person to whom the task has been delegated should find the answers, and the manager should not provide solutions.

5. Establish and maintain control. Without exercising excessive control, the manager should discuss the time frames and deadlines for the tasks. Establish checkpoints for review in consultation with the person. Be prepared to make changes when necessary. Above all, the manager should take time to review the submitted work.

6. Follow up and monitor the results. At agreed checkpoints, the manager and the person should review the project and offer feedback. Celebrate successes even if they are small. Avoid blame for failure and decide on the way forward.

7. Evaluate performance. At this point, evaluate the performance of the person. The strengths and weaknesses of the person being evaluated can be useful for future delegation.

When the medicine use review (MUR) was introduced by the National Health Service (NHS) in 2005, the pharmacists were busy trying to meet the financial targets of the pharmacy. In the process, all the tasks involved with MUR service (identifying patients, inviting them, conducting the review, preparing the report, communicating with the GP, and making entries in the computer) were all performed by the pharmacist. Dispensing took a longer time because the pharmacist was busy conducting MURs. The staff were dissatisfied, and eventually the pharmacist decided to delegate some tasks to the pharmacy technicians.

A useful worksheet for delegation is presented in Table 12.1. It shows how some of the tasks associated with the MUR service were delegated to the pharmacy technicians.

Table 12.1   Delegation of MUR Tasks

	Step	*Activity*	*Comments*
1	Identifying tasks	Identifying patients Inviting patients	When prescriptions are entered in the computer When medicines are handed over to the patient
2	When	Ongoing when the pharmacy is not busy	Pharmacist has time to delegate Perform at least one a day Risk of failure minimal and does not impact on other activities
3	To whom	Select a person to whom the tasks must be delegated	Pharmacy technician Pharmacy technicians have the necessary skills
4	How	Follow the steps	Expect to recruit at least one patient; target more as some will refuse Authority to identify suitable patients according to the protocol Pharmacy technician is responsible Limitations: Cannot conduct the MUR or write the report

(continued)

Table 12.1 Delegation of MUR Tasks (continued)

	Step	*Activity*	*Comments*
5	Establish and maintain control	Establish time frames, deadlines, and checkpoints for review	Daily activity; at least one patient should be recruited by the end of the day Daily review at the end of the day
6	Follow up	Follow up on previous day's activities	Determine the causes for refusal by the patients Check possibility of offering another date for the MUR to those who refused
7	Evaluate performance	Review the performance of the pharmacy technician in relation to the delegated tasks	How convincing is the pharmacy technician when the patient is invited? Can a sufficient number be identified from computer records?

12.7 Barriers to Delegation

Some managers are not keen to delegate for the wrong reasons (Leucke and McIntosh, 2009; Nichol, 2012), and some of these are listed below:

1. Fear of losing control. Managers who demonstrate an autocratic style of management are often reluctant to delegate for fear of losing control. When a task is delegated, a certain amount of discretion and authority is granted to the subordinate. But the manager remains ultimately responsible for the organization and for achieving the goals of the organization. This is not transferable.

2. Lack of trust in employees. The subordinates are unprepared to handle all the jobs handled by the manager, but they have skills and expertise in certain areas that the organization can utilize for the success of the enterprise. With proper instructions and some training, the subordinates are capable of accepting the challenge.

3. Lack of confidence in employees. Managers often assume that they are better suited to carry out the tasks than their subordinates. However, it is futile for a manager to do jobs for which the subordinates are skilled. By delegating these tasks to the employees, more time is available to focus on complex issues for which the manager is responsible.

4. Lack of time. An efficient manager always has time for subordinates. One of the functions of a manager is to develop the employees and their competencies. A good manager must be prepared to offer opportunities for the subordinates for new roles.

5. Failure to give up previous roles and accept new roles. When managers are promoted to new positions in the organization, they are quite comfortable doing what they have been doing previously, ignoring the new roles. They fail to give up previous roles, and the scenario cited in the beginning is a typical example. New managers must learn to let go of previous roles and embrace new roles to accomplish the goals of the organization.

12.8 Case Study of a Successful Delegation in Pharmacy Practice in the United States

Successful delegation is to teach, model leadership behavior, and free up one's time to get involved in the "big picture." Stewardship delegation leads to successful performance. It focuses on the outcome and not on the methods used to achieve the outcome. The leader establishes the vision and allows the employees to determine the methods. When tasks are delegated, the leader establishes accountability through timelines and criteria. Achievements are recognized and provision is made for advancement or development opportunities (Anderson, 2006).

A code cart (crash cart in UK terminology) is a cabinet on wheels containing medical supplies and equipment for emergency situations in the hospital. They are placed in strategic locations in the hospital for ready accessibility. Carts are checked daily or after an event and replenished. Generally, hospitals maintain code carts for adult, pediatric, and neonatal use. Participation of pharmacists in code events is essential because of the profound and evidenced impact they have shown on hospital medication errors and mortality rates in children.

The system vice president of pharmacy at Caritas Christi Health Care in Brighton, Massachusetts, has been actively involved in the code cart system in the healthcare center (Anderson, 2006). In his facility, the pharmacy plays a vital role on the code cart committee. The purpose of the committee is to formulate systems for responding to codes. The system vice president delegated the responsibility of serving on the committee to another pharmacist on the team. The delegated pharmacist enjoyed her role of influence, which benefited the nurses and physicians. Other professionals who serve on the committee have commented how "wonderful, knowledgeable, and helpful" the pharmacist was. The stewardship delegation saves time and enables staff development. It encourages delegated staff to become more capable of self-management.

12.9 Revisiting the Scenario

As mentioned above, Dianne has been reluctant to give up previous roles. All pharmacy technicians are familiar with the process of sending the prescriptions for pricing. Working through the worksheet, it is possible to delegate the following activities to pharmacy technicians:

- Classifying the prescriptions
- Endorsing the prescriptions—a useful recommendation is to endorse at the time of dispensing
- Preparing the documents for delivery
- Sending the prescriptions away

When these activities are assigned to pharmacy technicians, the manager can prepare the final report to be communicated to the top management. The manager's time is thus freed up to handle more complex managerial tasks in the pharmacy.

References

Anderson, E. (2006, June). The importance of delegation. *Pharmacy Practice News, 33.06.* Retrieved September 4, 2012, from http://pharmacypracticenews.com/ViewArticle. aspx?d_id=56anda_id=3755

Finch, L., and Maddux, R.B. (2006). *Delegation skills for leaders.* Boston: Course Technology.

Harvard Business School. (2008). *Delegating work.* Boston: Harvard Business School.

Leucke, A., and McIntosh, P. (2009). *The busy manager's guide to delegation.* New York: Amacom.

Nichol, G. (2012). The art of delegation. Quadwest Associates. Retrieved September 30, 2012, from http://www.leadershiparticles.net

Serrat, O. (2010). Delegating in the workplace. Knowledge solutions. Retrieved November 29, 2011, from http://www.adb.org/documents/information/knowledge-solutions/delegating-workplace.pdf

Sykes, E. (2006). Delegate to accelerate success. Managerwise. Retrieved November 28, 2011, from http://www.managerwise.com/article.phtml?id=520

Whetten, D., Cameron, K., and Woods, M. (2000). *Developing management skills for Europe.* Essex, England: Pearson Education.

Chapter 13

Empowerment

As we look ahead into the next century, leaders will
be those who empower others.

—Bill Gates

13.1 Scenario

Community Pharmacy Limited is a very busy pharmacy serving a large local community and providing all the necessary
services. To prevent a backlog of prescriptions, the technicians have to work overtime supporting the two pharmacists.
Overtime is arranged by the pharmacy manager in consultation with the supervisor. There is no input from the pharmacists or the technicians. Recently, extending the opening
hours of the nearby medical center resulted in a large influx
of prescriptions. To keep overtime under control, the pharmacy manager restricted the number of available hours for
overtime. Prescriptions could not be cleared on time, and they
accumulated for days. Patients were complaining. The manager did not take the complaints seriously, and the pharmacists
threatened to walk out if the issue was not resolved. The area

manager intervened and instructed the pharmacy manager to allow the staff to arrange overtime within the allocated budget.

13.2 Introduction

The word *empowerment* has been used since the 1980s, and the concept has been misused to such an extent that it is used to refer to anything from team building to decentralized organization structures. Empowerment is quite distinct from other related management behavior. In the 1950s, human relations organizations promoted the concept that managers should be friendly to employees. In the 1960s, managers were required to be sensitive to the needs and motivation of employees through sensitivity training. By the 1970s, organizations began to invite employees to join employee involvement schemes. Quality circles and teams evolved in the 1980s. Since then, the emphasis has been on employee involvement and empowerment. However, in actual practice, it was rarely seen (Whetten et al., 2000).

13.3 Definitions

The concept of empowerment must be understood in terms of the context in which it is used. It has different meanings in different sociocultural and political contexts. Often the terms *self-strength, self-control, self-power, self-reliance, own choice,* and *life of dignity according to one's own values* have been associated with empowerment. In broad terms, it means the expansion of freedom and choice, which increases one's authority and control over the resources and decisions that affect one's life (Narayan, 2002).

In terms of business, empowerment is the concept that employees make and take decisions on their own when authority is handed down to all levels of the organization (Hindle, 2008).

According to Carroll (1994), it is a two-way arrangement between the management and the workforce. It is a shared understanding between managers and employees that employees are trusted to assume responsibility for individual and team results and are able to take action and make decisions to meet the goals of the organization. The purpose of empowerment is to utilize resources in a competitive environment where speed, efficiency, innovation, and commitment to service are essential.

13.4 Benefits and Costs of Empowerment

Companies that have implemented empowerment no doubt have experienced benefits to the organization and its employees (Bodner, 2003). Among the benefits are employee commitment, quality products and services, efficiency, responsiveness, synergy, and management leverage. Employees are trusted and act responsibly to maintain trust between management and the employees. Small work units can overcome obstacles effectively. Empowerment results in committed and passionate employees who can easily respond to customer requirements. Employees control their work, and therefore can suggest alternatives to problems and become more innovative. They can easily coordinate projects across several departments. There is greater job satisfaction because they realize that they play a significant role in the success of the company.

Employee ownership programs have enabled the organizations to increase sales and employment figures, and decrease workers' compensation claims. Some U.S. companies that have empowerment programs have experienced strong employee relations and retention even during a recession.

Implementation of an empowerment program is not without costs (Bodner, 2003):

■ Unresolved conflicts disrupt creativity and motivation, and employees involved in such disputes fail to find solutions.

- In the absence of controls imposed by the management, deadlines may be missed or standards may be compromised.
- Even after training, empowered employees may not be able to know in advance the consequences of the decisions they have made.
- Managers may have to intervene to resolve conflicts to keep employees on track and aligned with company goals.

13.5 Creating a Path to Empowerment

Although empowerment has been acknowledged as a progressive step in business performance, there has been little progress during the past 30 years. Empowerment requires effective change programs (Argyris, 1998). Some of the reasons for lack of progress in empowerment are

- Change programs are ineffective in promoting innovation, motivation, and drive of employees.
- The command-and-control method inhibits its development.
- Employees are unsure about empowerment because they do not want to be held accountable.

Empowerment begins with commitment. It is about "generating human energy and activating the mind" (Argyris, 1998). Employees commit themselves in two ways: external commitment and internal commitment. They are externally committed when others define their tasks, expected behavior, and program goals and their importance. On the other hand, when management and employees jointly define the performance goals and employees define their tasks, behavior, and the importance of goals, internal commitment is promoted.

However, there are limits to internal commitment. When change programs that initiate internal commitment and empowerment are developed, the following factors should be considered (Argyris, 1998):

1. Companies may have both top-down controls and empowerment programs. Inevitable inconsistencies must be managed by encouraging individuals to discuss them openly.
2. Change programs that are intended to expand internal commitment actually produce external commitment. Management has to ensure that such programs deliver what is expected of them.
3. Empowerment has its limits. Management must have a clear vision of how much can be empowered, what can be accomplished, who has the right to change, and the limits of permissible change.
4. Organizations need both external and internal commitment of employees. Most routine jobs require external commitment. Employers should identify tasks that need internal commitment.
5. Improve working conditions that promote empowerment. Most employees are prepared to be internally committed if management is sincere about it, the type of work allows it, and rewards are offered for achievements.
6. Although morale, satisfaction, and commitment are important human resource policies, they should not be used as ultimate criteria for success in organizations. The management must focus on performance.
7. Support employees to determine the choices they make about their own level of commitment.

13.6 Effect of Control Systems on Empowerment

One of the dilemmas faced by managers today is maintaining control, efficiency, and productivity while empowering employees to be creative, innovative, and flexible. Companies such as Sears and Standard Chartered Bank, which have given too much autonomy to employees, have ended up in disaster situations. On the other hand, command-and-control models cannot be used in the modern business world. However, four control systems can be used to strike a balance between empowerment and effective control (Simon, 1995):

1. Diagnostic control systems
2. Belief systems
3. Boundary systems
4. Interactive control systems

Diagnostic control systems depend on quantitative data such as variance from the budget, overheads, overtime, etc. They are useful to detect some problems, but leave room for managers being manipulative and resorting to unethical practices.

Pharmacists have often been instructed by their managers to meet the targets set for medicine use reviews (MURs) conducted in the pharmacy. The National Health Service (NHS) has reported on such fraudulent cases where claims have been made without providing the service (Business Services Authority, 2010).

Managers are empowered to make claims for services delivered in the pharmacy. The system has been abused, and at present, primary care trusts are keeping a close watch.

Beliefs systems are employed to communicate the codes of corporate culture to every employee of the organization. They are only effective if employees can see the commitment of senior management to the key values and ethics of the culture.

Boundary systems can be considered the minimum standards necessary to safeguard the reputation and assets of the company. These systems allow the employees to create and define new solutions within the specified constraints. Generally they focus on profitability, productivity, and efficiency.

In one of the pharmacies where I was employed, the management of controlled drugs was a serious issue. Whenever an audit was done, discrepancies were detected, but they were not related to fraud. The issues were always resolved after several hours of investigation. Because I was empowered to improve the efficiency of the process, a new rule was imposed: do not receive or issue controlled drugs unless a physical check of the stock is done. No discrepancies were noted since then.

Interactive control systems involve regular dialogue between the management and the employees to monitor critical aspects of the operation. They differ from diagnostic control systems in that interactive control systems deal with constantly changing data, warrant regular monitoring to keep on track, and are best analyzed face-to-face with employees.

At the end of each day, the pharmacy manager discusses the dispensing figures (number of items dispensed and number of repeat prescriptions) with the pharmacy staff to monitor the progress of the pharmacy.

13.7 Dimensions of Empowerment

A number of dimensions have been proposed to measure empowerment. Most appropriate are the following eight dimensions (Bodner, 2003; Spreitzer et al., 1999):

1. Culture: Shared values, assumptions, and norms of the organization that guide the way the work is performed. It is also a measure of the fit between one's work role and one's beliefs, values, and behavior.
2. Trust: Extent to which the organizational members have confidence in each other and the organization.
3. Accountability: The obligation of an individual or a team to be answerable for the tasks, accept responsibility for them, and disclose the results in a transparent manner.

4. Leadership: The means of exercising power, authority, and influence at all levels of the organization and creating new roles to support the process.
5. Ability: One's capability to share and use critical information and perform work activities with skill and knowledge to enable decision making and task completion.
6. Commitment: The shared feeling of loyalty and responsibility between the employees and the organization.
7. Responsibility: The duty or obligation to manage, perform a given task, and make appropriate decisions satisfactorily.
8. Communication: The process of collecting, sharing, and attending to information required to perform the given tasks.

13.8 Steps for Developing Empowerment

The development of an effective implementation requires an implementation strategy. The following steps have been successfully utilized to create a culture of empowerment within the organization, thus enhancing the value of the business (McCoy & Associates, 2006):

1. Clearly define the outcome. Clearly define the two W's: what and why: The organization requires the employees to possess skills, competence, and authority to make decisions and take action to accomplish the company's goals within clearly defined job parameters. The employees are also required to understand and accept responsibility for their decisions and the outcome.

   The purpose of empowerment is to achieve the mission of the organization through empowerment.
2. Provide the necessary skills. Employees may not have all the necessary skills for the job. The management must be prepared to offer further education facilities, training, and coaching for the tasks as appropriate. At this stage, the

managers must demonstrate commitment to the empowerment program.

3. Develop the employees. Empowered employees have to accept greater responsibility for accomplishing the assigned tasks. Senior executives must develop the employees to accept more responsibility. The following tools are essential for the growth of the workforce:
   - Critical thinking skills such as setting goals, problem solving, decision making, and risk management
   - Performance analysis and feedback skills that involve the collection of necessary data and analyzing and acting upon them
   - Coaching skills that involve relationship skills and skills to influence others in the organization

4. Develop a common understanding. Empowerment is only effective when everyone in the organization shares the concept of empowerment, the performance objectives, and their role in the program. Everyone in the organization has to subscribe to the organization's beliefs and values because they are the foundations on which decisions are made and prioritized. The employees must feel that they can make a change. Clearly communicate the mission, vision, and goals of the organization because they give direction to the workforce. Celebrate even small accomplishments. Empowered employees must feel that their efforts are recognized, and this promotes motivation.

   All employees may not respond well to the program. The company must be prepared to address such issues as they arise.

5. Define accountability. Establish accountability for the tasks. Make the employees understand the limitations. Grant responsibility to match accountability. Some of the methods to develop a sense of accountability are
   - Define the expectations for all roles.
   - Communicate the purpose, mission, and service level agreements with each department.

- Create a list of responsibilities for each role.
- Construct an authority matrix.
- Encourage employees to practice and apply empowerment principles.

13.9 Patient Empowerment

With improvements in healthcare facilities, healthcare professionals face numerous challenges. There is an increasing demand for health services, and pressure to improve patients' quality of service, create more responsive organizations, and reduce costs. One way of improving the delivery of patient care is through patient empowerment. In the context of patient care, patient empowerment "is a process of helping people to assert control over factors that affect their health" (Lau, 2002).

The patient empowerment model is based on mutual respect between the patient and the healthcare provider. Issues of adherence are resolved in agreement with the patient. The important factors of patient empowerment are knowledge, behavioral skills, and self-responsibility. Initially, the healthcare provider should gain the patient's respect and determine his or her needs or preferences by soliciting the views and listening. An essential tool for patient empowerment is informed consent, which involves (Lau, 2002)

- ■ Disclosure: Nature of the condition, available options, potential risks, professional advice, and nature of consent.
- ■ Understanding: Communication of information in a manner that could be understood by the patient.
- ■ Volunteering: The patient must volunteer for the treatment or recommendation without coercion.
- ■ Competence: Consideration of patient's previous experience, age, responsibility, and the ability to understand and make decisions.
- ■ Consent: Authorization given to the healthcare provider.

The information should be made simple, and the patient must be given the opportunity to consider the decision and ask questions.

Managing diabetes has been a complex issue. Traditionally, the success of the management plan has been assessed on the basis of a patient's ability to adhere to the prescribed therapeutic regime. However, this approach has not proven satisfactory. An effective self-management plan must take into account the patient's priorities, goals, available resources, culture, and lifestyle (Funnell and Anderson, 2004). Table 13.1 shows an empowerment plan for patients with diabetes.

Table 13.1 Empowerment Plan for Diabetic Patients

Step	Description	How to Achieve
1	Define the problem	Ascertain the problems the patient is having with taking care of his or her diabetes
2	Ascertain the patient's beliefs, thoughts, and feelings	Clarify his or her feelings and meaning that support or obstruct the efforts
3	Develop long-term goals	Discuss what the patient wants, changes needed, time frame, options and barriers, provision for support, cost and benefits of each choice, and consequences of not taking any action
4	Commitment	Gain patient's commitment by giving advice on what he or she can do, when to do, and how the patient can measure the success of the program
5	Follow up	Ascertain the success or failure of the program, problems encountered, what lessons were learned, and what could be done in the future

13.10 Case Study: The Role of Pharmacists in Primary Care

The Institute of Medicine defines[*] primary care as "the provision of integrated, accessible health care services by clinicians who are accountable for addressing a large majority of personal health care needs, developing a sustained partnership with patients and practicing in the context of family and community." Primary care practice includes activities that foster patient well-being, prevention of chronic diseases and problems through diagnosis treatment, health promotion, disease prevention, health maintenance, patient counseling, and health education. A critical role in primary care is the effective management of medications that promote patient safety and quality care. Therefore, patient involvement and empowerment are essential components of primary care practice.

There are serious inadequacies in the U.S. healthcare system related to the provision of safe and effective medication management in primary care (Manolakis and Skelton, 2009). The necessities of primary care medication management are expected to increase in the future. Therefore, an effective primary care practice requires health professionals who are competent to manage patients' medication therapy and identify adverse drug reactions and drug-related problems. Pharmacists are qualified and trained to manage medication use in the primary care setting. They are able to enhance intended outcomes and educate patients on medication use.

The pharmacists can be empowered to play a wider role in the primary care setting. In fact, in the United States, many pharmacists have set up practices to provide primary ambulatory care, medication therapy management, and chronic and preventive care to patients.

---

[*] M.S. Donaldson, K.D. Yordy, K.N. Lohr, and N.A. Vanselow, *Primary Care: America's Health in a New Era* (Washington, DC: National Academy of Science, 1996).

The Department of Veterans Affairs (VA) has effectively empowered pharmacists to provide a multitude of services (Manolakis and Skelton, 2009). It is the largest integrated healthcare provider in the United States, with 600 healthcare facilities throughout the country. Each year, the VA serves over a half million inpatients and about 40 million outpatients. In its 157 hospitals and over 860 community-based clinics, the VA treats 50 million outpatients annually, dispensing over 100 million prescriptions.

The pharmacists fulfill the traditional roles of dispensing and quality assurance, and are empowered to utilize their clinical expertise in the primary care setting. The roles of pharmacists include

■ Make recommendations to prescribers.
■ Collaborate with other healthcare providers in inpatient and ambulatory care settings.
■ Prescribe under established protocol and help patients achieve expected outcome.
■ Provide preventive care, such as immunization, smoking cessation, polypharmacy assessment, and reconciliation of medication.
■ Provide home-based primary care and geriatric care.
■ Provide an effective health information service to healthcare providers that improves medication safety.
■ Manage the VA drug formulary.

The following benefits have been achieved as a result of pharmacists' contribution to primary care health service:

■ For every $1 invested in clinical pharmacy service, more than $4 in benefit was observed.
■ Ninety-two percent of the recommendations were accepted, which led to improved clinical outcomes in more than 30% of patients in each setting and prevented harm in 90% of cases. Overall, cost avoidance related to

all 600 recommendations was $700 each, with a total savings of $420,155.

■ At the San Diego VA facility, where pharmacists are involved in medication therapy, patients' outcomes were better than those reported for patients under Medicaid, Medicare, or commercial programs.

13.11 Barriers for Implementing Empowerment

The concept of empowerment may not be readily accepted by both the management and the employees. There are several barriers that can be classified as "myths" (Carroll, 1994):

1. The managers may not get credit for the achievements of the unit. The leaders of high-performing empowered teams gain more credit for the accomplishments because they develop talent in the organization and grow employees. Empowered employees have a higher commitment, leading to higher performance, and the top management soon becomes aware of the leader who works with high-performing teams.

2. Employees cannot handle decision-making authority. Employees cannot be expected to make important decisions without being provided with the necessary training and skills. However, when managers develop people for new responsibilities, employees master new tasks quickly, leaving very little need for supervision. An effective empowerment program can motivate even poor performers.

3. Close supervision is necessary for higher performance. This view is based on McGregor's theory X about employees who need constant supervision and control. However, when specific goals and measures that employees can use to monitor their progress are established, the efficiency of the team can be observed and improved.

4. When decisions are taken at a lower level, progress is slow. Although establishing goals and training employees

for decision making may take time at the start, empowered delegation frees up resources and improves the decision making in the short and long term.

5. Managers may have to take blame for mistakes made by employees. Employees must be allowed to take calculated risks and responsibilities. If they are not allowed to do so, employees will not be innovative or attempt difficult tasks. After the employees are empowered, managers should at all costs avoid providing solutions to problems and upward delegation (Oncken and Wass, 1999). Rescue must be attempted only in rare instances. Although employees are empowered to take risks and decisions, ultimate responsibility for achieving the goals of the organization rests with the manager.

   Although dispensary technicians are empowered to make some decisions, the responsible pharmacist concept introduced by the NHS in 2010 makes it quite clear that the pharmacist is accountable for all the pharmacy operations, irrespective of who performed them.

6. Personal freedom can lead to confusion. Empowered employees may take a different approach to handle tasks assigned to them. They may discover new ways of doing things that benefit the company.

7. Employees desire autonomy but do not like to accept responsibility. Most of the workforce would perform better when the authority given to them matches the responsibility. There will always be some who shirk responsibility, but such instances have to be dealt with according to company procedures.

8. People want the organization to look after them. No doubt people need security in their jobs, but material gains have a short-term "memory." People are motivated by challenges and the opportunity to contribute toward the success of the organization. Among the top five motivators are items that bring challenge, accomplishments, and skills development.

9. Empowerment does not always work. Empowerment programs that empower individuals and teams may look different in various industries and settings. However, they all have opportunities for decision making enabling empowerment.

10. Management roles may become obsolete when individuals or teams are empowered. With empowerment, the role of the manager changes. Instead of "firefighting," managers are needed to align goals, provide resources, train employees, and plan for the future. Some organizations may see the need to fill management roles that can support empowered teams.

13.12 Revisiting the Scenario

The pharmacy staff realized how critical the issue was. The team worked through the process of empowerment and arrived at a plan for overtime within the limits imposed by management.

Desired outcome: Arrange overtime to manage the backlog of prescriptions.

Skills: The pharmacy team has the necessary skills and resources and competence to manage overtime.

Development: Arranging overtime gives the team an opportunity to manage the financial budget for overtime.

Common understanding: The team has the common understanding of the need to meet the targets for prescription numbers and repeat prescriptions.

Accountability: The accountability to manage the overtime budget without exceeding the limits rests with the team.

Working with each of the members, the pharmacist assessed individual requirements and personal commitments and arrived at an effective overtime schedule to clear the backlog.

References

Argyris, C. (1998). Empowerment: The emperor's new clothes. *Harvard Business Review*, 76, 98–105.

Bodner, S. (2003). Dimensional assessment of empowerment in organizations. Master of Arts thesis, University of North Texas.

Business Services Authority. (2010). What does NHS fraud look like? Fraud awareness month June 2010. NHS. Retrieved December 4, 2011, from http://www.nhsbsa.nhs.uk/3112.aspx

Carroll, A. (1994). What's behind the "E" word: Myths about empowerment and why you need it. Interaction Design. Retrieved December 3, 2011, from http://interactiondesign.com/downloads/empwrart.pdf

Funnell, M., and Anderson, R.M. (2004). Empowerment and self-management of diabetes. *Clinical Diabetes*, 22(3), 123–127.

Hindle, T. (2008). *The economist's guide to management ideas and gurus*. London: Profile Books.

Lau, D.H. (2002). Patient empowerment: Patient centred approach to improve care. *Hong Kong Medical Journal*, 8, 372–374.

Manolakis, P.G., and Skelton, J.B. (2009). Pharmacists' contribution to primary care in the US: Collaborating to address unmet patient care needs. Paper prepared for the American Association of Colleges of Pharmacy. Retrieved September 4, 2012, from http://www.hrsa.gov/publichealth/clinical/patient-safety/aacpbrief.pdf

McCoy, T.J., and Associates. (2006). *Empowerment: Five steps that develop a high-involvement, high-performance workforce*. Problem Solver Series. Kansas City: T.J. McCoy & Associates.

Narayan, D. (2002). *Empowerment and poverty reduction: A source book*. Washington, DC: World Bank.

Oncken, W., and Wass, D.L. (1999). Who got the monkey? *Harvard Business Review.77*, 179–184.

Simon, R. (1995). Control in an age of empowerment. *Harvard Business Review*, 73, 80–88.

Spreitzer, G.M., De Janasz, S.L., and Quinn, R.E. (1999). Empowerment to lead: The role of psychological empowerment in leadership. *Journal of Organizational Behavior*, 20, 511–526.

Whetten, D., Cameron, K., and Woods, M. (2000). *Developing management skills for Europe*. Essex: Pearson Education.

Chapter 14

Motivation

Motivation is the art of getting people to do what
you want them to do because they want to do it.

—Dwight D. Eisenhower

14.1 Scenario

Community Pharmacy Limited has a high turnover of pharmacy staff. A dispensary technician has been on stress leave for several weeks. The manager, Dianne, has not made any permanent arrangements to fill the vacancy, and often the pharmacist has to work with little support. Susan, the technician, is very close to Dianne because she looks after Dianne's aged mother at times. Recently, Susan was offered a bonus for completing the stock audits well before the due date. Although other technicians supported her too, their contributions were not recognized. Important tasks were assigned to Susan, and therefore the other technicians did not know their responsibilities. At the monthly review, Max pointed out that Susan had been responsible for more near misses than others. Often, during the legitimate lunch break Dianne would interrupt and instruct Max to go to the dispensary for checking dispensed items. Twice during the previous six months, Dianne refused leave for Max to attend professional development courses during the daytime. Staff knew neither what they had to achieve nor their individual responsibilities. Morale was low and the dispensary staff developed bad work habits. Max, as the responsible pharmacist, realized that he had to motivate the staff, and for that he needed the support of the manager.

14.2 Introduction

Employers are challenged to motivate a workforce to motivate employees to realize the goals of the organization and achieve their personal goals. Organizations often struggle to meet these two requirements at the same time. In the healthcare environment, it is even more difficult because of the complexity of the organizations and the wide spectrum of employees employed to work with other healthcare providers providing optimum patient care. The types of employee range from highly skilled technicians/managers to unskilled workers. In addition, frequent changes in legislation, and pressure to dispense more items and deliver more services to the community lead to low levels of motivation, and it is the role of the pharmacy manager to motivate all employees, irrespective of their category (Shanks and Dore, 2012).

14.3 Definitions

White and Generali (1984) define motivation as the "state of being stimulated to take action to achieve a goal or to satisfy a need."

In terms of the ability within an individual, it is defined as "some driving force within individuals by which they attempt to achieve goals in order to fulfil some need or expectation" (Agomo, 2008).

Motivation is a combined process between an individual and the external environment. According to the 50–50 rule (Adair, 2009), 50% of motivation comes from within an individual and the rest from the environment, especially from the leadership encountered there.

14.4 Motivation Model and Phases of Motivation

Motivation as applied to the work environment means encouraging the staff to achieve their and the organization's goals and enhance performance. The basic model of motivation (Agomo, 2008) is represented in Figure 14.1. All employees have needs and expectations. Some behavior or action is needed to achieve the desired goals. The goals may refer to a personal fulfillment of some desire or an enhancement related to the job. Once the desires are fulfilled, feedback leads to further needs or expectations, or enhancement of what has been achieved.

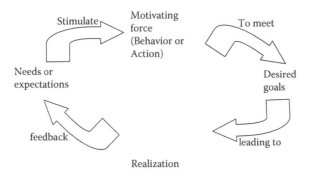

Figure 14.1 Basic model of motivation.

Nohria et al. (2008) have proposed a new model for motivation. According to their approach, there are four basic emotional needs:

1. Acquire: Material, travel, entertainment, social status.
2. Bond: Sense of belonging to the organization.
3. Comprehend: A desire to make a meaningful contribution to the organization.
4. Defend: Promotion of justice, security, and confidence and fear of change.

Figure 14.2 shows the six phases of the motivation process (Agomo, 2008):

Phase 1: Employee identifies the needs and expectations.
Phase 2: Employee seeks ways to satisfy the needs.

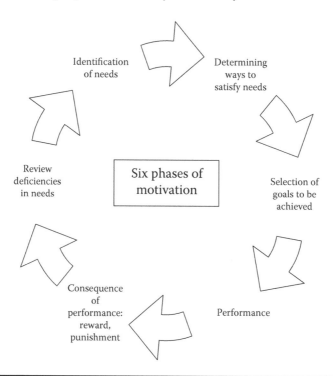

Figure 14.2   Motivation process.

Phase 3: Employee selects goal-oriented behavior.

Phase 4: Employee performs.

Phase 5: Consequences of performance—reward or punishment.

Phase 6: Review of deficiencies in needs.

14.5 Motivation Theories

Motivation has been a subject of research for many years, and psychologists have postulated numerous theories on human motivation. Some of the theories are described below (Shanks and Dore, 2012). The theories fall into three categories—theories that focus on (1) needs of employees, (2) extrinsic factors (external factors), and (3) intrinsic factors (internal thought process and views about motivation). Management theories are also cited here.

14.5.1 Needs-Based Theories

14.5.1.1 Maslow's Hierarchy of Needs

In 1954, Maslow (Adair, 1992) identified five needs that progress from the lowest subsistence-related needs to the highest self-actualization needs. When one level is satisfied, the individual motivates to satisfy the next level of needs (Figure 14.3).

The five levels of needs are

1. Physiological needs: Food, water, sleep, sex, and other needs essential for subsistence of the individual.
2. Safety needs: These needs are related to the safety of the individual and his family and include shelter, safe home environment, access to healthcare, money, resources, family health, and property.
3. Belonging needs: Desire for social contact, friendship, family, affection, love, and support.

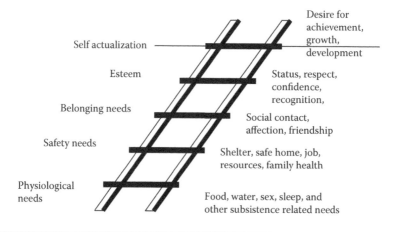

Self actualization — Desire for achievement, growth, development

Esteem — Status, respect, confidence, recognition,

Belonging needs — Social contact, affection, friendship

Safety needs — Shelter, safe home, job, resources, family health

Physiological needs — Food, water, sex, sleep, and other subsistence related needs

Figure 14.3   Maslow's hierarchy of needs.

4. Esteem: Status, recognition, confidence, positive regard, respect of others, and respect by others.
5. Self-actualization: Desire for achievement, personal growth, development, autonomy, morality, creativity, and problem solving.

Movement of progression from the lowest to the highest was termed satisfaction progression by Maslow. However, individuals do not seek satisfaction of their needs in this fashion of progression.

14.5.1.2 Alderfer ERG Theory

Alderfer reduced the five levels of Maslow's needs to three, which move forward as well as backward. The three levels are (1) existence, (2) relatedness, and (3) growth (Shanks and Dore, 2012).

Existence needs combine both the physiological and safety needs postulated by Maslow. Relatedness refers to the belonging needs. Growth needs combine the last two needs put forward by Malsow—esteem and self-actualization. According to Alderfer's theory, individuals move from one level to another, depending on the degree of fulfillment achieved by a need. This theory is compatible with real-life situations.

14.5.1.3 Herzberg's Two-Factor Theory

Herzberg postulated that individuals are motivated by two factors: hygiene factors and motivator factors (Agomo, 2008). According to Herzberg, satisfaction and dissatisfaction are independent. Elimination of dissatisfaction does not lead to satisfaction. The hygiene factors identified by Herzberg were low-level motivators that included company policy, administration, supervision, interpersonal relationships, working environment, salary, and job security. The fulfillment of hygiene factors does not lead to motivation (Figure 14.4). Motivator factors are higher-level needs that include achievement, recognition for achievement, growth or advancement, gaining recognition, responsibility, and challenging or stimulating work.

Herzberg's simple approach suggests that individuals have desires beyond "hygiene" needs and motivators are important.

14.5.1.4 McClelland's Acquired Needs Theory

McClelland suggested that needs are acquired throughout one's life, depending on his or her life experiences. His theory includes three types of needs: need for achievement, need for affiliation, and need for power. Achievement desires

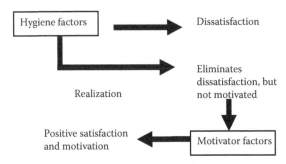

Figure 14.4   Herzberg's two-factor theory.

are achieving success, mastering skills, and attaining goals. The need for social contact and building relationships with others is identified as an affiliation need. The need for power refers to the desire for responsibility, control, and authority over others.

14.5.2 Extrinsic Factor Theories

14.5.2.1 Reinforcement Theory

The reinforcement theory postulated by Skinner focuses on the reinforcement of human behavior. According to him, individuals are motivated when their behavior is reinforced. He identified four types of behavior. Positive reinforcement and avoidance learning achieve desirable behavior, while punishment and extinction achieve undesirable behavior.

Positive reinforcement refers to actions that reward and recognize positive behavior. In contrast, avoidance learning refers to actions that reward behavior that avoids undesirable or negative behavior. Punishment refers to actions taken to reduce undesirable behavior and has negative consequences for the individual. The removal of positive rewards for undesirable behavior is termed extinction.

The reinforcement theory has limitation when applied to human behavior, in that it does not recognize an individual's ability to think critically and reason.

14.5.3 Intrinsic Factor Theories

14.5.3.1 Adam's Equity Theory

Individuals have the tendency to compare themselves with others in the community, and Adam's equity theory is based on the fact that individuals are motivated when they are treated equitably in comparison to others in the organization.

14.5.3.2 Vroom's Expectancy Theory

Vroom's expectancy theory is based on the expectations of individuals, and he postulates that they are motivated by performance and the expected outcome of their behavior.

14.5.3.3 Locke's Goal Setting Theory

According to Locke, individuals are motivated when they take action to achieve the goals. The key elements of the theory are (1) goals must be specific and challenging, (2) goals must be accepted and there must be a commitment to reach them, (3) goal priorities must be clarified, (4) management must provide regular feedback, and (5) accomplishments must be rewarded.

Locke's theory also has limitations. The goals established by the management may be different from those of the employees. Often the acronym SMART is used to establish goals: goals must be specific, measurable, attainable, realistic, and timely. Managers overlook the need to consult the individuals who are expected to perform the activities when setting goals. Employees are closer to the work, and they know the limitations of tasks. When financial goals are established in the pharmacy and medicine environment, it is possible for employees to focus on meeting financial targets without considering the ethical issues.

Medicine use reviews (MURs) have been a source of income for community pharmacies. Often, managers, in their eagerness to meet financial targets, apply pressure on pharmacists to conduct MURs for financial gain. Claims forwarded for payments for MUR service have received much attention in recent times. It is practically impossible at the same time to meet MUR targets and increase the number of items dispensed. The targets are purely arbitrary and there is ample room for abuse.[*]

---

[*] News Team, "Scrutiny around MUR Fraud to Rise," *Pharmaceutical Journal*, 286, 221, 2011.

At least 90 people died between 2004 and 2006 in Maidstone and Tunbridge Trust from the stomach bug *Clostridium difficile.* There was a catalog of serious errors, and according to Liberal Democrat Shadow Health Secretary Norman Lamb, "The report lays out in stark terms the danger of hospital staff chasing targets when they could be concentrating on caring for patients."[*]

14.5.3.4 Management Theories of Motivation

Management theories of motivation are those driven by aspects of management such as productivity, human resources, and other considerations. Two main theories in this category are the scientific management theory by Fredrick Taylor and McGregor's theory X and theory Y. These are discussed in Chapter 2.

14.6 Benefits of Motivation

A motivated workforce is an asset to any organization. In community pharmacies and hospital pharmacies where the tasks are aimed at proper patient care, it is essential that the management satisfies the needs and expectations of the staff to promote motivation and teamwork. Motivation provides several benefits for the organization (Bing, 2011):

1. Inspires individuals to perform better even in tough times.
2. Staff are able to set goals and stay on track to create a vision to achieve maximum outcome.
3. Improves networking among the staff that supports communication and enhances relationships among team members.

---

[*] V. Fletcher, "How Hospital Bug Killed 90 Patients," Express.co.uk, 2007, retrieved December 12, 2011, from http://www.express.co.uk/posts/view/21674/ How-hospital-bug-killed-90-patients.

4. Employees' efforts are rewarded, promoting strength and courage for creativity.
5. Organizes working strategies and develops key skills needed for handling the team.
6. Improves the behavior skills of the organization.

14.7 Motivational Strategies

Organizations employ various strategies to induce motivation among their staff. Some of the strategies are described below (Shanks and Dore, 2012):

■ Expect the best: Individuals live up to their and others' expectations.
■ Reward for desired behavior: Rewards should be offered for the desired behavior and not for undesired behavior.
■ Create a FUN (focused, unpredictable, novel) approach: Although financial benefits have a short-term "memory," they have a positive outcome, if used in an unpredictable way; for example, offering money for cinema tickets to the children of the staff during the holidays as a reward for exceeding some target can be a novel approach for the entire family to appreciate the organization.
■ Reward employees in ways that improve performance and motivation.
■ Tailor rewards to the needs of the individual: For example, paying annual tennis club fees on behalf of an individual who does not play tennis is a waste of money.
■ Revitalize employees: When employees work hard to achieve the goals and sometimes exceed them, it is necessary for management to recognize the efforts and offer inducements as a token of appreciation to prevent burnout and maintain enthusiasm.
■ Encourage employees to take responsibility for their own motivation: Difficult employee problems should be

resolved without delay. Managers must determine what motivates employees, understand their needs, and get them involved in problem solving.

■ Acknowledge employees' strengths, promote high performance, and focus on their learning methods. Management must assess individuals' strengths and weaknesses to enable appropriate tasks to be assigned. Learning methods will enable the managers to provide training and skills as an alternative method of encouraging and motivating them.

14.8 Principles of Motivation

A manager has to demonstrate leadership qualities to motivate the subordinates. Adair (2009) has presented eight principles for motivating others:

1. Be motivated yourself.
2. Select individuals who are highly motivated.
3. Treat each person as an individual and show empathy.
4. Set realistic and challenging goals.
5. Progress motivates.
6. Create an environment that fosters motivation.
7. Offer fair rewards for achievements.
8. Give recognition and praise when necessary.

One of the great challenges facing a manager when motivating his or her staff is developing the skill to help subordinates understand their needs and to help satisfy them effectively. The task is complex because each individual has a different set of needs that are constantly changing. But there are some guidelines that the manager can use to foster motivation among the team (Longest, 1984):

1. To motivate subordinates, the manager has to know what must be accomplished. He or she must clearly determine the objectives and purposes of the task to be completed.
2. The manager needs to demonstrate empathy with the staff so that their needs and expectations can be identified clearly.
3. The manager must communicate with the employees so that they can understand the expectations of management.
4. Employees have different needs, and it is the function of the manager to match the needs of the employee with those of the organization. The degree of success of the motivation depends on the extent of integration of an employee's objectives with those of the organization.
5. The manager should support the subordinates to accomplish the tasks by providing skills, training, and other resources.
6. Teamwork is an essential part of motivation, and the manager must promote this among the employees. Complex activities of a pharmacy always involve teamwork, and an individual is a part of the team. By careful planning, individuals can be motivated, and this will make the group more effective.

14.9 The Role of Incentives

Traditionally, incentives have always been associated with financial benefits. However, owing to current uncertain economic times, managers are cutting back on financial incentives. Individuals with higher salary packages are motivated by nonfinancial incentives such as long-term retention, job functions, and business contexts. A recent McKinsey quarterly survey has shown that praise from immediate superiors, the leader's attention, and the opportunity to lead a task or a project are the three most effective nonfinancial incentives

(Dewhurst et al., 2009). Although financial incentives only provide a short-term "boost of energy," banks and other high-turnover organizations still offer financial incentives even during tough times! The three highest rated financial incentives were cash bonuses, higher base pay, and stock options.

Contrary to the above view, a survey input from 145 U.S. organizations has shown that tangible incentives such as cash and awards work to different degrees according to the conditions in which they are implemented (International Society for Performance Improvement, 2002). The survey found that

■ Tangible incentives can dramatically increase performance by about 22%, if they are properly selected or administered.
■ Tangible incentives enhance interest in "incentivized" work tasks among the motivated employees.
■ Current research does not support the view that tangible incentives cause an unintentional decrease in the intrinsic personal value for work tasks.

However, tangible incentives are only effective under the following conditions:

1. Current performance on specific work goals is unsatisfactory.
2. Unsatisfactory performance is due to lack of motivation rather than a lack of knowledge, skills, or resources.
3. The desired level of performance can be measured and quantified.
4. The goals are challenging and achievable.
5. All other performance goals should continue to be achieved at or above the current level.

14.10 How to Motivate Pharmacy Staff

Pharmacies employ individuals from different communities with diverse views and opinions. Therefore, individuals will be motivated differently. The role of the manager is to take into account personality and diversity. The two factors that motivate most pharmacy staff are mutual respect and personal involvement (Agomo, 2008).

The rewards offered by employers for motivating their staff are of two types: intrinsic rewards and extrinsic rewards. Intrinsic rewards are derived from within the employee, and in the context of healthcare refer to the pride, satisfaction, and happiness derived by providing excellent patient care. On the other hand, extrinsic rewards are given by others in recognition of achievements, for example, the bonuses offered to the team for demonstrating quality and patient satisfaction (Shanks and Dore, 2012).

According to the model proposed by Nohria et al. (2008), there are levers that employers can use to fulfill the four emotional drives. Reward systems can be used to satisfy the employees' drive to acquire. Organization culture is the lever to employ to satisfy the need for bonding. The drive to comprehend can be met by proper job design. Finally, employees' drive to defend can be satisfied by demonstrating proper performance, management, and resource allocation processes.

Application of this model to the needs and expectations of pharmacy staff (Agomo, 2008) is shown in Table 14.1.

14.11 Motivating Pharmacy Staff for Continuing Education

A survey conducted among the Flemish community pharmacists regarding their views on continuing education (CE) has revealed that the three motivating factors for CE are (1) the need for extending their pharmacy practice knowledge, (2) social contact, and (3) the need for a syllabus. Barriers to

Table 14.1 Motivating the Pharmacy Staff

Emotional Drive	Primary Lever	Motivating Factors
Acquire	Reward system	Have a good working environment
		Provide breaks when necessary
		Look after their health
		Hire more staff to cope with heavy workload
		Have new technology
		Reward and celebrate achievements
		Recognize long service
		Occasionally take them for a treat
		Offer competitive salaries
		Support self-development and continuing education
		Consider partnership/franchise
Bond	Affiliation	Establish a family/friendly approach
		Encourage teamwork

(continued)

Table 14.1 Motivating the Pharmacy Staff (continued)

Emotional Drive	Primary Lever	Motivating Factors
		Frequently talk to the staff
		Provide support and encouragement
		Encourage staff to participate in community activities
		Introduce healthy competition of short duration
		Organize fun activities
		Encourage mentorship
		Promote collaboration with other healthcare providers
Comprehend	Job design	Promote a patient-oriented approach instead of target-driven approach
		Utilize job rotation to prevent monotony
		Involve the staff in setting the mission and goals
Defend	Performance, management, and resource allocation processes	Establish effective systems to manage the pharmacy
		Establish a system to tailor rewards to match the needs
		Establish a system to identify good performance

motivation are lack of time, family constraints, distance to the class, and uninteresting topics (Driesen et al., 2005).

14.12 Why Managers Fail to Motivate Employees

Managers who fail to motivate their staff have misconceptions about motivation and focus on the wrong things. As healthcare providers, it is important for pharmacy managers to assess and understand such misconceptions in order to be effective in their role. Often managers make wrong assumptions on what motivates their subordinates (Shanks and Dore, 2012; Dewar and Keller, 2011). Some of the misconceptions are cited below:

1. Employees do not care as much about the company as you think they do. There are five sources of meaning for humans at work: the impact of their work on society, customers, organization, team, and self. Most leaders do not focus on these primary motivators.
2. Less can be more when it comes to incentives. Big financial bonuses are less effective than unexpected gestures such as gifts. Bonuses are purely transactional, while gifts create a relationship between the parties.
3. Listen more, talk less. Commitment to the outcome is five times greater when individuals choose for themselves what to do instead of being told. Leaders should take time to listen to the staff to gather their views on improvements.
4. Do not forget the good stuff. Focus on the organization's and individuals' strengths to overcome barriers for progress and solve problems. Looking for opportunities to build on strengths fosters inspiration and motivation.
5. Leaders assume that individuals are motivated by extrinsic factors rather than intrinsic factors.
6. All individuals are motivated by intrinsic rewards.

7. Some people are not motivated.
8. Individuals are motivated by financial rewards.
9. Motivation is assumed to be manipulation of employees.
10. "One-size-fits-all" concept—not tailoring the rewards and recognition.
11. Motivation is an inborn quality and cannot be made.
12. There is one kind of employee satisfaction.

14.13 Motivation of Managers

A good manager should help subordinates feel strong and responsible and influence others' success. Good performance is rewarded, and subordinates feel that they know what must be done. He or she fosters a team spirit among them.

Managers can be classed into three motivational groups (McClelland and Burnham, 2003). The three characteristics that distinguish these groups are power, affiliation, and inhibition (controlled action). Affiliative managers have a higher need to be liked than for power. Their subordinates feel that they have little responsibility, believe that organizational procedures are not clear, and have no pride in their work. This type of manager has no regard for organized procedures, and that leaves the subordinates in a totally irresponsible position of not knowing what to do next. They are low in power and high in inhibition.

In contrast, personal power managers have little concern for affiliation but have a higher need for power. They are able to foster a sense of responsibility among the team and create greater team spirit. Subordinates are more loyal to them as individuals than to the organization. They are high in power and low in affiliation and inhibition. Power without discipline or controlled action is directed toward personal gain and not toward the benefit of the organization.

Research has shown that institutional managers are high in power, low in affiliation, and high in inhibition. Institutional managers build power through influence. By creating an effective work climate, subordinates feel they have more responsibility. They care more about the organization, are disciplined to get work done in an orderly manner, have a keen sense of justice, and are willing to self-sacrifice. The institutional management style is best suited to foster motivation among the staff.

14.14 Case Studies Based on the Model of Nohria et al. (2008)

The emotional drives to acquire, bond, comprehend, and defend are independent of each other. Fulfilling all four emotional drives is essential to motivate the employees. Major advancements compared to competitors occur through the combined effect of fulfilling all four drives because fulfillment of all reinforces the others. However, even if the organization demonstrates a slight enhancement in accomplishing one drive, an overall motivation shows a corresponding improvement. The following case studies, as reported by Nohria et al. (2008), illustrate the fulfillment of one or more emotional drives through organizational levers.

Sonoco, an industrial consumer goods manufacturer, established very clear links between employee performance and a reward system. The company set high business performance goals, but incentives failed to reward the achievements of employees. In 1995, the new vice president of human resources introduced a pay-for-performance reward system based on individual and group achievements. The net result, according to an internal survey, was employee satisfaction and improvement in performance. The organization was able to fulfill one of the emotional drives, the drive to acquire using a reward system as a lever. In 2005, Hewitt Associates placed Sonoco among the top 20 talent management organizations, which included companies such as 3M, GE, Johnson & Johnson, Dell, and IBM.

Wegmans supermarket meets the drive to bond (culture). This company appeared for decades on Fortune's list of "100 Best Companies to Work For." The business, owned by a family, has been a family-oriented organization. It has been able to cultivate a sense of belonging and teamwork among its employees. They regularly report on the caring attitude of management and among themselves.

Cirque du Soleil is a company that has met the drive to comprehend by making jobs challenging and fulfilling. It acknowledges the creativity of performers and drives them to perfection. Cirque du Soleil employees have a say on how performances are staged and get an opportunity to develop new skills by moving from one show to another and being exposed to world-renowned artists.

Aflac is an example of a company that has been successful in fulfilling all four drives. It is a Fortune 500 company with assets as of year-end 2011 of over $117 billion, with annual revenue of over $22.2 billion. It is represented in all 50 U.S. states and in Puerto Rico and the Virgin Islands.

Individual performance of employees is acknowledged and rewarded in transparent ways, thereby meeting the drive to acquire. Employee appreciation week has been introduced to create a sense of belonging and bonding among its employees, thus enhancing culture-bonding effects. The company invests significantly in training and development, fulfilling the drive to comprehend. Aflac management has a caring attitude toward its employees, offering benefits such as on-site child care, training, and scholarships and having a no-layoff policy. These benefits and the caring attitude of the company have improved the work–life balance and enhanced the quality of life of employees, meeting the drive to defend.

14.15 Revisiting the Scenario

There are a number of unresolved issues that have led to low morale in the pharmacy. Managers must realize that all staff must be treated fairly without favoritism. Susan's bonus may have been due to the close association between the manager and herself. It appears that the staff are under stress to perform, and this is borne out by the fact that a staff member is on stress leave. Max is confused and frustrated that nothing has been done to resolve the issues. The technicians may not be clear about who is responsible for certain tasks. Dianne has to identify the needs and expectations of the staff and allocate responsibilities in a fair manner. Staff shortages must be addressed to prevent a backlog of prescriptions. Management has to offer awards for achievements to all the staff in an equitable manner. Arrangements must be made for performing tasks in the pharmacy during legitimate breaks. Managers have to realize that professional development activities are essential for delivering effective services to patients. Dianne has to take advantage of review meetings to foster a sense of team spirit, demonstrate leadership qualities, identify the changing needs of the staff, recognize achievements, and clearly clarify what they have to achieve without suggesting how they should do it.

References

Adair, J. (1992). Leadership and motivation. In D.M. Stewart (Ed.), *Handbook of management skills* (2nd ed., pp. 133–151). Worcester: BCA.

Adair, J. (2009). *Leadership and motivation*. Philadelphia: Kogan Press.

Agomo, C. (2008). Understanding what motivates staff. *Pharmaceutical Journal*, 280, 545–548.

Bing, M. (2011). Employee motivation. Retrieved December 12, 2011, from http://www.bestmotivationtips.com/employee-motivation/employee-motivation-your-key-to-productivity/

Dewar, C., and Keller, S. (2011). Four motivational mistakes most leaders make. HBR Blog Network. Retrieved December 15, 2011, from http://blogs.hbr.org/cs/2011/10/four_motivation_mistakes_most.html

Dewhurst, M., Guthridge, M., and Mohr, E. (2009). Motivating people: Getting beyond money. McKinsey quarterly survey. Retrieved September 22, 2012, from http://www.mckinseyquarterly.com/Motivating_people_Getting_beyond_money_2460

Driesen, A., Leemans, L., Baert, H., and Laekeman, G. (2005). Flemish community pharmacists' motivation and views related to continuing education. *Pharmacy World and Science*, 27(6), 447–452.

International Society for Performance Improvement. (2002). Incentives, motivation and workplace performance: Research and best practices. Retrieved December 14, 2011, from http://www.loyaltyworks.com/incentive-program-research-articles/ispifullpdf.pdf

Longest, B.B. (1984). *Management practices for the health professional* (3rd ed.). Reston, VA: Reston Publishing.

McClelland, D.C., and Burnham, D.H. (2003). Power is the great motivator. *Harvard Business Review*, 81, 117–126.

Nohria, N., Groysberg, B., and Lee, L.E. (2008). Employee motivation: A powerful new model. *Harvard Business Review*, 86, 78–84.

Shanks, N.H., and Dore, A. (2012). Management and motivation. In S.B. Buchbinder and N.H. Shanks (Eds.), *Introduction to healthcare management* (2nd ed., pp. 39–52). Burlington, MA: Jones and Bartlett.

White, S.J., and Generali, J.A. (1984). Motivating pharmacy employees. *American Journal of Hospital Pharmacy*, 41(7), 1361–1366.

Chapter 15

Managing Cultural Diversity at Work

Cultural differences should not separate us from each other, but rather cultural diversity brings a collective strength that can benefit all humanity.

—Robert Alan,
American writer, artist, social activist

15.1 Scenario

Alfonso was a pharmacist from Spain with limited communication skills in English. He joined Community Pharmacy Limited during his preregistration period. Dianne Watts often instructed him to talk to patients, although he was reluctant to do so and found it difficult to get the message across. Max, the pharmacist, intervened whenever necessary to save embarrassment. Patients sometimes demanded to see a "pharmacist who could speak in English." Max recommended to Dianne that Alfonso should be allowed to work in the dispensary where his skills are not in question, until he gained the necessary confidence to talk to patients. Dianne refused and ultimately Alfonso left and joined another company to continue his training.

15.2 Introduction

England has always been recognized globally as a center for education and employment. People from all walks of life and from all over the world arrive in the United Kingdom for either employment or studies. Community pharmacies in the United Kingdom attract pharmacists from all over the world, including African and Asian countries, New Zealand, Australia, and those in the European Union. Regulatory requirements prohibit discrimination on the grounds of race, color, religion, or ethnic origin. The workplace has a mixed culture of individuals from different backgrounds. Individuals of any background other than white are classified as ethnic minorities. In 2009, the ethnic minority employment reached 60.9% of the workforce (Department for Work and Pensions, 2009). Ethnic minority groups include black African, black Caribbean, other black, Indian, Chinese, Pakistani, Bangladeshi, other Asia, and mixed. Progressive companies have embraced the policies of equality to make the workplace better and more challenging. The working environment in the community pharmacy has thus become multicultural. Therefore, pharmacy managers must have the skills to manage a diverse workforce to create an environment that promotes harmony and teamwork.

In the United States, even among the wider population, the number of people from distinct racial and ethnic backgrounds has been steadily increasing. "Minority" groups in the United States comprise African Americans, Native Americans, the Hispanic population, and Asians. Between 1980 and 2000, the white population increased by about 9%. In contrast, the African American population grew by 28%, Native Americans by 55%, the Hispanic population by 122%, and the Asians by 190% (Cohen et al., 2002).

According to Carla White Harris, RPh, director of the Recruitment and Diversity Initiative at the University of North Carolina Eshelman School of Pharmacy, the pharmacy profession is less racially diverse than physicians and other healthcare professionals (Scott, 2009). In the United States, 5.9% out of 247,000 registered pharmacists were African American, 2.5% were Hispanic, and 75% were Caucasians.

15.3 Definitions

15.3.1 Diversity

Diversity has been defined in terms of obvious differences in age, ethnicity, gender, physical disability, sexual orientation, religion, professional skills, values, culture, and social class language (Clements and Jones, 2008). These differences are observable in the workplace, and therefore to understand the significance of culture in a group, pharmacy managers have to consider the values held in the group. Culture has two dimensions: space and time (Hopkins, 2009). Individuals from a particular geographical location share common cultural values, and it is a dynamic entity that changes with time in response to economic and political pressure. A diverse workforce demonstrates varied perspectives and approaches to work (Thomas and Ely, 1996), and these could be used for the benefit of the organization. Green et al. (n.d.) define *diversity* as embracing the differences that exist among the various cultural groups. The terms *diversity* and *multiculturalism* have been often used synonymously.

15.3.2 Multiculturalism

Historically, multiculturalism refers to the philosophy of accepting and promoting people of different racial and ethnic backgrounds. Diversity broadens this view to include the differences that exist among various cultural groups.

15.3.3 Culture

Culture refers to a group or community whose members share common experiences and values that determine the way the members see the world. These groups may be based on gender, race, or nationality (Du Praw and Axner, 1997).

15.3.4 Values

Values are beliefs and judgments that are important and acceptable that individuals or groups hold. A high-ranking job that is a status symbol in Asian countries and working for a reputed organization are examples of values. These are based on one's or a group's ethnic background, racial origin, religion, gender, place of birth, or age (Greer and Plunkett, 2003).

15.3.5 Norms

Norms are acceptable forms of behavior or conduct within a community or a group. A group's conduct may not be the best way, and individual members are expected to conform to the standards set by the group. In a teamwork situation, group norms may stand in the way of carrying out work in the manner expected by the supervisor (Newstrom, 2007). Doing the job the way you are told without questioning or criticizing the work habits, even when they are not appropriate, are some examples of norms.

15.4 Key Cultural Indicators

According to cross-cultural psychologists, aspects of culture can be classified on the basis of several key indicators. However, this categorization has been much debated because (1) the studies focused on economically active societies, (2) the indicators are a reflection of Western bias, and (3) the cultures vary on the degree of importance placed on the indicators (Hopkins, 2009). Javidan et al. (2006) in their study revealed nine such indicators. In a community pharmacy, the individuals originating from various cultures may demonstrate work patterns contrary to what is expected by the management, depending upon the importance attached to the indicators by the individual. Therefore, the pharmacy manager must have a clear understanding of these indicators to resolve the issues. The key indicators are

1. Uncertainty avoidance: This is the extent to which a culture is encouraged or discouraged to take risks. People in countries such as Japan, Iran, and Turkey, which are high on uncertainty avoidance indicators, avoid uncertain situations, whereas individuals in countries such as Singapore, Hong Kong, and Sweden, which are low on uncertainty avoidance, accept creative ideas and are prepared to take risks.
2. Future orientation: This signifies the importance attached to the past, present, and future. People in past orientation countries place a high value on the past and venerate traditions. Examples of past orientation countries are France, China, and Japan. Individuals in present orientation countries believe in the present and enjoy the here and now. The United States is a future orientation country where people look forward to the future.
3. Power distance: This indicator measures the distance between the superior and the subordinate. The authority and power exercised by the manager is accepted by the subordinate staff. In countries such as Argentina and Spain, where power distance is high, inequality is accepted and bosses are powerful. People in Australia, Canada, and Denmark, where the distance between hierarchical levels is low, do not accept inequality.
4. In-group collectivism: People in this culture express pride, loyalty, and collectiveness in their organization and families.

5. Value orientation: This indicator is a measure of the degree of importance attached to human values. Euro-American cultures believe that some people are good and some bad. On the other hand, people in high-value orientation societies place importance on human values and believe that people are fundamentally good.
6. Institutional collectivism: Cultures high in institutional collectivism encourage and reward collective distribution of resources and achievements.
7. Performance orientation: This reflects the importance attached to the achievements of individuals.
8. Gender egalitarianism: This measures the degree to which gender inequality is minimized.
9. Assertiveness: Cultures high in assertiveness demonstrate assertiveness, confrontation, and aggression in their relationship with others.

15.5 Challenges of Diversity

A diverse workforce creates numerous challenges for management. These challenges have a significant impact on the work habit. A skilled manager is able to overcome the issues to promote a harmonious environment where all employees can take pride in their work irrespective of their ethnic origin. Broadly, the issues relate to work habits, communication, and attitudes of employees (Ngomsi, 2009; Du Praw and Axner, 1997).

1. Ethnocentrism: The belief that one's own culture is the best and must be followed. Some individual pharmacists, technicians, and managers from Western countries may view their work habits as the best.
2. History and stereotyping: Based on historical cultural experiences, employees and employers may be inclined to believe that all members of a culture or a group share the same values and norms. Stereotyping in this fashion

leads to a false understanding of others and prejudice. European pharmacists do not have a good command of English and may struggle to express their views. However, this is not true of all European pharmacists.

3. Generalization of groups and cultures: The term *Indian* is often associated with people with colored skin on the assumption that they originate from India. However, people from India, Pakistan, Sri Lanka, and Bangladesh are colored and vary in their cultures and values. In New Zealand, Chinese people are referred to as Asians, whereas in the United Kingdom the term *Asians* is used to identify people from India, Pakistan, Sri Lanka, Bangladesh, etc.

4. Communication style: Most countries around the globe are now independent colonies, and they have their own language and culture. Thus, immigrants from countries other than English-speaking countries may not possess adequate skills to communicate in English. This leads to frustration among co-workers. Nonverbal communication is also a characteristic of some cultures. In America and the United Kingdom, a raised voice is a sign of confrontation. But among some nationalities, conversation in a raised voice is a sign of excitement. A manager listening to a loud conversation between two non-white individuals may react with great concern.

5. Response to conflict: Some cultures consider conflict positive, while individuals in Eastern cultures tend to avoid conflict, which causes embarrassment to both parties. In these situations, a written response is preferred.

6. Attitude toward work habits: The significance attached to the resources needed for a task, rewards on completion, and the relationship between team spirit and the task may vary from culture to culture. Asian cultures often prefer to build relationships among the team workers before the commencement of the task. In Western society, tasks take priority and relationship building occurs as the work continues.

7. Decision-making styles: In some cultures, decision making is handed down to subordinates. But in other cultures, decision making is not delegated. In the United States, majority rule is the preferred method of arriving at a team decision. However, in Japan, the decisions are based on consensus.

8. Disclosure: Some cultures are sensitive to the display of emotions, disclosing personal information, or discussions on reasons behind a conflict or misunderstanding. In a conflict situation, managers must be aware of the values and norms of the people who are involved in the conflict.

9. Knowing: Different cultures have different ways of acquiring knowledge (Wood et al., 2006). The sources may be dialogue, experience, local knowledge, through symbols and nonverbal communication, through contemplation, and by doing.

15.6 Benefits of Diversity

A diverse workforce offers numerous benefits for the organization (Lockwood, 2005; Auckland Chamber of Commerce, n.d.; Department of Education and Early Childhood Development, 2002; Greenburg, 2004). Some of the benefits are

1. Improved team performance
2. Enhanced productivity and efficiency
3. Improved customer relations, community relations, and reputation
4. Broader base for recruitment
5. Reduced absenteeism, high staff morale, and increased retention of staff
6. Variety of viewpoints of solving problems
7. Creativity and innovation
8. Broader skill range

15.7 Healthcare Needs of Minority Groups in the United States

In order to meet the healthcare needs of the minority groups in the United States, a culturally competent workforce is essential. Racially and ethnically diverse healthcare professionals enable the provision of adequate healthcare to minority communities as well as the promotion of research in neglected areas of the communities and the availability of competent managers and policy makers to address healthcare issues.

15.7.1 Creation of a Diverse Healthcare Workforce

Cohen et al. (2002) propose that a diverse healthcare workforce can be established by (1) enhancing cultural competence, (2) increasing access to quality healthcare, (3) promoting medical research on health issues that affect minority groups, and (4) effective and efficient management of the healthcare system.

15.7.1.1 Enhancing Cultural Competence

Cultural competence refers to the acquisition of knowledge skills, attitudes, and behavior of healthcare professionals in order to provide effective and adequate care to people from various cultural and ethnic backgrounds. Such healthcare providers must have a greater understanding of the belief systems, cultural biases, ethnic origin, family structure, and other factors that influence their knowledge of illnesses and the response to medical advice and treatments.

Professionals who are culturally competent are aware of sensitive issues, such as English language barrier, various religious needs, alternate treatments, etc. Interacting with individuals from diverse backgrounds at the college level and at work enables them to acknowledge and understand the viewpoints of others and to realize their own viewpoints as seen by others.

15.7.1.2 Access to Quality Healthcare

Minorities are underrepresented in the healthcare workforce, and inadequate access to healthcare is observed mainly within minority populations. It is an observed fact that patients are more comfortable with services offered by a healthcare provider of their own racial and ethnic backgrounds. Healthcare biases and disparities can only be eradicated by making the services of diverse culturally competent healthcare professionals accessible to all minority groups.

15.7.1.3 Promotion of Medical Research

Clinical and health service research related to the neglected areas of health service is a vital necessity. Traditionally, research investigators conduct research on issues as they perceive them through their personal cultural and ethnic filters. Therefore, a racially and ethnically diverse research team is required to investigate health problems that affect minority groups. The logistics of how minority groups can be approached for participation in research must be worked out by the investigating team.

15.7.1.4 Effective and Efficient Management of the Healthcare System

The healthcare system in the future needs a pool of trained executives and policy makers to implement government efforts that address important health issues. At present, minority groups in medical management and policy-making roles are underrepresented. It must be acknowledged that provision of adequate healthcare to a diverse population is a difficult management issue that affects healthcare funders, program managers, and local, state, and national governments. Therefore, executives and policy makers must be drawn from a richly diverse talent pool.

15.8 Necessary Skills for Managing Diversity

Managers need to develop skills to manage a diverse workforce effectively. Apart from leadership skills, diversity management skills will enable the manager to create a harmonious environment (Clements and Spinks, 2009; Chang and Tharenou, 2004). The six essential skills are

1. Cultural empathy: Empathy refers to putting yourself in another person's "shoes" in order to understand how the other person thinks and feels. A joke about the accent of a person's speech may offend the other person. The person making the joke should be aware of how the other person feels about the joke. Cultural empathy includes cultural awareness and understanding, respecting values of others, treating people as individuals, and applying different perspectives in dealing with people.
2. Understanding: Closely associated with empathy is the need to develop an understanding of how your attitude affects the other person.
3. Enhanced awareness: The manager should be aware of his or her behavior that may affect the other person.
4. Building sensitivity: Being aware of the culture and the situation is an important transferable skill. People from different cultures have different ways of thinking, behaving, and different values and needs.
5. Awareness of consequences: Prejudicial behavior and lack of sensitivity or understanding may have serious consequences for other parties.
6. Being fair: The manager must treat all the staff in a fair manner, irrespective of cultural differences. This is achieved through equal opportunity and diversity policies that embrace differences in culture.

Chang and Tharenou (2004) in their study found five essential competencies for managing a multicultural workforce:

empathy (Section 15.8), learning on the job, communication, generic managerial skills, and personal style.

Learning on the job: This refers to the need for managers to learn about their diverse workforce to enhance their skills to adapt to new situations as they arise. The managers must be flexible and willing to learn by observation.

Communication: The manner of communicating with a multicultural work group is an essential competency to develop to manage a diverse team. Effective managers care to listen patiently, are approachable, and express their thoughts clearly.

Generic managerial skills: These include motivation, consulting, and conflict resolution.

Personal style: This style refers to the management style used by managers to manage the subordinate multicultural work group. To be an effective manager, managers should develop emotional stability by being calm and patient, respecting differences, focusing on common attributes, and being frank in all situations.

15.9 Managing Diversity

Within any organization there are culturally supportive and nonsupportive people, policies, and informal structures. The manager's role is to establish a pleasant environment where diversity is valued (Henderson, 1994). A good starting point is to evaluate the diversity climate in the workforce. Diversity perception can be measured by employing psychometric tests (Barak, 2005). Globalization of economy and changes in the workforce make it necessary for organizations to develop a strategy to manage the workforce that goes beyond recognizing individual differences and human resource policies. Essential steps for success are (McArthur, 2006) (1) understanding the economic consequences, such as loss of productivity, high employee turnover, lost opportunities, and legal battles, as a result of not having a clear strategy; (2) developing a strategy for managing diversity by communicating with employees, assigning responsibilities, allocating resources, and assigning accountability; (3) implementing the plan by communicating it, measuring the initial diversity perception, setting goals, and providing diversity training to all employees; and (4) monitoring the plan in order to measure its effectiveness and determining opportunities and threats.

A manager in a community pharmacy employing individuals of different cultural backgrounds has a significant role to play in developing a strategy. He or she must foster a culture (Thomas and Ely, 1996) that values diversity by the following:

1. The organization must understand that a diverse workforce will bring different perspectives and approaches to work.
2. The management must identify learning opportunities and challenges that arise as a result of different perspectives and approaches to work.
3. The organization culture must create an environment where a high standard is expected from all employees.
4. The management must encourage personal development and growth.
5. The organization culture must encourage open discussion.
6. The organization must create a culture where all employees feel valued.
7. The organization must have a clear vision that is understood by everybody.
8. The organization must establish an egalitarian and nonbureaucratic structure.

15.10 Guidelines for Multicultural Collaboration

In order to take advantage of diversity in the workplace, employees must acknowledge differences and embrace diversity. The following are some guidelines for multicultural collaboration (Du Praw and Axner, 1997; Auckland Chamber of Commerce, n.d.):

■ Learn from other cultures and avoid stereotyping.
■ Be aware of how best to communicate with a person of a different culture.
■ Listen actively and empathetically.
■ Respect the opinion of others.
■ Avoid judgment and view the situation as an outsider.
■ Be receptive to another person's perception of imbalance and dominance.
■ Articulate the organization's values of tolerance and respect.
■ Be flexible as much as possible in work arrangements.
■ Encourage employees to share individual needs with the management.
■ Ensure that bullying and harassment do not take place.
■ Offer diversity training to all employees.
■ Support out-of-hours interests of individuals.

15.11 Case Study from New Zealand

Waitakere City (WC), situated in West Auckland in New Zealand, has a vibrant community of people from diverse ethnic backgrounds. Ethnic minority groups in WC consist of Maoris, Pacific Islanders, Asians, Middle Eastern/Latin American/Africans, and Asians. Europeans make up the major group in the city. In 1995, Anoma De Silva, multicultural services librarian at Waitakere City, initiated a novel approach to foster diversity and promote library services among the ethnic groups.

The language barrier of the ethnic population and lack of enthusiasm to use library services were major obstacles to overcome. After she took over multicultural services, her first task was to introduce "Welcome" signage in all ethnic languages. As one entered the library, the welcome sign in his or her own language was clearly visible at the entrance. She visited community halls and churches where ethnic groups congregate to foster diversity and promote library services. A special budget was allocated to source ethnic reading material from reputed sources. Thereby, she established an international language collection of books and other resources in 30 languages. The special collection was a great asset to all international students and immigrants to enhance their English language communication skills. Another collection of material supported local business operators in their ventures in China, Japan, and Southeast Asian countries.

The multicultural services kiosk was highly visible at every event in the city to offer advice. Weekly conversation classes were held in the evenings in the libraries to improve communication skills in English. A multicultural society was established by De Silva to create better understanding among the community groups and promote individual cultures. The oral history project was very popular among the local immigrant community. The entire library staff supported her vision by participating in cross-cultural communication seminars and effectively serving a culturally diverse ethnic population. Policies relating to information resources and services to multicultural communities were reviewed and adopted by the library management team.

The diversity initiative was extremely popular, and soon the readership in the libraries increased. People began to appreciate diversity as a strength and not a weakness. For her contribution to the ethnic communities, the New Zealand government awarded De Silva the queen's service honor, the New Zealand Order of Merit, in 2002.

15.12 Revisiting the Scenario

In the scenario cited in Section 15.1, Alfonso did not get the support he needed to do his job. The manager should have encouraged him to attend communication classes and used him in dispensing rather than putting him in an embarrassing position of talking to patients before becoming fully conversant in English.

References

Auckland Chamber of Commerce. (n.d.). Managing diversity in the workplace. Retrieved November 18, 2010, from http://www.chamber.co.nz/Chamberfiles/5d/5df63470-eec-4150-a90-e8a30381a1450.pdf

Barak, M.E.M. (2005). *Managing diversity: Towards a globally inclusive workplace.* Thousand Oaks, CA: Sage.

Chang, S., and Tharenou, P. (2004). Competencies needed for managing a multicultural work group. *Asia Pacific Journal of Human Resources*, 42, 57–74.

Clements, P., and Jones, J. (2008). *Diversity training handbook: A practical guide to understanding and changing attitude* (3rd ed.). London: Kogan Page.

Clements, P., and Spinks, T. (2009). *The equal opportunities handbook.* London: Kogan Page.

Cohen, J.J., Gabriel, B.A., and Terrell, C. (2002). The case for diversity in the health care workforce. *Health Affairs*, 21(5), 90–102.

Department of Education and Early Childhood Development. (2002). Managing diverse and inclusive workplaces. State of Victoria. Retrieved November 18, 2010, from http://www.eduweb.vic.gov.au/edulibrary/public/hr/equalop/Manage-Diverse-Inclusive-Workplace.pdf

Department for Work and Pensions. (2009). *Monitoring the impact of the recession on various demographic groups.* London: Equality and Human Rights Commission.

Du Praw, M.E., and Axner, M. (1997). Working on common cross-cultural communication challenges. Public Broadcasting Service. Retrieved November 6, 2010, from http://www.pbs.org/ampu/crosscult.html

Green, K.A., Lopez, M., Wysocki, A., and Kepner, K. (n.d.). Diversity in the workplace: Benefits, challenges and the required managerial tool. University of Florida. Retrieved November 3, 2010, from http://edis.ifas.ufl.edu/hr022

Greenburg, J. (2004). Diversity in the workplace. Retrieved November 18, 2010, from http://ezinearticles.com/?Diversity-in-the-Workplace:-Benefits,-Challenges-and-Solutions&id=11053

Greer, C.R., and Plunkett, W.R. (2003). *Supervision: Diversity and teams in the workplace* (10th ed.). Englewood Cliffs, NJ: Prentice Hall.

Henderson, G. (1994). *Cultural diversity in the workplace: Issues and strategies.* Westport, CT: Praeger.

Hopkins, B. (2009). *Cultural differences and improving performance.* Surrey: Gower.

Javidan, M., House, R.J., Dorfman, P.W., Hanges, P.J., and de Luque, M.S. (2006). Conceptualizing and measuring cultures and their consequences: A comparative review of GLOBE's and Hofstede's approaches. *Journal of International Business Studies,* 37, 897–914.

Lockwood, N.R. (2005). Workplace diversity: Leverage the power of differences for competitive advantage. *HR Magazine* 50(6), A1–10. Retrieved November 18, 2010, from http://findarticles.com/p/articles/mi_m3495/is_6_50/ai_n14702678/

McArthur, E.K. (2006). Managing diversity for success. Diversity at work. Retrieved November 18, 2010, from http://www.diversityworking.com/employerZone/diversityManagement/?id=14

Newstrom, J.W. (2007). *Supervision: Managing for results* (9th ed.). New York: Mc-Graw Hill.

Ngomsi, E. (2009). Bridging cultures in the business workplace. Retrieved November 14, 2010, from http://www.yan-koloba.com/articles.html

Scott, A. (2009). Pharmacy faces diversity issues. Drug Topics E-News. Retrieved September 8, 2012, from http://www.modernmedicine.com/modernmedicine/article/articleDetail.jsp?id=596895

Thomas, D.A., and Ely, R.J. (1996). Making differences matter: A new paradigm for managing diversity. *Harvard Business Review,* 74, 79–90.

Wood, P., Landry, C., and Bloomfield, J. (2006). *Cultural diversity in Britain: A toolkit for cross cultural cooperation.* York, England: Joseph Rowntree Foundation.

Chapter 16

Performance Review

The man who does not take pride in his own performance performs nothing in which to take pride.

—Thomas J. Watson

16.1 Scenario

Max had not had a performance review for nearly two years. At that time, he reported to the pharmacy manager, who was a pharmacist. Since then, the managerial role was taken up by a nonpharmacist manager. Max was not happy to be interviewed by the present manager, who lacked technical skills. He requested the manager to invite the group pharmacist so that both of them could conduct the review. His request was refused. The manager opened the interview by briefly expressing her satisfaction with Max's commitment, accuracy, and dedication to work. However, there were no specifics. He was rated on several criteria, and the manager mainly focused on weaknesses according to her perception. Some of them were technical issues that were beyond the scope of the manager. Some critical incidents were presented to support her conclusions. But Max's comments on the issues were ignored. Suggestions for which he did not have any input for improvement were presented to Max. Finally, he was given a mediocre report, and he left completely demoralized and demotivated.

16.2 Introduction

Traditionally, employees view a performance review as a critical test of their performance, and it has been a stressful experience. Employers too feel the burden because they realize that their managerial skills are being tested. But, if the review is conducted in a fair, unbiased, and effective manner, it can be a source of inspiration and motivation to the employee, thereby benefiting the organization. There are diverse views on whether performance reviews are really beneficial in view of the fact that they are conducted annually or biannually. In this chapter, some of these views are discussed.

16.3 Purpose

The purpose of a performance review is to assess the performance of employees and determine how they can improve their performance and contribute to overall organizational performance.

Performance management is the creation of a management system in the workplace to bring together all the essential factors to enable all the employees to perform in an aligned and coordinated manner to the best of their abilities (Grubb, 2007).

16.4 Objectives

Performance appraisal has different objectives for the employees of the organization and for management. Employees expect

an assessment of their work in terms of personal development, work satisfaction, and involvement with the organization.
According to management, it serves to maintain organization
control and provides information about human resources and
their development, the efficiency with which human resources
are utilized, and the achievements for the purpose of offering
compensation packages. In addition, a performance appraisal
should identify mutual goals of the employees and the organization. They provide growth and development of human
resources and the organization, improve the effectiveness of
human resources of the organization, and enhance harmony
(Food and Agriculture Organisation, 1997).

In a survey sponsored by the Society for Human Resource
Management (SHRM) and Personnel Divisions International
(PDI) in 2000, the most important objectives were to (1) provide information to employees about their performance, (2)
clarify organizational expectations of employees, and (3)
identify needs for their development. The least important
objectives were to document preparation for employees and
collecting information for promotion decisions. Gathering
information for salary decisions and coaching was of moderate
importance (Fernberger, 2004).

16.5 Benefits of Performance Review

The subject of performance review has been controversial
since its introduction about 60 years ago. Those who hold the
traditional view see it as a means of developing the staff and
improving their and the organization's performance. The following are cited as benefits of performance reviews (Virginia
Tech and University of Georgia, 2008):

■ Enhance motivation to perform effectively
■ Improve staff self-esteem
■ Recognize the abilities of staff and supervisors

- Clarify job descriptions and responsibilities of staff
- Improve communication among the staff
- Promote self-understanding among the staff
- Recognize new development activities of value to the staff and the organization
- Offer rewards in a fair and equitable manner
- Clarify the goals of the organization
- Improve human resource planning, test validation, and development of training needs

In contrast to this view, many authors believe that performance reviews do not benefit the organization or its employees. Dr. Deming (2000), in his book *Out of Crisis*, wrote: "Evaluation of performance, merit rating, or annual review.... The idea of a merit rating is alluring. The sound of the words captivates the imagination: pay for what you get; get what you pay for; motivate people to do their best, for their own good. The effect is exactly the opposite of what the words promise."

Although performance appraisals are entrenched in management systems of most organizations, some quality professionals are advocating their demise (Juncaj, 2002). Tom Coens, principal at Quantum Paradigms, Inc., and Mary Jenkins present three reasons why performance reviews should be abolished (Coens and Jenkins, 2000):

1. They do not achieve the purpose for which they were created.
2. They do enormous harm to employee morale and self-esteem.
3. They are not in accord with organizational values.

Some additional problems of performance appraisals are presented by Grubb (2007). They fail because of difficulties in identifying performance and its measurement, various conflicts that arise in performance appraisal, using pay as a motivational tool, and the high cost of performance appraisals.

A similar view has been expressed by organizational psychologist Leanne H. Markus (2004). Common problems in performance management are

1. Design flaws: There is no link between objectives and organizational values, goals, and strategies. Most performance management systems disregard role-specific job requirements or do not address them adequately.
2. Lack of credibility: Most performance management systems do not provide honest feedback or set clear goals.

According to Samuel Culbert (2008), consultant, author, and professor of management at the UCLA Anderson School of Management at Los Angeles, performance is a dysfunctional pretense because it is a one-sided accountable, supervisor-directed approach. It is negative to corporate performance, an obstacle to effective relationships, and a cause of low morale at work. Performance reviews damage daily communication and teamwork. The following are other issues of performance reviews:

1. They are a review conducted by two people with two mindsets. The supervisor and the subordinate are at cross-purposes. The supervisor is thinking about lost opportunities, skill limitations, and relations that need improvement. He or she wants to see where performance should be improved. On the other hand, the subordinate is focused on issues such as compensation, job progression, and future career prospects and believes that he or she is negotiating a pay raise. The cross-purposes cause tension and achieve nothing.
2. Performance is not related to pay. Salary is primarily determined by current market forces, and most jobs are categorized into a salary range appropriate to the job at the time of recruitment. The review is a cover to justify the supervisor's decision on pay.
3. Objectivity is subjective. Performance reviews claim that the appraisal is objective and that is false. The outcome

depends on the evaluator's motives. Often the supervisor considers anonymous 360° feedback to support his or her judgment, which is illogical.

4. One size does not fit all. Individuals are unique, and no two people are identical in their characteristics and behavior patterns subsequently developed. All are assessed on a predetermined checklist. Performance reviews do not capture the unique features of the job or the quality of the person being evaluated.

5. Personal development is impeded. People resist help from those who cannot acknowledge their views, especially when their previous attempts have failed. Individuals do not want to pay a high price for acknowledging their need for improving their performance. Divulging crucial information can be used by the management for its own advantage.

6. Disruption of teamwork. Performance is generally one-sided, and the evaluator has all the power. The supervisor as the evaluator does not engage in teamwork during the review. The issue then becomes the individual's performance at stake rather than the joint performance of the supervisor and the individual.

7. Dishonesty of justifying corporate improvement. A performance review is conducted under the guise that it promotes individual performance while achieving corporate goals. It does not energize or motivate employees but creates cynicism. Instead of being direct, honest, and frank, the review becomes an effort to promote self-interest hidden as corporate activities. In effect, it is a violation of valuable resources.

However, some form of performance appraisal is a necessity. Performance appraisals are as good as the people using them—management team, employees, and supervisors. An effective performance appraisal, if conducted correctly and smartly, will support the coaching, feedback, and development of employees.

16.6 Performance Appraisal of Pharmacy Staff

The performance appraisal of pharmacists and technicians needs special consideration. Like any other business, pharmacies exist for the dual purpose of delivering services to the community while making a profit for the organization. However, ethical considerations must override any profit motive. Pharmacies are likely to achieve their goals and objectives when staff derive satisfaction from delivering services in an efficient manner. Pharmacists are under tremendous pressure to meet the financial goals of the organization while meeting the demands to increase the script volume, delivery of medicine use reviews (MURs), new medicine service (NMS), and other services that bring financial remuneration to the pharmacy and a higher degree of patient care. These trends require pharmacy managers to look for effective pharmacy appraisal systems for pharmacists and pharmacy technicians. Such programs have to consider certain values, such as commitment, dedication, reliability, and unselfishness, which are essential in the pharmacy environment. In addition, some aspects, such as autonomy and responsibility of pharmacists and support staff, call for alternate systems of appraisal (Desselle and Zgarrick, 2005).

16.7 Appraisal Methods

Several basic appraisal systems have been used by the organizations over the years. These are mainly traditional methods. There is no one best system. A method of appraisal used by one company may not suit another organization. As organizations change and mature, appraisal methods change. Managers have to identify the most suitable method or a combination of methods, depending on the circumstances (Desselle and Zgarrick, 2005; Jensen, 1997). Some commonly used appraisal methods are shown in Table 16.1. There are three categories of performance appraisal methods:

Table 16.1   Some Performance Appraisal Methods

System	Method	Concept	Advantages	Disadvantages
Absolute	Essay	The appraiser prepares a written statement of the employee's performance, particularly the strengths, weaknesses, prospects of job advancement, and development needs	Source of valuable information	Comments are generalized, review criteria are vague, lack of objectivity and differences across evaluators
Absolute	Critical incident technique	Evaluator keeps a daily log of critical incidents relating to both positive and negative behavior	Very specific	Subject to appraiser's bias and inconsistency; favoritism
Absolute	Trait/behavior checklists	Tailored to suit work situation; evaluator simply answers yes or no to questions concerning the selected characteristics to be evaluated; by assigning numbers, it can be quantified	Saves time, easy to complete, and tailored to individual work situations	Less precise; some employees dislike grading
Absolute	Graphic rating	Rating form is a scale on which the supervisor simply checks off employee's performance	Less time-consuming; quantitative comparison	Difference in rating by different supervisors; leniency, central tendency, use of traits

(continued)

Table 16.1   Some Performance Appraisal Methods (continued)

System	Method	Concept	Advantages	Disadvantages
Absolute	Behaviorally anchored rating scales (BARS)	Descriptive rating scale that indicates employee's tendency to show desirable behavior	Quantitative and enables feedback	Difficult to develop; central tendency
Absolute	360° feedback	Employees provide feedback anonymously from other employees in the team	Many points of view	Time-consuming; subject to role conflict, bias
Absolute	Forced choice	Evaluator is presented with a set of statements describing employee's performance	Minimizes bias	Tedious for evaluators; better feedback
Relative	Forced distribution ranking	Rank employees into various groups according to the quality of their work—best at the top and worst at the bottom; assume performance distribution follows normal distribution	Eliminates central tendency and the tendency to be lenient	Difficult to justify the ranking and the rank; can be biased

(continued)

Table 16.1   Some Performance Appraisal Methods (continued)

System	Method	Concept	Advantages	Disadvantages
Relative	Paired comparison	Each employee is compared with every other employee on each criterion	Situations where priorities are not clear and no objective data; helps set priorities	Limited feedback
Relative	Alternate ranking	Evaluator selects the best and the worst employee from the remaining pool of employees	Avoids leniency and central tendency	Bias and limited feedback
Outcome oriented	Management by objective	Supervisor establishes several specific objectives to be accomplished by the employee within a time frame	Employee participation, incentive driven, results oriented	Evaluated by different standards
Outcome oriented	Work standard approach	Evaluator sets a standard or an expected level of output and compares employee's performance against the standard or the level of output	Standardized approach	Standards may be considered unsatisfactory

1. Absolute methods: The evaluator rates the employee on predetermined criteria for performance using a scale or an index. This is the most commonly employed method.
2. Relative systems: This system involves comparison among employees.
3. Outcome-oriented systems: This system focuses on results and involves establishing quantifiable goals for the next period and performing a review at the end of it.

16.8 Nontraditional Appraisal Methods

16.8.1 Atlassian's Experiment

The employees of Atlassian, a software development company in Australia, had been appraised twice a year according to established human resources practices using the 360° feedback method on a 5-point scale. Managers determined the bonus on individual ratings. However, the results proved disappointing. Instead of inspiring employees toward better performance, it created disruptions, anxiety, and demotivated subordinates and managers. A significant amount of time was spent on conducting the reviews. Atlassian looked for a novel approach to evaluate employees (Luijke, 2011), and its lightweight continuous model is summarized below.

1. Traditional methods of evaluating performance reviews were discarded. The constructive aspect of one-to-one meetings of traditional methods was maintained. Atlassian managers conducted weekly one-to-one meetings with team members. Once a month, a meeting was dedicated to discuss how the individual could enhance his or her performance using his or her strengths. Unconstructive aspects of ratings and distribution curves were rejected.
2. Payment of bonuses for performance was stopped. Instead, competitive salaries were paid in keeping with

market forces. Stock options were also offered to employees to recognize their contribution toward the growth of the company.

3. Every month, one-to-one coaching topics were introduced. These coaching conversations were dedicated to improving the ability to succeed and help the employee move forward and take action. Separate sessions were allocated to discuss strengths, weaknesses, career developments, etc.

4. Performance was evaluated with some changes. Two of the monthly meetings were devoted to evaluating performance through manager's reports. The managers focused on honest feedback and how employees performed during the previous six months, particularly when they demonstrated outstanding performance. The performance was measured on two axes: demonstrating outstanding performance (y axis) and how often the employee stretched himself or herself to exceed expectations (x axis). This process provided opportunities to improve the frequency of certain behaviors.

5. Managers were trained on conducting coaching conversations. These sessions are different from normal everyday conversations. They focus on conversations that lead to the improvement of performance, enhanced performance capability, and improvement of relationships.

The program has been acclaimed a success, and the company has received several best employer awards, including a highly commended award in Australia for human resources leaders' employer of the decade.

16.8.2 Work Performance and Review (WP&R) Method

A year-long intensive test program of performance at General Electric has indicated clearly that the WP&R method of evaluating the performance of employees is a better approach for improving performance than annual traditional performance reviews (Meyer et al., 1965). The basic features of this method are summarized below.

The WP&R approach involves periodic meetings between the manager and the subordinate where the progress of past goals is reviewed, solutions are sought for job-related issues, and new goals are established. The aim of the method is to create an atmosphere where the manager and the subordinate can discuss job performance and much-needed improvements in detail without the employee becoming defensive. In particular,

- There are more frequent discussions of performance compared to traditional review methods.
- There are no summary judgments or scoring systems.
- The main focus is on goal planning and problem solving.

The WP&R approach has been shown to be better in defining what is expected of an individual and his or her progress on the job.

16.8.3 Positive Program for Performance Appraisal

A performance appraisal should achieve three objectives (Kindall and Gatza, 1963):

1. Improvement of performance in the current job, examination of the past, and preparation of plans for the future
2. Development of individuals to provide opportunities for those who are qualified to step into higher positions and support for individuals to acquire knowledge and abilities to become eligible for higher jobs
3. Providing honest feedback on how the individual is performing and how he or she can move forward

The proposed program has five essential steps:

1. The employee discusses the job description with his or her supervisor and agrees on the scope of the job and the relative importance of major duties, mainly what he or she is paid to do and accountable for.
2. The employee establishes performance targets for each of the identified responsibilities for the next period.
3. The employee meets with the supervisor to discuss the targets.
4. The employee and supervisor agree on checkpoints to monitor progress.
5. There is a meeting at the end of the period to discuss the outcome of the subordinate's efforts to meet the targets that have been previously established and agreed upon.

The main advantages of this method are

1. The employee knows in advance the criteria on which he or she is going to be judged.
2. Both the supervisor and the subordinate agree on the scope of the subordinate's job. Therefore, the supervisor has a better understanding of the problems associated with the job.
3. It strengthens the relationship between the supervisor and the subordinate.
4. The program has a self-correcting feature that tends to help employees set their own targets that are challenging and achievable.
5. The program provides an opportunity to identify training needs.
6. The program enables an individual's ability to identify organizational problems, plan methods of resolving them, implement the plans, incorporate new information as the need arises, and carry out the plans for completion.

16.9 Case Studies of Successful Performance Appraisal Systems

A subject matter expert for the American Productivity and Quality Center's national benchmarking study on best practices in performance appraisal identified companies that introduced novel methods of evaluating employee performance. The following case study reported by Grote (2000) demonstrates the active participation of employees in the performance appraisal system.

The Air Force Research Laboratory in Dayton, Ohio, conducted a formal performance appraisal of its 3,200 scientists and engineers with a view to lay off some staff. Except for one employee who was rated as marginal, all others were rated positive. No one was rated unsatisfactory or poor in performance. It was clearly evident that the performance appraisal process was flawed and needed review.

Managers discarded the traditional approach of assigning tasks that employees could successfully complete, which obviously generated high ratings. The scientists suggested a radically different approach of evaluating them on the basis of their contribution to the mission of the organization. With this approach, the scientists and engineers accepted more responsibility and difficult tasks. The salaries were linked to the value of their jobs to the laboratory.

Juncaj (2002) cites the case of Glenroy, which discarded traditional methods of performance appraisal and introduced a new approach. Glenroy, a manufacturer of packaging materials and thermal laminating films for pharmaceutical, food, and home products industries, was using traditional performance appraisal methods. Until 1989, all except the president received salary increases consistent with their annual performance appraisal ratings on a scale of 1 to 10. The employees perceived that the results were biased because of the subjective opinion of the supervisor.

A new concept of instant feedback was introduced where a worker or a supervisor can initiate an immediate dialogue with his or her supervisor. The leadership of Glenroy did not perceive the instant feedback process and do-it-now concept as difficult. Incentives were replaced with salaries linked to competitive market rates. Quarterly, it offered all its employees a company-wide bonus called the Glenroy Performance Award, a noncompetitive bonus. Simultaneously, the discipline process was also reviewed. During the 13 years since its introduction, the business quadrupled and the workforce increased from 42 to 142, with $40 million worth of goods.

16.10 Development of a Performance Evaluation System for Pharmacy Staff

The University of Texas Medical Care (UTMC) Correctional Managed Care Pharmacy developed quality indicators and measurement systems to evaluate departmental staff (Roberts and Keith, 2002). Its approach involves the following steps:

1. Identify the key performance indicators (KPIs).
2. Rank KPIs according to the importance and impact on the healthcare system.
3. Determine acceptable standards of performance for each indicator.
4. Develop a scoring system incorporating rank and acceptable standards.
5. Develop a system to collect data and monitor the results.
6. Develop a reporting method.
7. Continually review and modify the performance appraisal system to reflect the changing goals and objectives of the performance appraisal system.

16.11 A Proposed Method for Evaluating Pharmacists

Performance review is essentially a dialogue between the employer and the employee, and as such, communication, problem solving, and conflict resolution are important components of the performance appraisal system. At the performance appraisal session, the employer has to ask open-ended questions in a nonthreatening manner to elicit information. Problems and conflicts may have to be resolved to the satisfaction of the participants. These skills were discussed in earlier chapters.

No single method is suitable for evaluating the performance of pharmacy staff. The patients and the customers are totally dependent on the pharmaceutical services provided by the pharmacy. As such, biannual or annual appraisals of performance review are of little benefit to the effective delivery of services. Issues such as poor customer service or the inability to meet the MUR targets should be addressed without delay. Therefore, the supervisor should monitor the work performance regularly so that improvements can be made if the established targets have not been met. Thus, using a combined approach of frequent monitoring of work performance and biannual appraisal of leadership and management skills for growth and development, the performance appraisal is conducted in four parts (HumanResources.hrvinet.com. 2010a, 2010b; Chapman, 2011):

Part 1: Monitoring work performance regularly
Part 2: Biannual review of performance for growth and development
Part 3: Action plan
Part 4: Agreement

16.11.1 Part 1: Monitoring Work Performance

Part 1 involves a discussion between the supervisor and the employee to identify the roles and responsibilities and set goals, standards, and checkpoints for monitoring. Using KPIs (Roberts and Keith, 2002) and Kindall and Gatza's approach (1963), work performance is appraised at more frequent intervals. Table 16.2 shows the format for monitoring work performance, which is appraised in terms of whether the indicator exceeds, meets, or does not meet the standard. When the performance of the key indicator does not meet the standard, the employee is instructed to determine the causes of failure and submit an action plan for improvement. Therefore, the employee is in control of setting the goals and achieving them.

16.11.2 Part 2: Biannual Review—Evaluation of Managerial and Leadership Skills

The managerial and leadership skills are evaluated annually or biannually. At the annual or biannual review, the employee is provided feedback on the core competencies (HumanResources.hrvinet.com, 2010b) identified in Table 16.3. The definition of each core competency is clarified to the employee with detailed comments and supporting examples of how the competency can be demonstrated. In addition, they discuss how the competencies can be further developed (University of British Columbia, 2012). Each competency is ranked as E (exceeds expectations), M (meets expectations), or N (needs development).

Meeting expectations is not a measure of success. It is expected that some goals will be exceeded and some never attempted. Employees who always meet established targets are no better than those who always agree to unrealistic targets but fail consistently to reach them. When an employee fails to perform, it is the responsibility of the supervisor to support the subordinate by coaching, training, delegation, etc.

Table 16.2 Evaluation of Work Performance

Indicator	Number of Items	Description	Source of Information	Evaluating Frequency
Pharmacist's productivity		Number of items reviewed and authorized per day	Dispensing records	Daily
Support staff productivity		Number of items dispensed per shift divided by the number of support staff	Dispensing records and attendance data	Daily
Comments				
Stock takes		Stock takes conducted per week	Stock take audits	Weekly
Mis-shipment		Number of wrong deliveries to care homes	Complaint reports	Weekly
Comments				
Dispensing errors		Number of reported drug or dose errors per 100 items dispensed (%)	Complaint reports	Monthly
Near misses		Number of errors detected in the pharmacy before reaching the patient per 100 items dispensed (%)	Near-miss reports	Monthly

(continued)

Table 16.2 Evaluation of Work Performance (continued)

Indicator	Number of Items	Description	Source of Information	Evaluating Frequency
Clinical interventions		Number of interventions per 100 items dispensed	Intervention log	Monthly
Missing medications		Number of items missing per 100 dispensed	Complaint reports	Monthly
Medicine use reviews (MURs)		Number of MURs conducted per month	MUR reports	Monthly
New medicine service (NMS)		Number of NMS conducted per month	NMS reports	Monthly
Continuing Professional Development (CPD) activities		Completion of CPD activities	CPD records	Monthly
Comments				
Repeat Prescription Service (RPS)		Number of Patients Enrolled for RPS	RPS Record	Monthly

Table 16.3   Evaluation of Core Competencies

	Performance Factors	*Rating*
1	**Delivery of services:** The services required by the community are identified and provided efficiently and effectively. Ensure that staff are competent enough to deliver the services.	
Comments		
2	**Customer service:** Listen, understand, and respond to customers' needs in a pleasant manner. Provide relevant information needed by the patients and react to their queries in a problem-solving manner.	
Comments		
3	**Leadership skills:** Ability to lead the staff to accomplish their tasks. Create a clear vision for the pharmacy in accordance with the company's goals and objectives. Ensure that staff establish challenging goals. Maintain a safe working environment. Communicate the vision to all the employees. Build trust among the team. Provide opportunities for staff development.	
Comments		
4	**Planning, organization, and time management:** Organize the activities in a timely manner to accomplish personal and company goals. Able to make employees manage competing tasks and evaluate the amount of supervision required.	
Comments		
5	**Communication:** Able to express ideas clearly and professionally both verbally and in writing. Conduct open, honest communication. Convey information to supervisors, peers, and subordinates in a timely manner. Listen to others and receive feedback in a positive manner.	
Comments		

(continued)

Table 16.3   Evaluation of Core Competencies (continued)

	Performance Factors	Rating
6	**Problem solving and decision making:** Demonstrate independent thinking and effective problem-solving skills. Able to make sound and timely decisions and include appropriate people in the decision-making process. Weigh all options and select the most effective course of action.	
	Comments	
7	**Teamwork:** Communicate the plans with others in the pharmacy. Ready to provide help and offer support and help to those in need. Appreciate the achievements of others. Encourage group participation to resolve issues. Provide knowledge to the team to follow through with the assignments allocated to the team.	
	Comments	
8	**Reliability:** Commitment to effective and timely performance of tasks. Able to work independently and respond well to instructions and procedures. Demonstrate sincere approach in supporting staff to achieve their objectives.	
	Comments	
9	**Initiative and creativity:** Take initiative and create resourceful solutions to problems. Willing to take calculated risks to achieve excellence in performance. Look for new and creative ways of doing things. Able to start on one's own initiative, and encourage and promote the development of new approaches and methods.	
	Comments	

(continued)

Table 16.3   Evaluation of Core Competencies (continued)

	Performance Factors	*Rating*
10	**Competence:** Demonstrate competence in job duties and responsibilities with a high level of knowledge and skills. Work is accurate, thorough, and completed within the given time frame. Handle complex responsibilities and projects effectively. Aware of current developments and practices relating to the job. Follow the tasks to completion. Exhibit quality in any work undertaken.	
Comments		
11	**Financial awareness:** Aware of financial constraints and monitor expenses. Exercise controls to ensure that expenses are within the allocated budget. Manage resources effectively by providing the necessary resources and overtime.	
Comments		

16.11.3 Part 3: Action Plan

At this stage, the employee and the supervisor review the findings of the performance appraisal and agree on a common action plan as shown in Table 16.4.

Table 16.4   Action Plan

Performance Indicator	*Action Plan*	*Checking Dates*

16.11.4 Part 4: Agreement

Employee's name: Signature:
Reviewer's name: Signature:
Next review date:

16.12 Revisiting the Scenario

The manager has not performed appraisals regularly, and therefore has failed to identify opportunities for growth and development. In addition, both Max and the manager have not been aware of whether or not the company's goals have been met, and therefore improvements needed, if any, were not identified. Max's performance indicators are mainly technical, and therefore it is unlikely that a nonpharmacist manager woul be able to conduct a performance appraisal effectively. The nonpharmacist manager should have been aware of her limitations and in the interest of the organization should have invited the group pharmacy manager to perform the appraisal. Focusing on weaknesses as perceived by the manager is not beneficial for the organization or the employee. The manager has identified some of Max's strengths, but some specific examples would have strengthened the relationship between the employee and the manager. A performance review is essentially a dialogue between the manager and the supervisor, and Max should have been given the opportunity to express his views at the appraisal.

References

Chapman, A. (2011). Performance appraisal. Retrieved December 28, 2011, from http://www.businessballs.com/performanceappraisals.htm

Coens, T., and Jenkins, M. (2000). *Abolishing performance appraisals—Why they backfire and what to do instead*. San Francisco, CA: Berrett-Koehler.

Culbert, S.A. (2008, October 20). Get rid of the performance review! *Wall Street Journal*. Retrieved December 23, 2011, from http://online.wsj.com/article/SB122426318874844933.html

Deming, W.E. (2000). *Out of crisis*. Cambridge, MA: MIT Press.

Dessell, S.P., and Zgarrick, D.P. (2005). *Pharmacy management: Essentials for all practice settings*. New York: McGraw-Hill.

Fernberger, E. (2004). Employee coaching, evaluation and discipline. In A.M. Peterson (Ed.), *Managing pharmacy practice* (pp. 99–119). Boca Raton, FL: CRC Press.

Food and Agriculture Organisation. (1997). Performance appraisal. In V.N. Asopa and G. Beye (Eds.), *Management of agricultural research: A training manual. Module 5: Managing human resources (session 4)*. Rome: FAO.

Grote, D. (2000). Performance appraisal reappraised. *Harvard Business Review*. Retrieved September 8, 2012, from http://hbr.org/2000/01/performance-appraisal-reappraised/ar/1

Grubb, T. (2007). Performance appraisal reappraised: It's not all positive. *Journal of Human Resource Education*, 1(1), 1–22.

HumanResources.hrvinet.com. (2010a). Hospital pharmacists appraisal form. Retrieved December 25, 2011, from http://www.humanresources.hrvinet.com/hospital-pharmacist-appraisal-form/

HumanResources.hrvinet.com. (2010b). Community pharmacists appraisal form. Retrieved December 25, 2011, from http://www.humanresources.hrvinet.com/community-pharmacist-appraisal-form/

Jensen, J. (1997). Employ evaluation: It's a dirty job, but somebody's got to do it. The Grantsmanship Center. Retrieved December 23, 2011, from http://www.tgci.com/magazine/Employee%20Evaluation.pdf

Juncaj, T. (2002). Do performance appraisals work? *Quality Progress*, 35, 45–49.

Kindall, A.F., and Gatza, J. (1963). Positive programme for performance appraisal. *Harvard Business Review*, 41, 152–167.

Luijke, J. (2011). Atlassian's big experiment with performance review. Retrieved December 25, 2011, from http://www.managementexchange.com/story/atlassians-big-experiment-performance-reviews

Markus, L.H. (2004). Performance management—Problems and potential. Centranum Ltd. Retrieved December 22, 2011, from http://www.performancegroup.co.nz/pm.pdf

Meyer, H.H., Kay, E., and French Jr., J.R.P. (1965). Split roles in performance appraisal. *Harvard Business Review*, 43, 123–129.

Roberts, M.B., and Keith, M.R. (2002). Implementing a performance evaluation system in a correctional managed care facility. *American Journal of Health System Pharmacy*, 59, 1097–1104.

University of British Columbia. (2012). Performance evaluation. Retrieved January 8, 2012, from http://www.hr.ubc.ca/administrators/performance-development/

Virginia Tech and University of Georgia. (2008). *Performance review. A handbook of staffing practices in student affairs.* Retrieved December 20, 2011, from http://www.staffingpractices.soe.vt.edu/index.htm

Chapter 17

Quality Management Systems

Improving quality requires a culture change, not just a new diet.

—Philip Crosby, *Let's Talk Quality*

17.1 Introduction

Pharmacy practice has always been an integral part of any healthcare system. There is no room for error in pharmacy practice. An important aim of this practice is to improve the quality of the delivery of products and services to the community. A well-designed quality management system (QMS) ensures quality improvement in all aspects of products and services.

The military and nuclear industries have been implementing quality systems for many years, and it was only in the 1970s that similar systems were introduced into general manufacturing activities. Quality system standards are effective tools in the implementation of a quality management program. There are several international standards, and the one in use that has gained universal acceptance is the ISO 9000 series of standards.

Figure 17.1   Components of pharmacy practice.

Both community and hospital pharmacy practices are governed by four major components (Figure 17.1): regulatory requirements, code of ethics, internal procedures, and standard operating procedures (SOPs). While these components are essential for effective and efficient pharmacy practice, they do not promote quality improvement. Apart from these four components, there are no national or international standards for pharmacy practice similar to those in the ISO 9000 series (ISO, 2011). The principles of ISO 9000 can be equally well applied to the delivery of pharmaceutical products and services in retail shops and hospitals.

17.2 Definitions

Quality: Quality is a measure of the degree to which an item or a process meets a standard.

Quality control: Monitoring techniques and activities used to fulfill the requirements for quality.

Quality assurance: A set of procedures designed to ensure that the product that is manufactured or delivered conforms to specified requirements. Dispensing a prescription involves a series of steps, from accepting the prescription by a member of pharmacy staff to the delivery of medicines to the patient. Quality assurance of the process is managed by setting controls at each step in the process. Thus, quality control of the process of dispensing includes the following checks:

1. Personal information recorded in the prescription
2. Validity against regulatory requirements
3. Strength, dosage, and frequency of administration of medications
4. Significant interactions with the medications
5. Dispensed product and its strength against the prescription
6. Product label and bag label
7. Counseling
8. Delivery to the correct patient

Quality management: Management of activities designed to ensure that a product or service meets specified requirements.

Quality management system: A system that defines the management requirements to ensure quality.

ISO 9000 standards: Minimum guidelines to allow the development of an appropriate QMS, which can demonstrate product or service quality assurance to the customer.

17.3 General Pharmaceutical Council (GPhC) Standards

The GPhC of the Royal Pharmaceutical Society of Great Britain has created a series of standards that are outcome focused to ensure patient safety, thus enabling innovation. The following are the current standards (GPhC, 2012):

■ Standards of conduct, ethics, and performance
■ Standards for owners and superintendent pharmacists of retail pharmacy businesses

■ Standards for continuing professional development (CPD)
■ Standards for the initial education and training of pharmacists
■ Standards for the initial education and training of pharmacy technicians
■ Standards of proficiency

17.4 Quality Assurance Programs on Pharmacy Practice

17.4.1 NHS Quality, Innovation, Productivity, and Prevention Programme (QIPP)

QIPP is a transformational program involving the National Health Service (NHS) staff, clinicians, patients, and the voluntary sector and designed to improve the quality of care while saving £20 billion by 2014–2015, which will be reinvested in frontline care. Lead staff of the NHS develop plans that address quality and productivity challenge. The Department of Health has set up a number of work streams to deliver the QIPP. There are three main work streams: commissioning and pathways, provider efficiency, and system enablers. Table 17.1 shows the activities of each work stream (Department of Health, 2011). Although QIPP does not

Table 17.1 Activities of NHS Work Streams

Commissioning and Pathways	Provider Efficiency	System Enablers
Safe care	Back-office efficiency and optimal management	Primary care commissioning
Right care		
Long-term conditions	Procurement	Technology and digital vision
	Clinical support	
Urgent and emergency care	Productive care	
End-of-life care	Medicine use and procurement	

specify national standards to achieve quality of care, tools have been designed to meet the objectives of the NHS.

17.4.2 Australian Quality Care Pharmacy Programme (QCPP)

While the NHS QIPP is designed to improve the quality of care at the national level, the Australian QCPP establishes a set of quality assurance standards aimed at improving the standard of service that pharmacies provide to the public. The program was developed by the Pharmacy Guild of Australia and other industry stakeholders on the basis of business and professional standards (Pharmacy Guild of Australia, n.d.). The QCPP program includes 18 standards that cover the activities of pharmacies (Table 17.2). These activities cover the essential features of pharmacy practice, including the management of a profitable business. Provision has also been made for quality improvement in standard 7. However, it falls short of a comprehensive quality management plan as required by the ISO 9000 standard. Table 17.2 shows the comparison between the QCPP standards and the ISO 9000:2008 standards.

Missing from these standards are requirements related to quality policy, quality objectives, corrective and preventive action, internal audits, management reviews, and design and development activities. A new program to deliver medicines to care homes from the pharmacy is an example of a design activity (clause 7.3 of the ISO 9000:2008 standard).

17.4.3 Professional Practice Standards (PPS) and the Standards for the Provision of Pharmacy Medicines and Pharmacist-Only Medicines in Community Pharmacy

This program is the result of a review of the PPS by the Pharmaceutical Society of Australia, and a review of the

Table 17.2 **Australian Quality Care Pharmacy Programme Standards**

Standard Number	Title	Activities	Equivalent ISO 9001 Standard
1	Compliance with legal and professional obligations	Compliance with all statutory requirements and code of ethics	Clauses 4.2.1, 4.2.3
2	Supply of medicines, medical devices, and poisons	Distance supply, compounding, storing and repacking cytotoxic drugs, supplying pharmacy medicines and pharmacist-only medicines, supplying pseudoephedrine	Clauses 7.5, 8.3
3	Delivery of pharmacy programs and services		Clauses 7.5.1, 7.5.2
4	Advertising and promotions		Clauses 7.1, 7.2.3
5	Pharmacy premises and equipment	Pharmacy appearance, equipment calibration, temperature record, cold chain certification,	Clauses 7.6, 6.3
6	Operating an effective and profitable business	Customer survey, business plan	Clauses 5.2, 8.2.1
7	Complying with the program to improve quality	Quality care coordinator, procedure and template review schedule, incident register, incident report	Clauses 5.5.2, 8.5.1, 4.1

(continued)

Table 17.2 Australian Quality Care Pharmacy Programme Standards (continued)

Standard Number	Title	Activities	Equivalent ISO 9001 Standard
8	Department stock and consumable checks		Clause 8.2.4
9	Ordering, receiving, storing, and pricing stock	Receiving, unpacking, storing, and pricing stock	Clauses 7.4.1, 7.4.2, 7.4.3
10	Hiring equipment	Hire agreement, equipment data,	Clauses 7.1, 7.5.4
11	Customer service	Deliveries register, customer service charter	Clauses 5.2, 7.7.3
12	Employing staff	Employing staff procedure, job descriptor, offer of employment	Clauses 6.1, 6.2, 5.5.1
13	Inducting staff	Inducting checks	Clauses 6.2.1, 6.2.2
14	Managing staff	Staff roster, record of grievance resolution	Clauses 6.2.1, 6.2.2
15	Ongoing staff training	Training plan, training record	Clauses 6.2.1, 6.2.2
16	Dismissals and resignations	Staff counseling interview, statement of service	Clause 6.2
17	Maintaining safety and security	Description of offender, bomb threat checklist, loss prevention checks, testing safety systems	Clause 6.4
18	Information technology	Backup schedule and records, pharmacy information schedule	Clauses 4.2.3, 4.2.4

standards for the provision of pharmacy medicines and pharmacist-only medicines in community pharmacies by the University of Sydney (Pharmaceutical Society of Australia, 2010). While the QCPP is a set of standards required for the certification of the quality system of the pharmacy, the PPS have been aimed at individual pharmacists to assess their own professional practice. However, the QCPP requires the business enterprise to satisfy itself that all pharmacists working in the pharmacy complete their own individual assessment against the PPS. These standards are described below:

1. Fundamental pharmacy practice: Pharmacist demonstrates accepted professional behavior, maintains customers' and patients' rights to confidentiality and privacy, and promotes the quality use of medicines.
2. Managing pharmacy practice: Managing pharmacist addresses all management and organizational needs to ensure safe, effective, and efficient delivery of pharmaceutical care.
3. Counseling: Pharmacist counsels patients on the effective use of medicines and appliances.
4. Comprehensive medication review: Pharmacist reviews systematically the medication treatment regimen of the patient, takes action to achieve optimum therapeutic outcomes, and ensures regular medication reviews with the patient.
5. Dispensing: Pharmacist dispenses medicines accurately according to the instructions of the prescriber and the needs and safety of the patient.
6. Indirect pharmacy services: When face-to-face contact with the patient is not possible, pharmacist delivers the services in an ethical, safe, and effective manner while maintaining privacy.
7. Dose administration aids service: Pharmacist provides a comprehensive dose administering service that considers the needs and risk of the patient, selects the most appropriate device, and ensures that medications are correctly

dispensed and packed without compromising the stability and safety of medications. The dose administration service also includes regular reviews of medications with the patient.

8. Services to residential care facilities: Pharmacist provides an accurate and timely delivery of medicines and information to care homes and reviews the safety of facility systems with respect to medicines.

9. Continuing care through medication liaison service: Pharmacist provides a well-coordinated medication service to patients and healthcare providers when patients are transferred between healthcare settings.

10. Compounding: Pharmacist compounds preparation to ensure the integrity, quality, safety, and efficacy of the product.

11. Compounding sterile preparations: Pharmacist prepares and dispenses sterile products maintaining the sterility, quality, and safety and efficacy of the medication throughout its life cycle.

12. Provision of nonprescription medicines and therapeutic devices: Pharmacist is responsible for the safe and judicious provision of nonprescription medicines and appliances as required by the patient.

13. Health promotion: Pharmacist is actively engaged in promoting the health of the individual and the community.

14. Medicines information center: Pharmacist working in a medicines information setting provides accurate, timely, and relevant information on medicines and pharmacotherapy to the users of the service in order to optimize the health outcome.

15. Pharmacy services to Aboriginal and Torres Strait Islander health services: Pharmacist provides pharmacy services to these customers in a timely and culturally sensitive manner to ensure quality use of medicines and appliances.

16. Screening and risk assessment: Pharmacist uses evidence-based screening tests to systematically identify patients of a defined population who are at risk of diseases.

17. Disease state management: Pharmacist works with patients and other healthcare providers to manage the patient's disease condition, optimizes his or her health and well-being, counsels on risk factors, and encourages the patient to manage his or her health.

18. Harm minimization: Pharmacist follows established procedures to provide opioid substitution treatment and needle and syringe services aimed at optimum therapeutic outcome, improving the quality of life, and reducing the harm due to illicit drugs.

17.5 Quality Management Principles

The ISO 9000:2008 series is based on eight quality management principles. These principles can be used as a framework for improving the quality of products and services in an organization (International Organisation for Standardisation, 2011):

1. Customer focus
2. Leadership
3. Involvement of people
4. Process approach
5. System approach to management
6. Continual improvement
7. Factual approach to decision making
8. Mutually beneficial supplier relations

The ISO 9000 series comprises a set of standards required to establish and maintain a QMS of any organization. The current version is ISO 9001:2008. It is divided into a number of main clauses, and these are further subdivided into subclauses, some of which are further subdivided. The following are the main clauses:

Clauses 1–3: These clauses form the introduction and include the scope, normative reference, terms, and definitions.

Clauses 1–3 are not an "active" part of the standard (International Organization for Standardisation, 2009).

Clause 4: General requirements—develop and document the QMS, manage and control QMS documents, prepare QMS manual, and establish QMS records.

Clause 5: Management requirements—demonstrate commitment to quality, focus on customers, support the quality policy, establish quality objectives, plan QMS, define responsibilities and authorities, appoint management representative, promote internal communication, review QMS, monitor information about the QMS, and generate the outcome of management reviews.

Clause 6: Resource requirements—provide necessary resources for the QMS, appoint competent QMS personnel, ensure competence of the team, meet competence requirements, provide the necessary infrastructure, and provide suitable work environment.

Clause 7: Realization requirements—control the process for the realization of product or service, control customer-related processes, identify requirements unique to the product or service, review customer's product or service requirements, communicate with customers, control product or service design and development, control purchasing process and product, control product or service provision, and control monitoring and measuring equipment.

Clause 8: Remedial requirements—establish and perform monitoring and measurement processes, monitor and evaluate customer satisfaction, monitor and measure QMS processes, monitor and measure product features, identify and control nonconforming products/services, collect and analyze QMS data, and take corrective and preventive action and improve the QMS.

Standards and SOPs alone do not make an effective QMS. The drivers of a properly designed QMS are the mission statement, quality objectives, and strategic planning. These components are essential for the organization to move forward in an ever-changing business environment. The SOPs and the current standards can be incorporated into a QMS for pharmacy practice, and Chapter 18 deals with the development of a QMS.

References

Department of Health. (2011). Quality, innovation, productivity and prevention. Retrieved July 28, 2011, from http://www.rpharms.com/current-campaigns—england/qipp.asp#workstreams

GPhC. (2012). Standards and quality. Retrieved February 4, 2012, from http://www.pharmacyregulation.org/standards

International Organisation for Standardisation. (2009). ISO 9000:2008 requirements explained. Retrieved February 2, 2013, from http://www.iso9000checklist.com/management_review_sample.pdf

International Organisation for Standardisation. (2011). Quality management principles. Retrieved September 12, 2012, from http://www.iso.org/iso/qmp_2012.pdf

Pharmaceutical Society of Australia. (2010). *Professional practice standards* (Version 4). Retrieved February 4, 2012, from http://www.psa.org.au/download/standards/professional-practice-standards-v4.pdf

Pharmacy Guild of Australia. (n.d.). Quality Care Pharmacy Programme: QCPP maintenance check list. Retrieved February 4, 2012, from http://www.qcpp.com/iwov-resources/documents/QCPP/QCPP/Standards/Implementation%20and%20Rulings/ImplementationandRulings.pdf

Chapter 18

Quality Management System for Pharmacy Practice

A useful motto during the start-up phase is, "Think big—start small."

—Ernst & Young

18.1 Introduction

Designing and implementing a quality management system (QMS) requires the leadership to establish goals for the delivery of products and services to customers and then provide resources so that people can meet these goals. The ISO 9000 standard is a useful one to evaluate a QMS. By 2009, 178 countries had embraced the ISO 9000 standard, and worldwide 1,064,785 certificates had been issued (International Organisation for Standardisation (ISO), 2011). Chapter 17 described the standards and quality assurance measures adopted by pharmacies to deliver services to the public. These standards and quality assurance measures form the backbone of the QMS. ISO 9000 guidelines provide a comprehensive model for QMS with competitive advantage. The following are the benefits of implementing a QMS for pharmacy practice (Jackson, 2005):

■ Create a more efficient, effective organization
■ Increase customer and patient satisfaction and retention
■ Minimize errors
■ Enhance marketing
■ Promote employee motivation, awareness, and morale
■ Increase profit
■ Reduce waste and increase productivity

However, for small businesses that do not require certification to international standards, there are a few standards developed by certifying bodies. One such standard is the Small Business Standard (SBS) developed by the Chartered Quality Institute (2007).

18.2 Small Business Standard (SBS)

The SBS is a program specially designed for small and medium-size organizations and is based upon the ISO 9000 quality system standards. Pharmacies, both community and hospital, are small to medium-size enterprises that lack resources to implement a QMS based on the ISO 9000:2008 standard. The SBS enables these pharmacies to implement a basic management discipline to assure the quality of its products and services. Small to medium-size businesses such as pharmacies have the following characteristics:

■ Most employ less than 10 people.
■ They do not employ quality management professionals.

- The owner is a pharmacist who has a hands-on approach and spends long hours on paperwork.
- They usually do not have a documented system of quality management, nor a procedures manual.
- Standard operating procedures (SOPs), if present, have not been professionally designed.

The aims of the SBS code are to enhance the quality of products and services, reduce errors and failures, improve productivity and competitiveness, and provide a basis for further development of a QMS.

18.3 The Key Elements of the SBS

The SBS focuses on the critical elements of operating an effective management system. These key elements are

1. Management responsibility
2. Business reviews
3. Customer care
4. Staff and employees
5. Work environment and processes
6. Suppliers
7. Documentation
8. Preventing and correcting product or service problems
9. Records

18.3.1 Management Responsibility

Most pharmacies in the United Kingdom are managed by pharmacists. However, in the community pharmacy environment, and particularly in chain pharmacies, nonpharmacists who do not possess management skills manage the pharmacies. In hospital pharmacies, the managers have always been pharmacists. None of the managers are quality professionals. The SBS code requires management to

- Define management's policy related to the provision of products and services required to meet customers' needs and expectations
- Identify regulatory or sector requirements that are associated with the products and services
- Identify financial and activity performance targets, and provide the physical and human resources needed to achieve the targets
- Identify appropriate training requirements for people management, customer contact, processing, and verifying personnel

18.3.2 Business Reviews

Regular reviews of the plans must be undertaken by management. Records of the reviews must be maintained. The reviews must compare results with targets to provide a basis for improving customer satisfaction, business success, and management/process methods.

18.3.3 Customer Care

Management's policy for meeting customers' needs and expectations must be displayed to the public or communicated to employees and customers. Only products, services, and conditions must be offered to the public that can be provided in full. When accepting orders from customers, the processes used must ensure that the customers' needs and expectations are known and that the products or services can be supplied in accordance with those requirements. There must be an effective communication system for handling customer complaints, and opportunities must be provided for customers to make any unfavorable comments. Customer satisfaction must be assessed when a business review is conducted. Adequate care must be taken to protect the customers' property in the care of the organization from damage or loss.

18.3.4 Staff

All people employed in the business must be provided with written contracts. Hours of work and remuneration are to be, at a minimum, in accordance with national and local requirements. All employees must understand their responsibilities and how they should achieve the required results.

18.3.5 Working Environment and Processes

Management must provide a suitable and safe working environment. The equipment necessary for the production of products and services must be provided and properly maintained in accordance with regulatory requirements and the manufacturers' instructions. Regulatory requirements and instructions related to the operation of equipment must be readily available to the relevant people. Persons using the equipment must have had appropriate training. Methods or processes must be in place to provide the customer with what management and the customer expect. Storage facilities will be provided that protect materials and products from deterioration or damage. Products with a defined shelf life will be controlled and removed from stock and disposed of when date expired.

18.3.6 Suppliers

Suppliers of products and services will be selected on the basis of quality of products, reliability of service (including timely delivery), and cost. Purchase orders may be verbal or written, as agreed upon between the business and the particular supplier. Adequate information should be provided when ordering to ensure delivery in accordance with requirements.

Any supplier shortcomings that arise should be considered during the business reviews.

18.3.7 Documentation

Management must be aware and have access to the relevant regulatory documents. Documents given out to customers and other external parties must, at a minimum, contain all normal contact details.

18.3.8 Preventing and Correcting Product or Service Problems

Annual plans must consider the effect of any changes in business conditions, objectives, or targets relating to customer satisfaction, and the quality of processes, products, and services. Appropriate actions necessary to prevent problems must be included in the plan. Where a problem arises, action must be taken to rectify the problem and prevent recurrence. This action will depend on the seriousness of the problem and the risk to which the business is exposed.

18.3.9 Records

In addition to the annual plan, management must assess what records should be kept to minimize exposure to risk, for example, contract documents, personnel records, etc.

Management will decide on the period for which these records are held.

18.4 Process for Designing a QMS

In designing an effective and efficient QMS, it is necessary to identify the processes required to establish an organization that can meet its customers' requirements. Core processes, support processes, and assurance processes form the foundation on which the QMS is built. Building a foundation with these processes using quality assurance principles is more beneficial for the organization than developing a system around the clauses of the ISO 9000:2008 standard. The process for designing a QMS is shown in Figure 18.1.

Quality assurance in pharmaceutical care is defined as a set of activities carried out to monitor and improve performance so that the healthcare provided is as effective and safe as possible (Wiedenmayer et al., 2006).

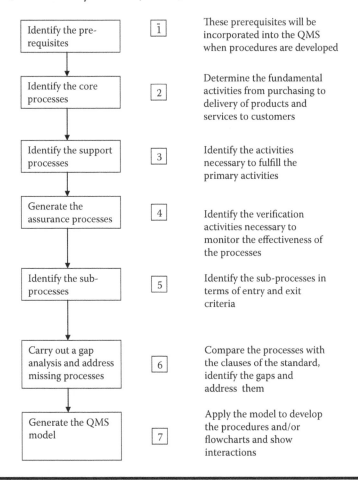

Figure 18.1 Process for designing a QMS.

18.4.1 Prerequisites

Long-term survival of the QMS depends on the organizational environment in which it is created. To be successful in business, organizations have to deliver what the customer wants, be reliable, and be able to adapt to an ever-changing business environment. In order to recognize the needs of customers and gain staff commitment, the organization has to fulfill four prerequisites: mission statement, strategic plan, top management commitment, and quality culture (De Silva, 2004).

Mission statement: The mission statement outlines the purpose or the reason for the existence of the enterprise. Its creation involves the people in the organization and different constituencies that it hopes to affect. Above all, it must inspire commitment, innovation, and courage. A mission statement must define the purpose, the business, and the values of the organization (Radtke, 1998).

The purpose statement focuses on the outcome and includes a phrase that indicates a change, such as *increase to, decrease to, prevention, elimination*, etc., and the recognition of the issues to be changed. Its business statement outlines the activities or programs of the organization to be implemented to achieve the purpose. The value statement includes the beliefs that the staff share in common, and these guide them in performing their work for the organization.

The mission statement of Pharmfinders UK Limited includes all the elements of a good mission statement: "To lead the UK pharmacy recruitment market through a specialist and professional service delivered within a culture of teamwork and integrity."

Change aimed at: Lead through a specialist and professional service.

Business statement: UK pharmacy recruitment market.

Value statement: Culture of teamwork and integrity.

Strategic planning: It has been known since the time of spiritual leaders that change is inevitable. This is particularly so in a competitive environment. If the organization does not change, someone else will. Those who do not change with the changing environment will be left behind. The business environment is constantly changing, demographically, economically, and culturally. The process of responding to these changes and creating an organization's future within the context of change is known as strategic planning. It allows the organization to control its future. The stages of strategic planning (Schumock and Wong, 2005) are

1. Create a mission and a vision for the organization.
2. Critically look at the current situation.
3. Develop strategies, goals, and objectives, and map approaches to be taken and specific and general results expected.
4. Outline the strategic direction, goals, and objectives. Prepare, draft, review, consult senior members, revise, and make final plan.

The planning process involves all the stakeholders: board of directors, staff, clients, and external shareholders. The board of directors should be involved in processing environmental information and approval of mission, values, and priorities. The employees of the organization have a wealth of information and can translate the vision to day-to-day activities. How well clients' needs are addressed will determine the success of the business. Their involvement in the planning process provides guidelines for future needs.

Management commitment: A necessary source of commitment is the genuine belief in the values of the project. Without commitment from top management, there is little motivation for staff to accept changes. The designing and implementing of a QMS is the responsibility of the quality professionals in the organization. But the senior management team must be aware of the fundamental requirements of the QMS, so that the team can commit the necessary resources and have a positive approach to the project. Its role then is to influence the project's success. Senior management can demonstrate commitment by

- Promoting the concepts of total quality management
- Establishing employee involvement
- Showing openness, patience, and trust
- Participating in quality management activities
- Regularly communicating with the staff
- Walking through the workplace
- Promoting the mission and vision of the organization

Building a quality culture: An effective and efficient QMS can only be built on a solid foundation of a quality culture. The environment within which the staff work must be such that they can develop a sense of ownership and urgency around the business, welcome innovation, and take risks. Sharing information gives the staff a sense of belonging to the organization, and customer satisfaction starts with staff satisfaction.

Culture can be defined as shared beliefs, values, attitudes, institutions, and behavior patterns that characterize the members of a community or organization (Woods, 1996). In the development of a quality culture, the company's expectations are integrated with those of the customers, so that they become the accepted norms of the organization. To develop a quality culture, managers have to take a proactive approach. Some guidelines to transform the culture of the organization to a valued quality culture are as follows (Travalini, 2001):

1. Seek complete executive support for quality.
2. Solicit buy-in from the staff.
3. Carefully arrange plans and align them with actions.
4. Select employees to lead key initiatives and support them.

5. Integrate quality into all aspects of training and as a part of daily activities.
6. Focus on customers for planning, action, and improvement.
7. Share information.

The creation of a quality culture is essential to develop a sense of belonging, so that they participate and contribute most positively. Clearly, such an environment is a prerequisite for designing and implementing a QMS.

18.4.2 *Identifying Core and Support Processes*

The set of processes from receiving inputs to delivery to customers can be considered a value chain. In this value chain, the key processes that are essential to performing assembly and transformation, bringing improvement, or maintaining integrity or reliability of the product or service are the core processes. These are the core processes that define the primary activities of the organization. Those processes that support the core processes to ensure that they are working are the support processes, while the assurance processes ensure that the organization is meeting its objectives. Table 18.1 shows the core processes of a pharmacy.

The core processes of purchasing, supply medicines, goods and appliances, delivery of services, medication review, counseling, and customer service are common to both the community pharmacy and the hospital pharmacy environment. In addition, community pharmacies deliver a multitude of services, including smoking cessation; a weight loss program; monitoring of blood pressure, cholesterol, and blood glucose; etc. Also, the sales of medicines, goods, and appliances are core processes of a community pharmacy. Apart from these activities, the hospital pharmacy also provides activities such as drug monitoring and discharge planning (Stuchbery et al., 2007; Clark, 2001).

Essential to fulfilling the core processes are the support processes listed in Table 18.2. Irrespective of the size of the

Table 18.1 Core Processes

Core Processes	Process Activities
Purchase medicines, goods, and appliances	Evaluate suppliers and purchasing data, confirm order, verify purchased product, check back orders
Supply of medicines, goods, and appliances	Compounding, dispensing, ward pharmacy, preparation of sterile products, preparation of cytotoxics, preparation of radiopharmaceuticals, supply of methadone
Sale of medicines, goods, and appliances	Patient counseling, sale of OTC products, and medical appliances
Delivery of goods	Delivery of medicines and appliances
Delivery of services	Screening for medical conditions, clinical pharmacy, clinical trials, disposal of unwanted medicines, discharge planning, drug monitoring
Medication review	Patient/family/carer interview, review history, observation chart and therapy chart, check allergy, review dosage
Counseling	Review medication, check interactions
Storage and distribution	Storage and distribution of medicines and appliances
Repeat dispensing	Processing repeat dispensing prescriptions

pharmacy, information technology (IT) plays a significant role in the activities of a pharmacy. Technical as well as nontechnical staff are essential to run a pharmacy. Recruitment, induction, dismissal, training, and performance reviews are included in the human resources (HR) package. Other support services are financial management, sales and marketing, and the management of the QMS. Health promotion activities are conducted by the sales and marketing team.

Table 18.2   Support Processes

Support Processes	Process Activities
IT	Purchasing, competence of staff, training pharmacy staff, document and record control
HR	Recruitment, induction, training, dismissal, staff training, performance review, internal communication
Sales and marketing	Pricing, accounts, health promotion, advertising, design of services
Accounts	Payroll, accounts payable, accounts receivable, taxes, Value Added Tax (VAT) payments, financial reports, financial budgets
Management of quality system	Quality planning, implementation of QMS, provision of resources, continual improvement
Communication	Internal communication with the staff and managers, external communication with customers and other healthcare providers, provision of health information
Self-care	Support for self-care

Note: IT, information technology; HR, human resources; QMS, quality management system.

18.4.3 Assurance Processes

The pharmacy generates several reports at periodic intervals to monitor its performance. These reports monitor not only the financial performance, but also the efficiency and effectiveness of pharmacy activities, such as dispensing, stock control, customer complaints, medicine use reviews (MURs), and other services. They are listed in Table 18.3.

The relationship among these processes is shown in Figure 18.2.

Table 18.3   Assurance Processes

Monitoring Activity	Verification
Effectiveness of activities	Audits, nonconforming work reports, corrective action, preventive action, equipment calibration, financial audits, management reviews
Availability of medicines and appliances	Stock control
Timeliness of delivery	Audits, waiting times, supplier evaluation, performance figures
Feedback	Customer satisfaction surveys
Accuracy of payments	Financial audits, annual reports, budget reports
Evaluation of training	Competence records, performance reviews
Effectiveness and accuracy of therapy	Drug interaction reports, adverse drug reaction reports

18.5 Process Approach

A process can be defined as a set of interacting activities that transforms inputs to outputs. This transformation requires human and material resources. There are four main types of processes (ISO, 2008):

1. Processes for the management of the organization: These relate to activities such as strategic planning, policies, and objectives.
2. Processes for managing the resources: The activities necessary to acquire resources to meet the goals and objectives of the company are defined by these processes.
3. Realization processes: They include the processes required to achieve the outputs.

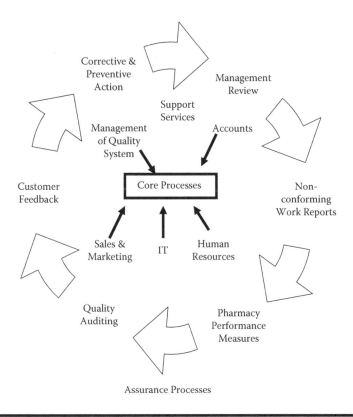

Figure 18.2   Management of processes.

4. Measurement, analysis, and improvement processes: The
   activities needed to measure and monitor data are defined
   by these processes. They include the assurance processes
   defined earlier.

Any management system has many interacting activities.
The output of one process may be an input into another process. The interaction among the various processes can best
be illustrated in the form of an interaction matrix as shown in
Table 18.4 (Kaganov, 1994). The table shows the interactions
in the form of arrows (up or down), P, or I. For example, the
counseling process is an input into the sales of the medication process, whereas sales of medications provide input into
the purchasing process. Less defined interactions are shown as

Table 18.4 Process Interaction Matrix

Process	Process No.	Process name	Purchasing	Supply	Sales	Delivery Goods	Delivery Services	Medication Review	Counseling	Storage and Distribution	Repeat Dispensing	IT	HR	Marketing	Accounts	QMS Management	Communication	Self-Care
Core	1	Purchasing		→	→					−		→		−	→	←	−	
	2	Supply	←		P	←	P	P	→	P	←	→	→	P	P	←	−	←
	3	Sales	←	P			P	P	→	P		→	→	←	→	←	−	←
	4	Delivery goods		→							P						−	
	5	Delivery services		P	P				→		P			→			−	P
	6	Medication review		P	P				→		P	−	→		−		→	P
	7	Counseling		←	←		←	←					P				→	←
	8	Storage and distribution	−	P	P							→				←		
	9	Repeat dispensing	−	→		P		P				−			−		P	

(continued)

Table 18.4 Process Interaction Matrix (continued)

Process	Process No.		Purchasing	Supply	Sales	Delivery Goods	Delivery Services	Medication Review	Counseling	Storage and Distribution	Repeat Dispensing	IT	HR	Marketing	Accounts	QMS Management	Communication	Self-Care
Support	1	IT	↑	↑	↑			I		P	I		P		↑	↑	P	
	2	HR		↑	↑		↑	↑	P		P	P			P		↑	
	3	Marketing	I	P	↓										↓		↓	↑
	4	Accounts	↑	I	↑			I				↓	↓	I		P		
	5	QMS management	↓	P	↓				P	P		↓	↓		P		P	
	6	Communication	I	↑	I	I	I	↑	↑				↓	↑	↑	↑		↑
	7	Self-care		↓	↓		P	P	↓				P	↓			↓	

Note: ↑, sales has input into the purchasing process, for example; ↓, counseling has input into the sales of medications, for example; P, participates in the process; I, information only.

P (participation) or I (information only). The sales of medications during counseling or medication review process and the storage and distribution process provide information to the purchasing process.

Each page of a process document contains the following features:

1. **Header:** Includes section, title, date released, page number, issue number, reference, date reviewed, and the signature for approval.
2. **Subheadings:**
   a. Purpose and scope: The purpose of the procedure and its scope.
   b. Responsibility: Who is carrying out what?
   c. Associated documents: Samples of all documents relevant to the procedure. For example, the documents associated with the dispensing process are a sample prescription, a product label, and a bag label.
   d. Resources: All resources needed to carry out the activities are listed here.
   e. Measures/controls: Quality assurance measures necessary to monitor the effectiveness of the procedure are classified under measures and controls.
   f. System description: All activities needed to carry out the procedure are described here. Any reference to flowcharts is included.

18.6 Structure of the QMS

All the elements necessary to establish the QMS are now complete. The core, support, and assurance processes have been identified. Figure 18.3 shows the structure of the QMS.

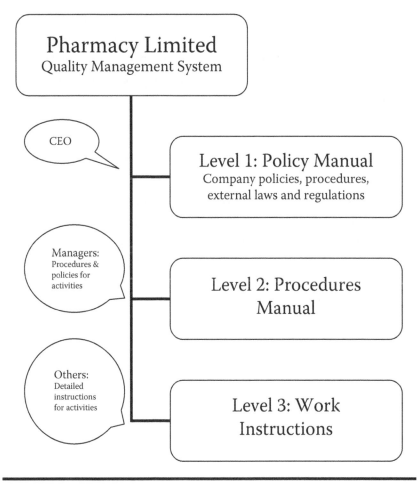

Figure 18.3 QMS structure.

Essentially there are three levels of documentations:

Top level—policy manual: This manual defines the policies relating to the codes of the standard. It includes policies relating to management responsibility, planning, communications, resources, purchasing, product/service realization, customer service, and verification. The CEO must demonstrate his or her commitment by defining the policies of the organization. Each policy document refers to associated procedures and reference to the SBS.

Middle level: The procedures manual describes the procedures of the organization identified earlier as core, support, and assurance processes. This manual forms the backbone of the organization. Each procedure makes reference to work instructions as necessary to be followed by the staff.

Bottom level: Work instructions comprise the instructions in the form of flowcharts that describe the details of the activities to follow. These instructions are written in a style easily understood by the staff (language of "things"). In contrast, the CEO who lays down the policies understands the language of "money." The middle managers, that is, pharmacy managers, are responsible for the procedures, and they communicate with the CEO and the working staff, and therefore must be conversant with the financial implications and work instructions so that they can guide and support the staff in the pharmacy.

18.7 Operations Manuals

18.7.1 Policy Manual

Appendix A shows the contents of a policy manual of a pharmacy. This manual includes the policies relating to each of the requirements of the SBS code. Each policy document includes the SBS code relevant to the policy and reference to appropriate quality procedures. For example, PM 3.8 is the policy document on continual improvement, and the relevant SBS code is business review. Policy PM 3.8 also refers to the procedure document 14.1 (continual improvement) in the procedures manual. Some policy documents, such as objectives, scope, and quality management administration, do not have related procedures.

Appendix B shows a sample policy document for the realization of products and services. Company policies on all the activities necessary to satisfy customer requirements are included in this policy document.To avoid any repetition, the policy manual makes provision for adding references to corporate policies or company policies that are relevant to it, such as quality policy, objectives, company profile, and budgets and goals.

18.7.2 Procedures Manual

The second hierarchy of documentation is the procedures manual. In this manual, individual procedures needed to meet customer requirements are described in detail. Appendix C shows the contents of this manual. Each procedure includes the requirements described under Section 18.5.

Appendix D shows the procedure for dispensing. It describes the requirements, from the receipt of the prescription from the patient to the delivery of items. The responsibilities of healthcare assistants, pharmacists, and dispensary assistants are described. Associated with this procedure are three documents: the prescription, product label, and bag label. Samples of each should be attached to the procedure. Resource requirements are the computer program necessary to add the patient's details, the details of the prescription and generating the necessary labels, medicines and equipment, presence of a pharmacist (legal requirements), and reference material such as the British National Formulary (BNF), Merck Index, pharmacopeias, and product information from suppliers. Item 5 of the document describes the measures and controls necessary to assure the quality requirements: (1) legality of the prescription, (2) clinical checks, (3) accuracy of product label and bag label, (4) accuracy of assembly, and (5) accuracy of labeling. The final section of the procedure QP 1.1 is the system description, which refers to the flowchart FC 1.1 (Appendix E), which is often described as SOP or work instructions.

Policy documents, procedures, and flowcharts without a header including the approval signature are not control documents and for all practical purposes are useless.

18.7.3 Work Instructions

The third level of documentation is work instructions that represent all activities relating to the procedure in the form of a flow diagram. Each work instruction document has a header similar to the procedure document and policy document, including the signature of the person who approved the document. The input to the work instruction FC 1.1 is the receipt of the prescription from the patient, and the output is the delivery of the items to the patient. All activities necessary to accomplish the patient's needs are represented by flowchart symbols. The person who carries out the activities and a brief description of the tasks are also shown.

18.8 Completing the Manuals

1. **Create/refine SOPs:** The first task of a pharmacy manager is to create SOPs as required by the regulations. It is a good starting point. These SOPs may have to be refined to meet the standards described earlier. Some new SOPs may have to be created, and these form a work instructions manual.
2. **Policy manual:** The next step is to create this manual using existing policy documents. Most pharmacies have policies relating to activities such as purchasing, dispensing, customer complaints, etc. These existing policies form an excellent foundation to create policy documents. To avoid repetition, existing policies can be referred to in the policy document. Some policies in Appendix A may not be applicable. On the other hand, it may be necessary to add policies not listed in Appendix A.
3. **Procedures manual:** The second step of the process is to create this manual. Not all procedure documents may have associated flowcharts. Procedures must be created for all activities in the pharmacy. The contents pages

in the appendices are only guides. Some procedures in Appendix 2 may not be applicable. On the other hand, it may be necessary to add procedures not listed in Appendix B.

References

Chartered Quality Institute. (2007). Small Business Standard. Retrieved September 20, 2011, from http://www.thecqi.org/Documents/knowledge/small_business_standard.pdf

Clark, C. (2001). *Review of clinical pharmacy services in Northern Ireland*. Department of Health, Social Services, Public Safety.

De Silva, K.T.Y. (2004). Designing a quality management system for a manufacturing organisation in New Zealand using process mapping supported by knowledge management. Unpublished doctoral thesis, California Coast University.

ISO. (2008). *Introduction and support package: Guidance on the concept and use of process approach for management systems* (Document ISO/TC 176/SC 2/N54R3). Retrieved September 22, 2011, from http://www.inlac.org/documentos/N544R3-Guidance-on-the-Concept-and-Use-of-the-Process-Approach.pdf

ISO. (2011). ISO 9001 certification top one million mark, food safety and information security continue meteoric increase. Retrieved August 11, 2011, from http://www.iso.org/iso/pressrelease.htm?refid=Ref1363

Jackson, T.L. (2005). Ensuring quality in pharmacy operations. In S.P. Desselle and D.P. Zgarrick (Eds.), *Pharmacy management: Essentials for all practice settings* (pp. 125–149). New York: McGraw-Hill.

Kaganov, M. (2004). A process interaction matrix. *Quality Progress*, 37, 194–198.

Radtke, J.M. (1998). *Strategic communications for non-profit organizations: Seven steps to creating a successful plan*. New York: John Wiley.

Schumock, G.T., and Wong, G. (2005). Strategic planning in pharmacy operations. In S.P. Desselle and D.P. Zgarrick (Eds.), *Pharmacy management: Essentials for all practice settings* (pp. 65–78). New York: McGraw-Hill.

Stuchbery, P., David, C.M., Kong, G.N., Giovanna, N., and Desantis, S.K.L. (2007). Identification by observation of clinical pharmacists' activities in a hospital inpatient setting. *Pharmacy Practice*, 5, 1–16.

Travalini, M.M. (2001). The evolution of a quality culture. *Quality Progress*, 34, 105–108.

Wiedenmayer, K., Summers, R.S., Mackie, C.A., Gous, A.G.S., and Everard, M. (2006). *Developing pharmacy practice: A focus on patient care: Handbook*. Geneva: World Health Organisation.

Woods, J.A. (1996). The six values of a quality culture. Retrieved August 12, 2011, from http://my.execpc.com/~jwoods/6values.htm

Chapter 19

Audits and Reviews

Twice and thrice over, as they say, good is to repeat and review what is good.

—Plato

19.1 Scenario

At the opening time of 9.00 a.m., Wendy Richardson, a pharmacist from a local branch, arrived in the pharmacy. She signed the visitor's book and commenced her work in the rear section of the pharmacy. Max, the pharmacist in Community Pharmacy Limited, was not aware of why she was there or what she was doing. Dianne, the manager, arrived shortly afterward, and only then was Wendy introduced to Max. Dianne said, "Wendy is going to look at our processes and suggest improvements."

Wendy worked in the pharmacy until its closure that day without communicating with Max. At the end of the day, Dianne and Wendy had a discussion behind closed doors. Max was not invited. About an hour later, Wendy and Dianne invited Max to talk with them. Wendy presented her findings without any input from Max. The findings were presented in a threatening manner; for example, "This branch is not operating efficiently because no one takes the lead. You as pharmacist should direct the staff..."

Dianne was completely exonerated and Wendy did not consider that Max was working under Dianne's supervision. There was no opportunity for Max to express his views.

19.2 Introduction

The scenario cited above demonstrates the need to conduct audits and reviews in a professional manner. These must be carried out in an impartial manner to be effective. Business processes in a pharmacy are aimed at adding value for the customer, and the outcome is increased effectiveness and efficiency. Audits and reviews are essential tools necessary to identify and improve company performance.

19.3 Definitions

Audit: A systematic assessment of policies and procedures of an organization associated with the administration, use of resources, and planning and improving employee and organization performance. It is conducted against a set of standards or procedures (Askey, 1994). In a community pharmacy setting, an audit involves all the activities as specified in company procedures. Its objectives are to
- Determine the implementation and effectiveness of procedures
- Ascertain the compliance or noncompliance with specified processes
- Provide a basis for improvement
- Meet legal requirements
- Specify standards for future performance

Auditor: The person/organization conducting the audit.
Auditee: The client being audited.

19.4 Management Review

Management review is an analysis of business activities against specified processes to identify gaps and opportunities for improvement. It is "an activity undertaken to determine the suitability, adequacy and effectiveness of the subject matter to achieve established objectives."*

The management review is conducted to ensure that adequate business processes are in place to meet the goals and objectives of the company. To maintain a competitive advantage, goals and objectives need to change with time, and all business processes should reflect these changes. A review can also be considered an assessment of process efficiency. The aims of a review are to

- Redesign ineffective and inefficient jobs
- Analyze and make improvements to processes that are ineffective in meeting company objectives
- Make recommendations for improvement
- Change the organizational structure to meet changing needs of customers and the strategic plan

Essentially, the difference between an audit and a review is that an audit is conducted against existing processes, whereas a review is carried out to determine the processes needed for improvement.

---

* ISO 9000:2005 3.8.7.

19.5 Auditing Styles

The style of auditing or reviewing the management system significantly affects the outcome of the activity. Audits and reviews should be a positive experience both the auditor and the auditee. A successful audit or review results in a win–win situation. There are three main styles of auditing, outlined in the sections below.

19.5.1 Inspectorial Style

All auditors conducting the audit in this manner assume the role of an inspector deliberately trying to find noncompliances. The auditee is threatened, and it is not possible to carry out an open and honest discussion. Very little information is provided to the auditor voluntarily, just like a person visiting the GP (general practitioner) for a medical examination at the request of an insurance company.

19.5.2 "Show and Tell" Style

In this style of audit, the auditee attempts to "show off," distracting the auditor from conducting a proper audit. Activities that do not comply are rarely brought to the focus of the auditor. Unless the auditor is assertive, the outcome is not beneficial to both parties.

19.5.3 Collaborative Style

A collaborative style of audit is beneficial to both parties, and the end result is a win-win situation. An open and honest discussion takes place between the auditor and the auditee. Noncompliances are handled in a nonthreatening manner. Necessary information is provided by the auditee voluntarily, just like a person consulting his or her GP for an ailment.

19.6 Types of Audit

Essentially, there are three types of audits: product, process, and system (Russell, 2005).

19.6.1 Product Audit

A product audit involves an assessment of hardware, processed material, software, or service to determine whether it conforms to specified requirements. When conducted on a service, it is referred to as a service audit. Examples of service audits are those performed on blood pressure monitoring services, blood glucose monitoring services, and medicine use reviews (MURs).

19.6.2 Process Audit

Community pharmacies regularly require that their operating procedures be verified to ensure that they are working correctly. Such audits are known as process audits. Inputs, actions, and outputs are examined to determine whether they comply with requirements defined in the operating procedures. The focus of this audit is mainly on activities directly affecting the customers. Process audits take much less time than system audits. The dispensing process, handling of customer complaints, and delivery of medications to homes are some examples of processes that are audited in community pharmacies.

19.6.3 System Audit

A system audit is an examination and evaluation of a documented activity to verify that the processes are effective, appropriate, and properly implemented to meet the expectations of customers and company objectives. A system audit may reveal that the dispensing process is not efficient enough to meet the rapid inflow of prescriptions to the pharmacy. It may also show that the process of maintaining controlled drugs does not meet regulatory requirements. A system audit specifies what must be done and not how it is done. How an activity should be performed is the responsibility of the organization.

19.7 Classification Based on Who Carries Out the Audit

There are three main types of audits, depending on who performs the audit: first-party, second-party, and third-party audits (Russell, 2005).

19.7.1 First-Party Audits

These audits are mainly internal audits conducted by the company itself by the auditors assigned by the organization. For example, a pharmacist from another branch of the company may visit another pharmacy to examine the dispensing process. The results of these audits are documented. The company may limit the scope of the audit to activities that are important for customers, such as handling of complaints, services provided, delivery of medications to homes, etc. In consultation with the auditee, recommendations are made, if necessary, and followed up by the auditor.

19.7.2 Second-Party Audits

Second-party audits are carried out by a contracted party who receives a product or a service from the company. Supply of medications to care homes is the norm these days and is done on a contractual basis. Before the contract is awarded, the manager of the care home may require an audit to be performed on activities affecting the service. These audits are more formal than internal audits. The report may highlight areas for improvement that must be addressed before the contract is awarded.

19.7.3 Third-Party Audits

Third-party audits are performed by an independent body. A care home may nominate an accredited auditing agency to perform the audit on its behalf. These audits are performed against a specified standard. To date there are no international standards, such as International Organisation for Standardisation (ISO) standards, that can be applied directly to the activities of community pharmacies. Instead, an independent body can perform the audit against regulatory requirements. Third-party audits are very formal and the auditors come from certifying bodies.

System, process, or first-party audits are generally carried out to evaluate performance against specified requirements and identify areas for improvement.

19.8 Specific Purpose Audits

Specific purpose audits are special audits conducted to monitor the management of the audit program. Two types of specific purpose audits are document review audits and follow-up audits. The former are performed prior to visiting the site to ensure that the documents required to manage the activities of the company meet specific requirements. Auditees are not interviewed and operational activities are not observed.

Follow-up audits are conducted to ensure that corrective actions relating to noncompliances are completed within a given time frame. Depending on the significance of the corrective action, follow-up audits are done either at the end of the time frame or at the next audit visit, usually after one year.

In the community pharmacy environment, commonly carried out audits are process, first-party, and system audits.

19.9 Audit Skills

A skilled auditor is a person who has completed an accredited audit program conducted by a certifying body. Although there is no regulatory requirement to employ registered auditors, training programs offer the skills necessary to perform an effective and successful audit. Auditing is a challenging profession, and may not appeal to everybody. An auditor may need to work in a stressful environment and question people throughout the audit (Business Training Schools, 2010). The auditor may uncover mistakes and frauds at early stages. Essentially, three types of skills are necessary for auditors: behavior, technical, and management skills (Chartered Institute of Public Finance and Accounting, 2010).

19.9.1 Behavioral Skills

Negotiating: There may be differences of opinion between audit findings and recommendations, and therefore a skilled auditor needs to negotiate a successful outcome.

Influencing: A change is most effective when it is done by influence rather than by control.

Oral and written communication: During the course of the audit, the auditor needs to interact with those involved with the audit by questioning them in a nonthreatening manner and demanding documents and answers in a nonthreatening manner. The auditor needs to communicate clearly in a manner that is understood by the recipient, avoiding technical jargon. Listening skills are also essential to gather all the information.

Assertiveness: An auditor may encounter a difficult situation where the auditee may not provide the information voluntarily. In such instances, the auditor must be assertive to obtain the relevant information.

Enthusiasm and initiative: The individuals who are involved with the audit are more cooperative when the auditor demonstrates initiative and enthusiasm. An audit is also a learning experience for the auditee and the auditor. A skilled auditor must be prepared to learn new challenges when encountered.

Teamwork and professionalism: The auditor interacts with all levels of staff, and therefore he or she must demonstrate professionalism and the ability to work as a team in order to gain their confidence.

Interview skills: The auditor needs to interact with managers and other staff, and has to ask appropriate questions to gain the desired information.

19.9.2 Technical Skills

An auditor must have the skills to analyze a series of sometimes disconnected events and draw some preliminary conclusions from the data. The data may also need to be tested to determine whether the objectives of the audit have been met (Moeller, 2009).

Knowledge of audits and scope: Auditors carry out different audits, and they should be able to apply audit principles, processes, and techniques to each type of audit to perform the task consistently and systematically.

Analytical skills: The auditor has to analyze and comprehend the data and draw valid conclusions. He or she may have to use statistical tools to analyze the data. Testing and sampling may also be necessary.

IT skills: Currently, IT is applied to almost every business function in the workplace. A basic knowledge of the IT environment of the organization is essential to understand the broad technology issues and to evaluate and communicate technology risks and opportunities to the management of the organization.

19.9.3 Management Skills

Audit management: The audit process is unique to the organization being audited and must be managed efficiently against the audit program in consultation with the client.

People skills: Generally, an audit is considered a threatening experience by the auditee. Exceptional people management skills are necessary to deal with various types of behavior. The auditor must put the auditee at ease and understand how the auditee feels. Demonstrating respect throughout the audit process is an essential quality of an auditor.

Leadership skills: An audit is teamwork between the client and the auditor. A competent auditor has accomplished the skills needed for auditing and should be able to demonstrate these to the client and the audit team. Leadership skills are essential to convince the client that the audit will lead to continuous improvement.

19.10 Audit Process

The audit process involves four distinct phases (Stebbing, 1993):

1. Planning
2. Conducting the audit
3. Audit findings and audit report
4. Follow-up

19.10.1 Planning

During the preparation phase, the following activities are performed:

- Appoint an auditor
- Inform the auditee

- Agree on the audit plan
- Collect all the necessary documents for preview
- Brief the audit team
- Prepare a checklist

The plan of the audit must be agreed upon between the client and the auditing organization or the auditor (Arter, 2003; Russell, 2005). A typical audit plan for a community pharmacy is presented in Table 19.1.

Table 19.1   Audit Plan

Audit No.	
Purpose	
To assess the conformance and effectiveness of the activities of Community Pharmacy Limited against the standard operating procedures (SOPs) and regulatory requirements.	
Scope	
All dispensary activities and shop floor activities are included in the audit.	
Requirements	
As specified in the SOPs and regulatory requirements in the code of ethics.	
Applicable documents	
SOPs of Community Pharmacy Limited	
Code of ethics	
Other regulatory standards	
Schedule	
(Insert the schedule here)	
Signed: Auditor	Client

19.10.2 Conducting the Audit (Figure 19.1)

Step 1: Entry meeting. A brief entry meeting is conducted between the auditor and the client. The persons involved with the audit are invited to be present at the meeting. Generally, in a community pharmacy, the manager, the pharmacist, and the supervisor should attend the meeting. Its purpose is to (1) introduce the audit team; (2) explain the scope of the audit, timetable, and plan; (3) explain the tools used for auditing; (4) agree on the time frame and the time for conducting the exit meeting; (5) explain how noncompliances are addressed; and (5) arrange for a person to accompany the team.

Step 2: Gathering evidence. The audit is done against the prepared checklist. An auditor uses three tools for performing the audit: checking the documents, observation of activities, and talking to the staff as necessary. During the interview, open-ended questions are posed to elicit correct information. The reasons for noncompliances are explained and agreed upon between the auditor and the client.

Step 3: Evaluation of evidence. At this stage the auditor has collected all the relevant information to complete the audit. Previous noncompliances and corrective action reports are reviewed. The noncompliances are classified according to the agreed criteria.

Step 4: Exit meeting. All those who attended the entry meeting are invited to be present at the exit meeting. It should not be a meeting only between the auditor and the manager behind closed doors. The meeting begins by emphasizing the activities observed to have been effective, thereby creating a positive environment. A brief summary is given; for example,

> The purpose of our audit was to evaluate the effectiveness of pharmacy activities against the SOPs. There was evidence to indicate that the

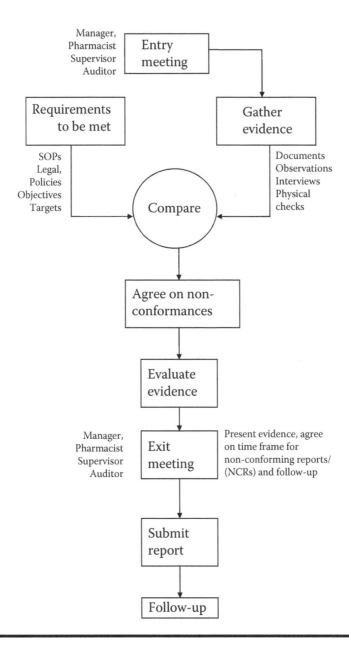

Figure 19.1   Audit process.

previous noncompliances have been addressed
and were found to be effective. Generally, the
activities are being carried out according to
the SOPs. There were a few areas that needed
attention.

An overview of the results is presented and an
opportunity is given for clarification of any issues.
Noncompliances are explained and a time is agreed upon
between the auditor and the client to address them. It
is important to present the findings in a nonthreatening
manner. The findings should be addressed to the team
rather than to an individual. For example, an auditor who
finds that the pharmacist is not directing the assistants in
the morning should avoid a statement such as

You, as the pharmacist, should ensure that the
assistants are appropriately directed to carry out
their functions every morning, and I have no evidence that it is taking place.

A more positive way of presenting the findings is as follows:

The assistants are performing their activities efficiently. However, it is necessary to direct them
in the morning as specified in the SOPs. This is
a noncompliance that should be addressed.

If a deviation is observed and the current procedure
has been shown to be effective, the auditor may make
a recommendation rather than recording the activity as
noncompliance. For example, the SOP requires weekly
audits of controlled drugs. However, the auditor finds that
weekly audits are not performed. Instead, the discussion
between the pharmacist and the auditor revealed that
physical checks of stocks are verified whenever receipts

and issues are made. Documents clearly confirmed the verification. Therefore, in the opinion of the auditor, the current procedure appears to be effective, and as such, he or she may make the following recommendation:

> I see that weekly stock takes of CDs are not being done. But, I find that the physical verification done during receipts and issues has been equally effective. I'll therefore recommend the SOP to be reviewed to reflect the current practice.

19.11 Audit Report

Following the exit meeting, the auditor should prepare and submit the audit report (Stebbing, 1993). It should include the following:

- Organization/branch audited
- Scope of the audit
- Audit schedule
- Management representatives and auditor(s) present at the entry meeting
- Audit criteria
- Audit tools
- Summary of the audit
- Audit finding
- Record of nonconformances
- Result of the audit
- Follow-up
- Distribution list

A sample audit report is shown in Table 19.2.

Table 19.2   Audit Report

Name of the audit company and contact details:
Date of audit:
Audited company, branch: Company Pharmacy Limited, Branch 721
Scope of the audit: Dispensary activities
Audit schedule: (Audit timetable)
Audit criteria: Standard operating procedures and regulatory requirements relating to dispensing activities
Audit tools: Observation of activities being preformed, checking the documents, interviewing the staff responsible for the activities, and checking the physical stocks of samples of controlled drugs
Present: (Give names of those present at the entry meeting)
Summary: The purpose of the audit was to verify the effectiveness of dispensing activities covered by SOPs 001–050. The audit finding indicates that, generally, the SOPs are being adhered to. Some areas need closer attention and review. Deviations were identified in the following activities: (State the activities for which nonconformances were raised.) The procedure employed to control the stocks of controlled drugs has been effective, although it deviates from the SOP, and as such, SOP 025 (stock control of controlled drugs) needs reviewing.

Audit findings:			
(An example is given below.)			
SOP No.:	*Description*	*Audit Finding*	*Compliance*
SOP 023	Receipt of CDs	Receipts have been correctly recorded. Records between January 1, 2009, and January 6, 2009, were checked.	Complies

(continued)

Table 19.2   Audit Report (continued)

SOP 025	Stock control of CDs	Physical stock is checked against the balance whenever receipts and issues are made. SOP 025 required weekly stock takes to be done. However, the current procedure has been shown to be very effective.	Does not comply; SOP 025 needs revision
SOP 030	Methadone issues	Entries have not been made in the order in which methadone has been dispensed.	Does not comply with legal requirements and the SOP; nonconformance

Summary of nonconformances:

(List the nonconformances here.)

Result of the audit:

Except for the nonconformances listed above, dispensary activities comply with the SOPs and regulatory requirements. There is no risk to the patients as a result of the nonconformances. The previous nonconformances have been addressed and the corrective actions have been effective.

Follow-up:

A follow-up visit is not necessary and corrective actions will be checked at the next scheduled audit.

Signature of the auditor:

Signature of the client:	Date:

19.12 Revisiting the Scenario

In the scenario cited in the beginning, Wendy has been requested to carry out a review of activities in Community Pharmacy Limited. In carrying out the review, her approach was unprofessional. The review conducted by her had the following shortcomings:

1. Wendy did not introduce herself and did not explain the purpose of her visit. There was no entry meeting.
2. The audit/review was conducted without any input from the pharmacist, Max. No issues were discussed with him at any stage.
3. The findings were discussed behind closed doors with the manager, who is a nonpharmacist. Max was not given any opportunity to discuss the issues raised by Wendy.
4. Wendy's findings were presented in a threatening manner.
5. A summary was not presented, and there were no positive comments on the activities carried out effectively in the pharmacy.

An audit or a review should be a positive and challenging opportunity for both the auditor and the client. Unless it is conducted in a professional manner, the findings are not beneficial to the organization.

References

Arter, D.R. (2003). *Quality audits for improved performance* (3rd ed.). Milwaukee, WI: Quality Press.

Askey, J.M. (1994). Internal quality management auditing: An examination. *Managerial Auditing Journal*, 9(4), 3–10.

Business Training Schools. (2010). Essential skills for auditors. Retrieved August 30, 2010, from http://www.business-training-schools.com/a/auditor/essential-skills-for-auditors.html

Chartered Institute of Public Finance and Accounting. (2010). Overview: Audit skills framework. Retrieved August 30, 2010, from http://learning.cipfa.org.uk/alc/overview/default. asp?more=2

Moeller, R. (2009). *Brink's modern internal auditing* (7th ed.). Hoboken, NJ: John Wiley.

Russell, J.P. (Ed.). (2005). *The ASQ auditing handbook* (3rd ed.). Milwaukee, WI: American Society for Quality, Quality Press.

Stebbing, L. (1993). *Quality assurance: The route for efficiency and competitiveness* (3rd ed.). West Sussex, England: Ellis Horwood.

Chapter 20

Dispensing Errors and Near Misses

Mistakes are the usual bridge between inexperience and wisdom.

—Phyllis Theroux, *Night Lights*

20.1 Scenario

One morning, Mrs. Tina Green, a patient who regularly collects medications from Community Pharmacy Limited, arrived in the pharmacy and wanted to speak to the manager, Dianne Watts. Dianne invited Mrs. Green to the consultation room. She was very agitated and produced a pack of Xalacom® eye drops from her handbag. It had been dispensed the previous day. She complained that she had been given Xalacom instead of Xalatan®. Fortunately, she said she detected the mistake when she was about to use the drops. Dianne went to the pharmacy and collected the dispensed script. The prescription had been for Xalatan, and the pharmacist and the dispenser had dispensed Xalacom in error. Dianne apologized for the error and corrected the mistake immediately. Mrs. Green accepted the apology with the assurance that it would not happen again. Dianne then called Max and the dispenser to her room and sternly warned them that it should not have happened and their performance was not acceptable. Dianne was not interested in finding out how it occurred or how it could be prevented in the future. Max and the dispenser left the room disheartened.

20.2 Introduction

According to the National Health Service (NHS) Business Services Authority, there were 10,951 community pharmacies in England as at March 31, 2011. In 2010–2011, the community pharmacies dispensed 850.7 million items (NHS Information Centre, 2012). The average number of items dispensed per day per pharmacy across England is about 249.* In the community pharmacy environment, dispensing errors occur, some of which are detected before the medication reaches the patient.

Dispensing error is a discrepancy between what has been prescribed by the medical practitioner and what has been delivered to the patient. Unprevented dispensing errors are those that had not been identified in the pharmacy and were detected only after the medication had been given to the patient. On the other hand, a near miss (prevented dispensing error) is an error identified before the medications reach the patient. In a community pharmacy, dispensing errors and near misses are critical.

Figure 20.1 shows the dispensing process. Errors can arise at any stage in the process.

---

* Assuming a 6-day week and 52 weeks per year.

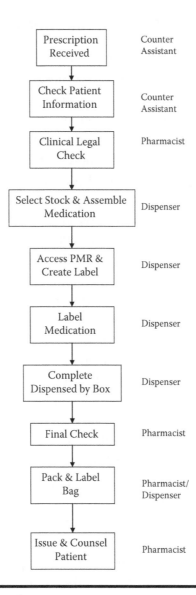

Figure 20.1 Dispensing process.

20.3 Incidence of Dispensing Errors and Near Misses

20.3.1 Dispensing Errors in the United Kingdom

James et al. (2009) have conducted a comprehensive review of the literature on incidence, type, and causes of dispensing errors in hospitals and community pharmacies across several countries. The incidence of near misses in community pharmacies in the United Kingdom (four studies) varied from 0.22% to 0.48% of the number of items dispensed. Unprevented dispensing errors occurred at the rate of 0.04% to 3.32%. The most common errors were supply of the wrong drug, drug with wrong strength, wrong quantity, wrong form, and wrong directions on the label. In a further study by Ashcroft et al. (2005), selection errors and errors due to labeling, bagging, and selection of the wrong medication record were found to be the common dispensing errors. The incidence of these errors varied from 7.6% to 60.3% of the total number of errors (Ashcroft et al., 2005).

In nine studies in hospitals in the United Kingdom, the incidence of unprevented dispensing errors varied from 0.008% to 0.02%. Near misses (prevented dispensing errors) in eight hospital pharmacies occurred at a frequency of 0.11% to 2.7%. The most common errors were associated with the wrong drug, wrong strength, wrong formulation, wrong quantity, and incorrect label (James et al., 2009; Chua et al., 2003).

Analysis of 135 near misses over a 32-day period (Table 20.1) in a community pharmacy has shown that wrong name and wrong address accounted for 25% of near misses. Forty-one percent of the near misses were due to wrong strength, wrong form of medication (e.g., capsules or tablets), or wrong drug. In three instances, the near misses were due to picking errors. For example, 300- and 100-mg tablets of bisoprolol and pravastatin, and allopurinol had been stored in the same compartment. Wrong directions, such as two times daily instead of three times daily, or one capsule daily instead

Table 20.1 Study of Near Misses at Branch 1234

Type of Near Miss	Number of Near Misses	Percent
Wrong directions	33	24.4
Wrong strength	23	17.0
Wrong address	20	14.8
Wrong form	19	14.0
Wrong drug	14	10.4
Wrong quantity	11	8.1
Wrong name on bag	8	5.9
Wrong name	6	4.4
Wrong dose	1	0.7
Total	135	99.7

of two capsules daily, were found in 33 instances of near misses (De Silva, 2010).

There is no peak time during which near misses occurred. Generally, most near misses occurred between 10 a.m. and 6 p.m., during which the surgeries were open. One to four near misses occurred over 20 days, and 10 to 12 near misses were identified on 2 days. Figure 20.2 shows a near-miss log.

Near-Miss Log

Date: Time:

Nature of near miss:

Time of occurrence:

Circumstances: Busy ☐   Interruptions ☐   Staff shortage ☐
        Storage issue ☐   Fatigue ☐   Other ☐

Title of the person responsible for the near miss:

Preventive measures:

Figure 20.2   Near-miss log.

20.3.2 Dispensing Errors in the United States

Unprevented dispensing errors in community pharmacies in the United States occurred at a frequency of 0.08% to 24%. Near misses happened at a frequency of 1.28%. The most common errors were labeling errors, supply of wrong strength, dosage form of medication, and wrong directions on the label. Near misses in U.S. hospitals occurred at a rate of 0.75% (one study). According to 16 studies in U.S. hospitals, unprevented errors occurred at a rate of 0.06% to 18% (James et al., 2009). The most common dispensing errors associated with both manual and automated dispensing systems were supply of the wrong drug, dosage form, strength and quantity, and wrong directions on the label.

Review of the literature by Chueng et al. (2009) on dispensing errors in community and hospital pharmacies in both the United States and the United Kingdom has shown similar results.

Figure 20.3 shows a dispensing error report.

20.4 Causes of Dispensing Errors

Currently, all community pharmacies operate a manual dispensing process, and errors can arise due to human failure. Preventive action can only be resolved by management, if the causes are properly understood. Factors that contribute to errors are (James et al., 2009; Chueng et al., 2009): (1) the staff, (2) prescription, (3) procedures, and (4) others.

Staff:
- Shortage and workload
- Inadequate training, experience, and knowledge
- Working long hours without breaks
- Hunger, fatigue, and stress
- Poor communication
- Lack of concentration

Dispensing Error Report

Date: Report No:

Form of complaint: Written/Verbal
Patient Details: Attach a bag label from the patient's record

Details of the complaint:

Dispensed by: Checked by:

Responsible pharmacist:

Has the patient taken or used the medication?   Yes ☐   No ☐
If "YES," is the patient OK?   Yes ☐   No ☐
Describe the patient's condition:

Has the patient reported or likely to report the incident to higher
authorities?   Yes ☐   No ☐
Probable cause of error:

Resolution:

Written response required: Yes ☐   No ☐

Corrective action to prevent a recurrence:

Signed (Pharmacist):   Manager:

Figure 20.3   Dispensing error report.

- – Job dissatisfaction
- – Interruptions

Prescriptions:

- – Illegible handwriting
- – Nonstandard directions, for example, ASD for "as directed"
- – Many items on the prescription

Procedures:
- Unclear or lack of procedures
- Lack of controls
- Failure to check before handing over the medication
- Failure to follow SOPs

Other factors:
- Look-alike or sound-alike drug names
- Similar packaging
- Poor design of the dispensary
- Inefficient computer software
- Storage issues
- Poor lighting

Human error cannot be eliminated completely. However, if action is taken to address the factors that contribute to errors, dispensing errors and near misses can be minimized.

20.5 Use of Bar Code Technology and Automatic Dispensing

Ros and de Vreeze-Wesselink (2009) have carried out a business process redesign to evaluate the effectiveness of a computerized prescriber order entry (CPOE) system together with a bar code-assisted dispensing process (BAP) in Gelre Hospital, the Netherlands. In this study, the dispensing error rate decreased from 3.1% to 1.7% when compared with the pre-CPOE system implementation. Application of a BAP resulted in a further decrease from 1.7% to 0.84%. Although the study was carried out in a hospital setting, these concepts are applicable to community pharmacies too.

In a further study (Agrawal, 2009), bar coding drugs in a hospital pharmacy reduced dispensing errors by 31% and adverse events by 63%.

Bar code technology to identify drugs has been in use in Australia for several years. After the details of the prescription have been entered in the computer, the bar code of the selected medication is scanned to verify the product. According to the Pharmacy Board of South Australia, mandating bar code scanners has reduced medication errors by 50% at the point of dispensing (Gertskis, 2009). In the United Kingdom, an electronic prescription system has been in use across many community pharmacies. In the United States, a sevenfold reduction in prescribing errors was observed following the implementation of electronic prescribing (Kaushal et al., 2010).

Bar code technology and an automatic dispensing system can minimize or eliminate the number of dispensing errors, for example, errors related to the prescription, errors due to packaging and selection, and errors associated with software.

20.6 Application of Crew Resource Management

Crew resource management (CRM) is a tool that has been widely used in the airline industry following a spate of accidents in the 1970s and 1980s (Seal, 2007). It is defined as "effective use of all available resources to ensure flight safety and operational effectiveness." When the CRM concept is applied to a community pharmacy setting, flight safety and operational effectiveness can mean medical safety and healthcare effectiveness. Six factors contribute to the CRM concept:

1. Understanding personalities to get the best out of them
2. Effective management of errors
3. Being aware of all available resources, including personnel
4. Involving everybody in the decision-making process and prioritizing and regularly reviewing the decisions
5. Good leadership skills to get the best out of the staff
6. Effective communication by building rapport

CRM involves management skills as well as creating layers of defenses against potential errors.

20.7 Management of Errors

A dispensing error is a disturbing experience to the pharmacist and others involved in the process as well as to the patient. With increasing regulatory requirements to monitor the proficiency of pharmacists, pharmacists have to be alert at all times. However, to a nonpharmacist manager a dispensing error is not a harrowing experience because such managers are not directly accountable, unlike the responsible pharmacist. Both the pharmacy manager and the manager must develop adequate skills to manage dispensing errors effectively. This effectively means shifting from a culture of blame to a culture of fairness (Seal, 2009).

20.8 Preventive Measures

Every dispensing error has to be treated as a learning experience. By analyzing the factors that contribute to the error, future errors of such types can be eliminated. An approach to prevent dispensing errors is based on their classification. The three types of errors are: (1) prescribing errors, (2) dispensing errors, and (3) administration errors (Williams, 2007).

20.8.1 Prescribing Errors

Prescribing errors arise when an inappropriate drug, wrong quantity, incorrect dosage, or nonstandard abbreviation is included in the prescription. The handwriting may be illegible or the prescription is communicated verbally. Electronic prescribing (Kaushal et al., 2010) has been shown to improve medication safety. In a hospital setting, Ros and de Vreeze-Wesselink

(2009) found that computerized CPOE and bar code-assisted dispensing systems have improved patient safety.

20.8.2 Dispensing Process

Dispensing errors that occur during any stage between the receipt of the prescription and delivery to the patient can be minimized (Williams, 2007) by implementing basic steps such as (1) efficient and effective dispensing procedures; (2) separating look-alike packages; (3) identifying high-risk drugs such as cytotoxics; (4) addressing staff issues such as work overload, stress, and interruptions; (5) providing adequate breaks and avoiding long working hours; (6) efficient computer systems with provision for warnings, cautions, and significant drug interactions; and (7) effective counseling at the time of delivery of medication and having a good understanding of medication.

Improved designs of the dispensary (Adcock, 2007) and bar code scanning systems (Gertskis, 2009) have been effectively used to prevent dispensing errors. A new approach is the use of robotic dispensing (Dermott, 2006). In this approach, the bar coded prescription is scanned in the pharmacy with a bar code reader that downloads the information to the patient medication record. The data flows into the selection area where the correct product is selected and delivered to the counter by the robot. Robotic dispensing improves patient safety and reduces human error of selecting the wrong medication. In addition, the pharmacy can order stock as and when required.

20.8.3 Administration Errors

Administration errors mainly occur in hospitals or surgeries when the medication is administered to the patient. With pharmacies taking over vaccinations, pharmacists must be aware of errors such as incorrect administration technique and administering an outdated product.

20.9 Management Responsibility

Although the pharmacist is directly responsible for dispensary errors, the manager must play a significant role to prevent errors from happening. Occupational well-being of the pharmacists must be improved to avoid errors due to stress and workload (Willis and Hassell, 2010). Demonstrating leadership qualities, supporting the staff to perform their job effectively, addressing staff issues, resolving and following up on complaints without blaming the staff, and providing resources to prevent errors are some of the functions that create an environment to achieve patient care.

A small rural pharmacy in Wanganui, New Zealand, has been supplying medication trays to the elderly population in the area. Once a fortnight, patients visit the pharmacy to collect their trays. One day, the technician prepared two trays, packed in bags ready for collection. The trays were signed off by the pharmacist. Because the patients were well known to the staff, the technician did not make any attempt to check the name and address, and the wrong tray was handed over to one of the patients. After taking a single dose of a medicine, the patient realized that he had been given the wrong tray. When the error was brought to the attention of pharmacy staff, the manager conducted an immediate investigation. The mistake was detected and the manager made arrangements for the patient to visit the pharmacy with the wrong medication. He apologized for the error on behalf of his staff, and information was provided for the patient to contact the regulatory authorities, if necessary. The manager contacted the general practitioner (GP) and explained what happened. The patient was sent to the GP for an examination. In the afternoon, the patient visited the pharmacy smiling, saying, "I'm alright. The doctor said there is nothing wrong with me." Even at this stage the manager explained his right to bring the matter to the attention of higher authorities. But, the patient simply said,

"Young man, I've been in production for many years. Mistakes do happen. Let's learn from them."

The incident cited above illustrates the correct actions taken by the manager: (1) acknowledged that the mistake occurred, (2) apologized for the error, (3) explained the patient's right to bring the incident to the attention of higher authorities, (4) initiated a consultation with the GP, and (5) implemented corrective action to prevent a recurrence.

20.10 Revisiting the Scenario

In the scenario cited in the chapter, the manager's response to the complaint was to affix blame. This attitude is counterproductive. A better approach would have been to get the staff involved in a quick problem-solving session. When Max invited the staff to resolve the problem, it was discovered that Xalacom and Xalatan were both stored in the same refrigerator and in the same compartment! Moving one set to another refrigerator in the pharmacy minimized the picking error.

References

Adcock, H. (2007). Design for a safer dispensing process. *Pharmaceutical Journal*, 279, 644–645.

Agrawal, A. (2009). Medication errors: Preventing using information technology systems. *British Journal of Clinical Pharmacology*, 67(6), 681–687.

Ashcroft, D.M., Quinlan, P., and Blenkinsopp, A. (2005). Prospective study of the incidence, nature and causes of dispensing errors in community pharmacies. *Pharmacoepidermology and Drug Safety*, 14(5), 327–332.

Chua, S.S., Wong, I.C., Edmonson, H., Allen, C., Chow, J., Peacham, J., Hill, G., and Grantham, J. (2003). A feasibility study for recording of dispensing errors and "near misses" in four UK primary care pharmacies. *Drug Safety*, 26, 803–813.

Chueng, K.C., Bouvy, N.L., and De Smet, P.A. (2009). Medication errors: The importance of safe dispensing. *Journal of Clinical Pharmacology*, 67(6), 676–680.

Dermott, R. (2006). Automated drug provision. Manufacturing and Logistics IT. Retrieved October 6, 2010, from http:// www.logisticsit.com/absolutenm/templates/article-critical. aspx?articleid=1713&zoneid=31.

De Silva, K.T.Y. (2010). A study of near misses at branch 1234. Unpublished paper.

Gertskis, M. (2009). Barcode scanning halving errors. Pharmacy e-News. Retrieved November 11, 2009. Pharmacynews.com.au

James, K.L., Barlow, D., McArtney, R., Hiom, S., et al. (2009). Incidence, type and causes of dispensing errors: A review of the literature. *International Journal of Pharmacy Practice*, 17, 9–30.

Kaushal, R., Kern, L.M., Barron, Y., Quaresimo, J., and Abramson, E.L. (2010). Electronic prescribing improves medication safety in community based office practices. *Journal of General Internal Medicine*, 25(6), 350–356.

NHS Information Centre. (2012). General pharmaceutical services: England 2001–2002 to 2010–2011. Retrieved March 16, 2012, from http://www.ic.nhs.uk/statistics-and-data-collections/ primary-care/pharmacies/general-pharmaceutical-services-in-england-2001-02-to-2010-11.

Ros, H., and de Vreeze-Wesselink, G. (2009). Reducing the number of dispensing errors by implementing a combination of a computerised prescriber order entry system and a bar code assisted dispensing system: The BAP concept. *European Journal of Hospital Pharmacy*, 15(4), 86–92.

Seal, C. (2007). How to harness all your resources. *Pharmaceutical Journal*, 279, 593–596.

Seal, C. (2009). We should move from a culture of blame to a culture of fairness. *Pharmaceutical Journal*, 282, 743–744.

Williams, D.J.P. (2007). Medication errors. *Journal of the College of Physicians of Edinburgh*, 37, 343–346.

Willis, S., and Hassell, K. (2010). Pharmacists' well-being needs to be improved in order to avoid dispensing errors. *Pharmaceutical Journal*, 285, 371.

Chapter 21

Patient Complaints

> Your most unhappy customers are the greatest source
> of learning.

> **—Bill Gates**

21.1 Scenario

Mrs. Green walked into the community pharmacy and complained that she had not received her medication for weeks, although the script was with the pharmacy. The counter assistant referred the complaint to the manager, Dianne, who greeted the patient, listened to the complaint, and excused herself to obtain more information relating to the problem. She returned shortly afterward and informed the patient that the particular item, Sinemet® Plus, was not available because of manufacturing problems. No further action was taken. Mrs. Green collected the script and walked off an unhappy customer.

21.2 Introduction

The community pharmacy is the first port of call for patients. It offers a wide variety of services, ranging from blood pressure measurement to emergency hormonal contraception. Patient complaints are a true reflection of dissatisfaction with the services received. With increasing expectations of patients, community pharmacies need to establish a closer relationship with their customers.

21.3 Significance of Patient Complaints

The greatest asset of any organization is its reputation. In the community pharmacy environment where patient care is a fundamental goal, any complaint, however minor, can have serious consequences. The process by which high-quality services are delivered to patients is known as clinical governance (Royal Pharmaceutical Society of Great Britain, 2010). It is defined as "a framework through which NHS organisations are accountable for continuously improving the quality of their services and safeguarding high standards of care by creating an environment in which excellence in clinical care will flourish."

A survey carried out in the United States (i-Sight, n.d.) has shown that

- About 50% of the time, dissatisfied customers do not complain.
- Nine out of ten unhappy customers will never return and take their business elsewhere.
- Fifty percent of dissatisfied customers who complain are not satisfied with the resolution.
- One dissatisfied customer will tell seven to nine others about his or her experience.
- Negative information carries twice the impact of positive information on buying decisions.

Patients as consumers have a far greater influence on the business. Unresolved complaints will damage the reputation of the organization and adversely affect future business. A problem that affects a patient may have serious consequences. Therefore, prompt resolution of patient complaints is essential for the well-being of the patient and the future of the business.

21.4 Benefits of an Effective Complaints Management System

An effective complaints management system offers several benefits for the organization (Consumer Affairs Victoria, 2007):

- Has better-quality products and services
- Reduces error rate, resulting in less time in resolution
- Has better awareness of customers' needs
- Promotes customer loyalty
- Attracts more customers through satisfied customers, and less time is spent on attracting new customers
- Improves reputation of the organization
- Improves profit

21.5 Why Do Patients Complain?

Pharmacists should be aware that the public is tolerant of occasional lapses. However, repetition of the failure is not acceptable. Patients complain about the services they receive for a variety of reasons. In a retail pharmacy setting, complaints relate to dispensing errors, delivery of services, and shortage of medicines. Dispensing errors can be a cause for major dissatisfaction and may lead to a serious situation regarding the well-being of the patient. Chapter 20 discusses the management of dispensing errors. Defective products purchased, such as a faulty blood pressure monitor or a poor service delivered, can also be cause for concern. In a primary healthcare clinic in Singapore, Lim et al. (1998) found that in 1994 and 1995, 28.8% of patients complained about the attitude and conduct of the staff, and 17.8% of the complaints were due to lack of professional skills. Among the patients, 16.2% said their expectations were not met by the clinic. Long waiting times (10.0%) and communication problems (7.8%) were also causes of dissatisfaction.

Similar results were also shown in a study conducted by the Pharmacy Board of Victoria (Newgreen et al., 2007). While 45% of the complaints were due to dispensing errors, 55% referred to a nonerror type of complaints. In this study, which spans nine years from July 1, 1998, to June 30, 2007, 281 complaints out of 514 were due to nonerror types of complaints. Major reasons for complaints were (1) receiving incorrect information or advice; (2) violating confidentiality and privacy; (3) refusal to supply a medication for ethical reasons or refusing to provide an identification when requested; (4) administration of methadone, buprenorphine, and naltrexone; (5) substitution of brands by cheaper brands or patients refusing to pay the premium price for the brand prescribed; and (6) unprofessional attitude and rudeness of the staff.

21.6 How to Handle Complaints

Progressive companies have systems in place to ensure that the customers are satisfied with the products and services offered by the company. Although preventive measures exist, complaints are unavoidable and should not be viewed as a negative experience. Handled correctly, a complaint can lead to satisfied customers. The following are some guidelines for handling customer complaints efficiently (Consumer Affairs Victoria, 2007):

1. Appoint a customer lead. This can be the pharmacy manager, supervisor, or pharmacist. It is the responsibility of the customer lead to follow up the complaint until a resolution is achieved.
2. Ensure that information is available to the public on how to address any issue with products and services offered by the company.
3. Train the frontline staff to receive complaints without offending the customer. They should be aware when a complaint should be referred to a higher authority and how to handle more complex cases and difficult customers.
4. Designate an area where the issue can be discussed confidentially. Normally, in a community pharmacy this will be the consultation room.
5. Acknowledge the complaint. Complaining causes inconvenience to the customer; and if the customer is a patient, health issues may also be involved. Listen carefully without interruption and clarify any issues. Apologize to the patient even if you feel that you are not at fault. Sometimes, a patient who has experienced poor service may demonstrate aggression. If you respond in an aggressive tone, the situation can escalate to abuse. It is important to stay calm and keep your voice down (Bridgen and Memon, 2004). Be assertive, but let the patient "let off steam." Ask open-ended questions to clarify the problem. If the patient does not calm down, say clearly that you do not tolerate aggressive behavior or abuse and you are unable to resolve the problem until the patient calms down. In rare instances it may be necessary to inform the police.
6. Investigate the complaint. If a mistake has been made, acknowledge the mistake and assure the patient that steps will be taken to prevent it from happening again.
7. Resolve the complaint in accordance with company guidelines. If a resolution cannot be achieved immediately, keep the patient informed throughout the process. In case of complaints received over the phone, by email, or by

letter, communicate with the customer within 48 hours even if a resolution has not been made.

8. Record the complaint for future reference. Keep careful notes of verbal communications. The information that should be recorded is shown in Table 21.1.
9. Promptly inform the customer about the proposed solution.
10. Follow up. Find out whether the customer is satisfied with the solution. If the complaint has been referred to a third party, such as the professional body or primary care trust, cooperate fully, and provide all the information relevant to the case and the proposed action.

It is important to demonstrate professionalism and be honest throughout the complaint-resolution process. Do not hide any facts.

Table 21.1 Complaint Report	
Date:	Report No.:
Name of the patient/customer:	
Contact details of patient/customer:	
Name of the staff member who handled the complaint:	
Description of the complaint:	
Notes on investigation:	
Resolution:	
Was the customer satisfied with the solution? If not, why?	
Preventive action:	
Follow-up:	
Further information:	
Action completed by:	Date:

21.7 Management of Complaints

Complaints should be viewed as a source of learning experience. The company must develop a system to manage the complaints effectively, and it should include a policy of welcoming complaints, training of staff to handle complaints effectively, and monitoring and reviewing complaint reports regularly to identify ongoing problems.

21.8 Revisiting the Scenario

In the scenario described earlier, Mrs. Green was clearly dissatisfied with the response given by the manager. Dianne should have requested permission from Mrs. Green to contact the General Practitioner (GP) regarding the issue. It is possible that the GP may have amended the script for the generic version of Sinemet Plus, which was available. Community pharmacies exist to serve patients, and as such, all efforts should be made to provide adequate service.

References

Bridgen, D.N., and Memon, M.I. (2004). *Dealing with aggressive patients* (occasional paper, Mersey Deanery Education Matter Sheet 19). Retrieved February 1, 2013, from http://www.doc stoc.com/docs/702999540/M-ersey-D-eanery-Mersey-Deanery

Consumer Affairs Victoria. (2007). Complaints handling. Retrieved February 8, 2012, from http://www.consumer.vic.gov.au/businesses/fair-trading/complaint-handling

i-Sight. (n.d.). *Consumer complaints management guide.* Retrieved September 19, 2011, from http://www.customerexpressions. com/CEx/cexweb.nsf/Consumer_Complaint_Management_-_ The_Guide_for_Businesses.pdf

Lim, H.C., Tan, C.B., Goh, L.G., and Ling, S.L. (1998). Why do patients complain? A primary healthcare study. *Singapore Medical Journal*, 39(9), 390–395.

Newgreen, D.B., Pressley, J., and Marty, S.H. (2007). What do clients of pharmacies complain about? *Australian Pharmacist*, 26(12), 908–1001.

Royal Pharmaceutical Society of Great Britain. (2010). Clinical governance. Retrieved February 8, 2012, from http://www.rpharms.com/best-practice/clinical-governance.asp

Appendix A: Policy Manual

Name of the Pharmacy

Contents: Policy manual	Reference: PM
Title: Contents	Date released:
Page: 1 of 3	Date reviewed:
Issue no.: 01	Approved:

Section	Description	Small Business Standard Clause	Quality Procedures
1 Introduction			
PM 1.1	Introduction	—	
PM 1.2	Abbreviations	—	
PM 1.3	Definitions	—	
PM 1.4	References	—	
PM 1.5	Quality policy	1	
PM 1.6	Company profile	—	
2 Administration			
PM 2.1	Objective	1	
PM 2.2	Scope	—	

Section	Description	*Small Business Standard Clause*	*Quality Procedures*
PM 2.3	Quality manual administration	—	
PM 2.4	Copyright	—	
3 Management responsibility			
PM 3.1	Requirements	—	
PM 3.2	Implementation and responsibility	1	
PM 3.3	Budget and goals	—	
PM 3.4	Structure of the QMS	—	
PM 3.5	Organization structure	1	
PM 3.6	Process interactions	—	
PM 3.7	Management commitment	1	
PM 3.8	Continual improvement	2	QP 14.1
PM 3.9	Documentation requirements	7, 9	QP 11.1– QP 11.2
4 Planning			
PM 4.1	Quality objectives	1	
PM 4.2	Quality planning	1	QP 14.2
5 Communication			
PM 5.1	Internal communication	4	QP 8.6
PM 5.2	Customer communication	3	QP 9.5
6 Resources			
PM 6.0	Provision	1	QP 8.2, QP 11
PM 6.1	Work environment	5	QP 8.4
PM 6.2	Staff competence and training	4	QP 8.1, QP 8.3, QP 8.5
PM 6.3	Infrastructure	1	QP 8.4

Section	Description	Small Business Standard Clause	Quality Procedures
7 Purchasing			
PM 7.0	Purchasing process	6	QP 2
PM 7.1	Purchasing information	6	QP 2
PM 7.2	Verification of purchased product	6	QP 2.6
8 Product/process realization			
PM 8.1	Processes	5	QP 1, QP 3
PM 8.2	Project management	—	QP 4
PM 8.3	Calibration of equipment	5	QP 13.2
PM 8.4	Preservation of product	—	QP 5
PM 8.5	Data analysis	2	QP 13.4
PM 8.6	Monitoring and measurement	2	QP 13.3, QP 10
9 Customer service			
PM 9.1	Sales and merchandising	3	QP 9.1, QP 9.4, QP 12
PM 9.2	Self-care	3	QP 9.3
PM 9.3	Handling complaints	3	QP 9.3
PM 9.4	Customer satisfaction	3	QP 9.2
10 Verification activities			
PM 10.0	Internal audits	8	QP 13.5
PM 10.1	Control of nonconforming product	8	QP 13.6– QP 13.7
PM 10.2	Corrective action	8	QP 13.8
PM 10.3	Preventive action	8	QP 13.8
PM 10.4	Management reviews	2	QP 13.1

Appendix B: Sample Products and Services Department

Name of the Pharmacy

Section: Product/service realization	Reference: PM 8.1
Title: Processes	Date released:
Page: 1 of 1	Date reviewed:
Issue No.: 01	Approved:

(Name of the company) shall plan and develop the processes needed for product/service realization consistent with other processes of the Small Business Management System. In planning product/process realization, (Name of the company) shall consider the following, as appropriate:

- Quality objectives and requirements for products/services
- Processes, documents, and resource requirements for product/process realization
- Verification, validation, monitoring and measurement, inspection, and test activities specific for the product/service and the criteria for product/service acceptance
- Appropriate records to demonstrate the realization of product/service according to the specified requirements

Associated procedures are

QP 1 Supply of medicines and equipment
QP 3 Delivery of services

Appendix C: Sample Procedures Manual

Name of the Pharmacy

Contents: Procedures manual	Reference: QP
Title: Index	Date released:
Page: 1 of 4	Date reviewed:
Issue No.: 01	Approved:

QP 1 Supply of medicines and equipment
QP 1.1 Dispensing
QP 1.2 Compounding
QP 1.3 Sterile preparations
QP 1.4 Preparation of cytotoxics
QP 1.5 Preparation of radiopharmaceuticals
QP 1.6 Repeat dispensing

QP 2 Purchasing
QP 2.1 Approval of suppliers
QP 2.2 Offering contracts
QP 2.3 Purchasing data
QP 2.4 Purchasing computer hardware and software
QP 2.5 Amendments to purchase orders
QP 2.6 Verification of purchased product

QP 2.7 Control of customer-supplied product

QP 2.8 Receipt of medicines, appliances, and other goods

QP 3 Delivery of services

QP 3.1 Screening for medical conditions

QP 3.2 Clinical pharmacy

QP 3.3 Ward pharmacy

QP 3.4 Clinical trials

QP 3.5 Provision of substances of abuse

QP 3.6 Medicine use reviews

QP 3.7 Disposal of unwanted medicines

QP 3.8 Delivery to homes

QP 4 Design of services

QP 4.1 Design planning

QP 4.2 Design input

QP 4.3 Design output

QP 4.4 Design review

QP 4.5 Design verification

QP 4.6 Design validation

QP 4.7 Design changes

QP 5 Storage

QP 5.1 Handling and storage

QP 6 Patient counseling

QP 6.1 Patient counseling

QP 6.2 Handling drug interactions

QP 6.3 Handling adverse drug reactions

QP 7 Discharge planning

QP 7.1 Planning for discharge of patients

QP 8 Human resources

QP 8.1 Training and induction

QP 8.2 Recruitment

QP 8.3 Dismissal

QP 8.4 Welfare and security

QP 8.5 Performance review

QP 8.6 Internal communication

QP 9 Customer service

QP 9.1 Sales

QP 9.2 Customer satisfaction

QP 9.3 Customer complaints

QP 9.4 Merchandising

QP 9.5 Self-care

QP 9.6 Customer communication

QP 10 Accounts

QP 10.1 Payroll

QP 10.2 Accounts receivable

QP 10.3 Accounts payable

QP 10.4 Taxes, VAT

QP 10.5 Financial reports, budgets

QP 11 IT

QP 11.1 Document control

QP 11.2 Record control

QP 11.3 IT procedures

QP 11.4 Security

QP 11.5 Data maintenance

QP 11.6 New software

QP 11.7 Maintenance of computer programs

QP 12 Marketing

QP 12.1 Health promotion

QP 12.2 Advertising

QP 13 Assurance processes

QP 13.1 Management review

QP 13.2 Calibration of equipment

QP 13.3 Monitoring and measurement

QP 13.4 Analysis of data

QP 13.5 Internal audits

QP 13.6 Nonconforming work reporting

QP 13.7 Disposal of nonconforming goods

QP 13.8 Corrective and preventive action
QP 13.9 Supplier performance

QP 14 Management of the quality system
QP 14.1 Continual improvement
QP 14.2 Quality planning

Appendix D: Dispensing Procedure

Name of the Pharmacy

Section: Supply of medicines and equipment	Reference: QP 1.1
Title: Dispensing	Date released:
Page: 1 of 3	Date reviewed:
Issue No.: 01	Approved:

1.0 Purpose and Scope

The purpose of this document shall be to describe the procedure for dispensing a prescription in the pharmacy. It includes all activities, from receiving a prescription from the patient to handing over the medication.

2.0 Responsibility

Healthcare assistant/technician/pharmacist shall

- Receive the prescription
- Check contact details and amend, if necessary

- Confirm whether the patient is waiting or calling back for the medicines
- Hand over the prescription to the pharmacist or dispenser
- Hand over the dispensed items to the patient

Pharmacist shall

- Check the legality of the prescription
- Carry out a clinical check
- Contact the prescriber or the patient for clarification, if necessary
- Hand over the prescription to the dispenser to enter the prescription in the computer
- Communicate with the customer regarding missing items
- Check the assembled items for accuracy against the prescription
- Make relevant records as necessary
- If a dispenser is not present, carry out performance of all activities to dispense the prescription
- Sign off "checked by," place the items in the bag, and label the bag with patient's details

Dispenser/pharmacy technician shall

- Enter the prescription in the computer
- Assemble the medications and equipment
- Order any items missing and communicate with the supplier
- Communicate with the customer regarding missing items
- Label and sign off "dispensed by"
- Hand over the assembled items for checking by the pharmacist

3.0 Associated Documents

Prescription (Doc 001)

Product label (Doc 002)
Bag label (Doc 003)

4.0 Resources

XXXX computer program
Medicines and equipment
Pharmacist
Reference material

5.0 Measures/Controls

Legality of the prescription
Clinical check
Accuracy of the product label and bag label
Accuracy of assembly
Accuracy of labeling

6.0 System Description

6.1 System Description

The procedure for dispensing is shown in flowchart FC 1.1.
[Attach sample prescription, product label, and bag label here.]

Appendix E: Standard Operating Procedures

Name of the Pharmacy

Section: Supply of medicines and equipment	Reference: FC 1.1
Title: Dispensing	Date released:
Page: 1 of 3	Date reviewed:
Issue No.: 01	Approved:

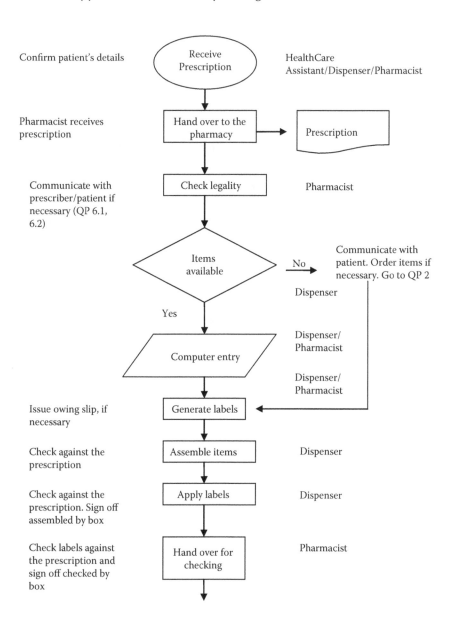

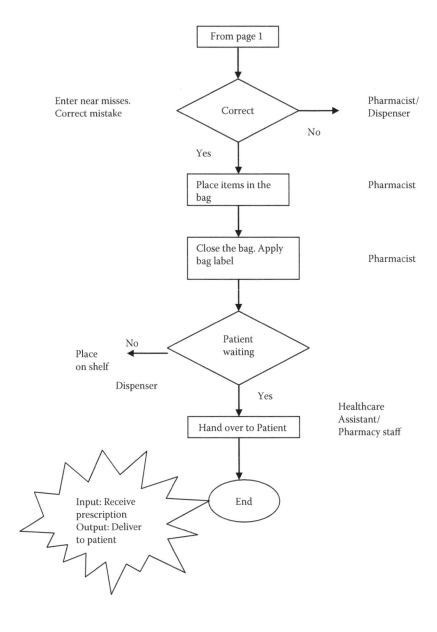

Index

X